Into
the

C000265313

Into the Wadi is the story of Michèle, a young Australian woman who meets and then marries a fellow scholarship student at an American university. He is Jordanian, and Michèle returns with him to his country to live with his family.

Michèle Drouart's memoir is a sensitive, compelling exploration of cultural similarity and difference, written against the versions of Arab and Muslim culture to be found in such popularist texts as *Not Without My Daughter*, *Princess* and *Sold*.

It is also a beautifully written and moving book about family, exile and belonging, about memory, and the complexities of human relationships.

Michèle Drouart was born in Sydney. Now residing in Perth, she has lived a large part of her life in France, the United States of America, the Middle East and Scotland.

Into The Wadi is her first book. She has read extracts from this work on Radio National's 'Arts Today' program, and as a featured writer at WEB (a women writers and performance network) readings in Perth.

Into the Wadi

Michèle Drouart

FREMANTLE ARTS CENTRE PRESS

First published 2000 by
FREMANTLE ARTS CENTRE PRESS
25 Quarry Street, Fremantle
(PO Box 158, North Fremantle, 6159)
Western Australia.

Reprinted February 2000.

Consultant Editor Janet Blagg.
Production Coordinator Cate Sutherland.
Cover Designer Marion Duke.

Typeset by Fremantle Arts Centre Press
and printed by Sands Print Group, Western Australia.

National Library of Australia
Cataloguing-in-publication data

Drouart, Michèle Eliane Françoise, 1947 -.
Into the wadi

ISBN 1 86368 275 9.

I. Title

A823.3

The State of Western Australia has made an investment in this project
through ArtsWA in association with the Lotteries Commission.

Publication of this title was assisted by the Commonwealth Government
through the Australia Council, its arts funding and advisory body.

For the people of
Kufr Soum

To protect the people concerned, the names of the characters in this book are fictional, although the scenes and events presented here are reconstructed from personal experience and from memory.

Contents

Family Tree   8

Prologue   11

Opening   15
Present and Past   21
North to Kufr Soum   61
Wall   103
The Sharers   145
You   187
Bidoun Kaalima   225
Rihaab Dances   261
Marriage   295
Noor   327

Epilogue   357

Maps
  Levant   364
  Jordan   365
Note on Transliteration   366
Translation   367
Glossary   368

Acknowledgements   374

Family Tree

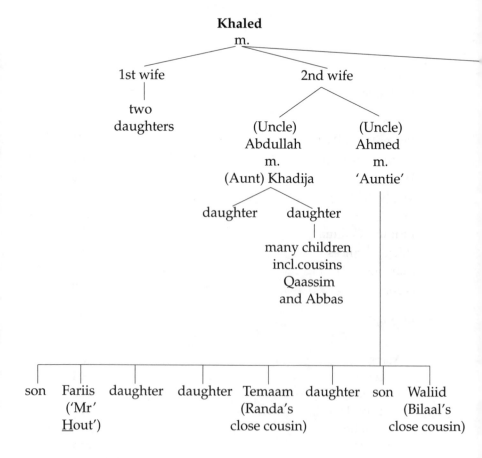

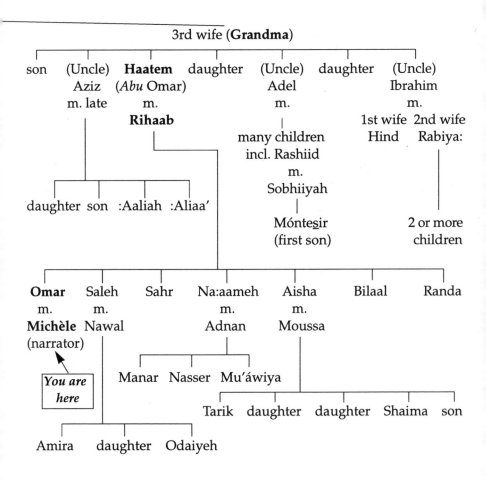

Prologue

Movement

In the beginning was movement. God's breath on the void. A stirring, readying to pronounce the Word. Movement is our own first mirror. New born, I see the batting and kicking of four pudgy tentacles, each with tiny projections of its own, that have a life of their own. Yet I know I am attached to them.

In childhood I learn not to move. Something — parental anxiety? an inner voice of caution? the sense of being female? — tells me to avoid all action, even speech. This pure nought, 0, certifies my innate absence of badness. But the mind cannot be still. Something gives, and the dreaming begins. Travels in fancy.

I was nineteen years old when I made my first actual trip. That was to the island of New Caledonia in a French semi-cargo ship. Its trading enterprises allowed me to spurn the luxury liner (which I couldn't have afforded anyway) for the romantic, bohemian voyage of a hard-up student. My accommodation was a third-class cabin near the hold, which I shared with my first love.

It was so hot that on many nights we lay on the deck.

The silhouettes of the cranes stood out like the shadowy masts of old sailing ships, and behind them the Milky Way flowed by. Or we'd lean over the deck rails looking down at the Pacific Ocean's own flecks of stars churned up by the bow.

Milky skies and starry seas. And other things I couldn't untangle.

We stopped at two ports of call in Vanuatu, then officially named the New Hebrides or *Les Nouvelles Hébrides*, depending on which of the two colonial administrations you were talking to. A true sharing.

That was only the beginning, but beginnings matter. I thought I would remember best the coral reefs, the coloured fish, the amazing turquoise water. But it's the events that stand out for me now, what we did: the two of us walking along a bright, white beach near Vila and 'borrowing' a small outrigger canoe. We lost the paddle. When we made it back to shore we looked around for the owner. There were only palm trees, water, the fine white beach, and that small canoe we replaced where we had found it. The emptiness made it easier for us. And harder.

In Santo, I stood with him one evening — that same first love — on an upper deck of the ship looking down on a throng of handsome island men who had come aboard. They were near naked, with wonderfully strong thighs, and were slashing open — with knives that flashed in the sun — great burlap sacks full of shelled coconuts, which they then sent thundering into the hold.

In Noumea I learnt to dance the *tamouré*, and in the New Caledonian mountains I bathed in hot sulphur springs and swam in cool flowing streams that ran alongside them. On the Isle of Pines we made love.

Still, with all that, my cocoon floated about me like an unburst amniotic sac. Only in later travels did its edges lightly brush against me as the tiny pinprick of a thought grew that it could not be a perfect nought with me inside. I existed. I took my place in the world, however small.

Movement. Separation of time and space. Irreversible disruption of 'is'. And still and for ever the smallest breath, stir or deed flashes out, ripples, repercusses throughout the cosmic weave: the stroke of my hand, the step of my foot, the walk, the run, the dance.

The journey.

And the mind remembering, and telling its memories.

Opening

Going Somewhere

Every morning I took the same village bus. Yet every morning was new, different. So much to see, inside and out, and detail mattered. I wrote it all down as it was happening. Wrote it in my head.

The bus spent up to half an hour doing the rounds of the village before taking to the road out. It retraced the same route over and over, or nearly the same route, each time adding one small street or turning one corner sooner. Then it set off on its sixteen-kilometre run into the city that is itself an overgrown village.

The passengers, the driver, the places passed, even the lurches of the bus, its speeding into bends, its loud engine, stopping, starting — all this I turned into flowing language, meaning.

One of the many villagers that I recognise only from these bus trips is waiting by the road. Mona, I think, a second cousin of one of our neighbours. Yesterday she had her four-year-old daughter with her, and she wore a tailored dress patterned in black and white. She had stockings on and shiny black shoes with narrow high heels, and she carried a matching leather handbag. Her long black silk scarf bore a silver leaf design along one edge; both ends had been thrown loosely back over her shoulders. She wore make-up yesterday too. Lots of make-up.

Today she's alone. Not even a handbag. She's in a blue *dish-dásha* — a long shift that hangs almost to the ground. It has a great red and gold flower embroidered down the front and tiny flowers in the same colours around the sleeves. This is her casual dress. A small blue scarf is tied tightly at the back of her neck; there's not even any *ko̱hl* around her eyes, and she has only the simple, flat *khofái* on her feet. I think to myself as she takes the seat in front of me: she will leave the bus long before we reach the city today. With her right hand she puts a salted pumpkin seed between her front teeth, cracks it expertly and blows the husk into her left hand. She gets off at a house two kilometres outside the village. Behind it I glimpse a garden of fruit trees, and behind that the land falls away steeply into a wadi or valley, scattered with dry grass and bushes, running down, down and off into the distance.

There's an elderly couple towards the back of the bus. The man gets up and helps the woman, his hand on her bent elbow as he guides her up the aisle to the front. He alights first, then turns to help her down the steps. It takes a long time, but no one hurries him. He is solicitous, dignified in his care, and our patience takes on his concern — and something of his dignity.

And who is this old man clambering aboard carrying a young lamb? Why is he taking this lamb into the city? Is it sick? Does he care for it so much? He is tall. His cloak and his red-and-white-checked *kefiiyeh* — the headcloth that men wear — make him look even larger and taller. His rough hands are big and strong, cradling the lamb in the folds of his cloak. I commit the picture to memory.

Going home in the late afternoon, I wait at the company bus station, where over forty small Mitsubishi buses arrive and depart from their own special stop to over forty northern villages. Sometimes my bus is already standing there with plenty of people on board, waiting to fill up before it will leave. Then I am not only the watcher. It is I who am observed, commented on. I find a seat where I can. An older woman in the traditional dark-coloured dress, called a *shrsh* in these parts — loose and long and straight-hanging — turns to her fellow passenger after I pass up the aisle.

'Who is she?'

'I don't know.'

Someone in front of them answers.

'It's the wife of Omar.'

'Where's she from?'

'From America. He brought her back from America.'

I don't correct them. I don't say, 'No. I'm Australian.' It's true, after all, that we met in the States.

These older women don't know what to make of me. Besides, they have all the time in the world to look, and wait, and see how I behave.

But sometimes the younger passengers talk to me in English.

On the bus it was easy to transform everything I saw and heard into words: variations, renditions, translations. Easy because I was there, and the bus and my words were surely going somewhere. I felt I was singing the eulogies in my head, in time to the Arabic music that blared from the bus driver's radio and heightened my receptiveness to every small thing. The bus itself became pliable under that influence, sure of its twists and turns and swayings to the rhythm. And I was ecstatic in my certainty of not losing a moment of the world around me, promising myself to transfer it later to pen and paper.

Whatever plans and projects were made on the bus, every evening on my return to the house other things distracted me. Life had to be lived, not written. 'Come and meet Sobhiiyeh and her sister.' The family believed it was unhealthy for me to remain alone with my thoughts. All did their best to keep me occupied. 'Would you make some tea for the guests?' If I stayed by myself for too long, even to write letters, then it was, 'We are going to Na:aameh's. Aren't you coming?'

The words have been fading, and the scenes that produced them.

With every visit I have renewed my acquaintance with the Arabic letters on the side of the bus. From right to left, one at a time, I pronounce them anew and inch forward to an automatic reading:

K–F–R–S–W ... no, not W ... it's O, or OU, then M. And now this other word: A ... no, I. That's it. I–R–B–D. Yes, those are the letters that together give the name of our village and the name of the city.

كفر سوم – إربد

Kufr Soum — Irbid

Once back in Australia, I copy out the whole address as I think I remember it.

Addresses, names, words of greeting, words for food, plants, clothes, places ... They're fading, all fading. Will they soon be gone?

Present and Past

Present: The Celebration

I have no idea where this drum came from, this tabla, played with so much ease. The bagpipe too. Things turn up here as if by magic, prepared quickly and quietly, without fuss. All effort is hidden from view. Only when everything is ready can commotion enter, and then it's the commotion of joy, just as now these young women are singing all around me and suddenly the tabla joins them. Its hollow *doum tac-a-tac* and the drone of the pipe echo across the courtyard and over the front wall into the street, but the singing we have all to ourselves, netted in flight by this thick cover of vines.

I look about me and notice that the older women are not with us. They have gone to other parts of the house and garden, and there's one group of them dressed in black from head to foot, sitting on the bench on the far side. Crones. Or crows, like the old women in a sunlit Greek village I stayed in many years ago; groups of skeletal, wing-damaged silhouettes against the whiteness of their domed church and chalky streets. The women on the bench are fatter. They would fit the stereotype perfectly if it were not for their extra weight. Still, they all look the same from here. Faceless, nameless. But not these around me, in their teens or early twenties, barely more than girls, each eager to make her mark on the evening. I am the oldest one here, almost twice their age, but they treat me as one of themselves.

I clap with them, fascinated, as they burst into another wedding song. Here is Shareen, round-faced, with tight curls. She does not stay with us for long, but keeps leaving and returning. Shareen and her brother are Omar's English students, and I think they must be fond of him as a teacher. It is her brother who will be married in a couple of days, in a climax to these festivities. Tonight Shareen is looking after her professor's wife, has taken it upon herself to be my personal hostess. She is busy with many things, and many people, but comes to me often. She knows that although I am married to Omar, I do not live here, am only paying a visit. Yet her dimpled smile, her gestures, the look in her eyes, express wholeheartedly the time-honoured greeting,

أهلاً و سهلاً

áhlen wa sáhlen
Welcome and be at ease.

We are sitting on chairs arranged in a semicircle, and at the other end is Rima, with the long lashes. She gets up to help May with her hair, replacing four thick black coils fallen down her neck. Next to them Nancy sings and claps wildly. Her hair is not pinned up. It is not even just down. It floats in long dark waves about her shoulders and often in front of her face, accentuating its strong structure. Her face appears sensual and self-willed. Nancy is constantly saying something in the ear of one of the others, then returning with a toss of her head to the words and rhythm of the song as if she had never left them.

And here beside me is Sahr, my sister-in-law. She appears a little older and more modestly dressed than the others, but she sings lustily and with authority. Exuberance shines from her eyes, from her whole face, though not a single strand of hair peeps out from under the floral-patterned scarf.

I suppose I should not have been surprised on this visit to see more of Sahr than anyone else in the family, even Omar. Kufr Soum is in the north, and I am staying at Omar's campus apartment in the university where he teaches. The nearest town of any size is this one, Karak, where the wedding is taking place. We are some way south of the capital, and far from his own home. Sahr made the trip south to look after his apartment for the few weeks of my visit, and she spends much of each day with me while he is teaching the special midsummer courses. She has also joined us on several outings. Of all the people here with me, Sahr is the only one I know from the village, besides Omar of course. I won't see much of Kufr Soum this time round.

Turning to face Sahr as she sings, I am enthralled by her joy of the present. Her participation is total. That's Sahr. She throws herself into everything. Not like Omar, who stands back, observing. They may be brother and sister, but although in their village Sahr is known for her singing, Omar never sings or dances. He only chats quietly with the other men, holding his head high with a dignity that is exactly the right degree short of exaggeration, a self-esteem teased almost — but not quite — to the edge of comedy.

Tonight Omar is beyond the gate with all the men, beyond the gate and around the wall, just beyond view, and the women relax here and enjoy each other's loveliness.

Not for the first time I wonder why it is that my own response to the celebrations is so intense, as it is to everything here. I have not yet found an answer that wholly satisfies me, especially since this complete engagement is so out of character, for me, who still looks most of the time as if I have come into the world unwillingly. As a baby, if there was a beetle moving through the grass, I entered its very microcosm, became engrossed in what it was doing and where it was going. If there was a star moving across the sky, I spotted and tracked it till it went down at the edge of the horizon, or, if not so long, till my mother shook, scolded and shoved my arm into the sleeve of the yellow velvet coat I used to wear. As for 'being there', being mentally in the place where my body was located, that must have been some kind of duty I resented. It took my mother forever to dress me. And yet now, in everything I see and do in this country, I feel quickened, emerging into life as I participate, desire and satisfaction coming together. Tonight, with these fat clusters of green grapes hanging above us, I plunge into the exultation of connectedness of being here among the clapping and trilling of the beautiful young women sitting beside me.

Do they know of Sahr's reputation in her own village for her knowledge of traditional wedding songs? They must by now. Several times they have cast about for a new song and it is Sahr who suggests one, or simply begins to sing. Ah! Now she is throwing her voice into those high-pitched, near-nasal notes that never descend, verse after verse, so common to weddings. Those around me are responding with repetitions and refrains, in a unison of recognition.

I look from Sahr in her coloured scarf to Nancy on the other side of our circle, Nancy with her abundant hair. She is no doubt one of the many Christian guests at this Christian wedding. The two women are smiling broadly as they sing, and their eyes meet, dancing. There is no difference. As I watch, I think of the weddings in Kufr Soum, far to the north, where no woman would step out of doors with her head uncovered. The younger ones, in long-sleeved blouses and ankle-length skirts, wear scarves pinned beneath the chin or, more adventurously, with the ends thrown over the shoulders. But the older women — clothed from neck to foot in the shapeless, dark-coloured *shrsh* — wear on their heads a piece of black material with a hole for the face, a sort of close-fitting cowl. Called an *:assaaba*, it covers the head, the ears and every wisp of hair at the sides before tucking under the chin, its lower folds pulled across the neck and chest like a wimple. Over this comes a bright cloth drawn over a pointed head comb, or the red-checked *kefiiyeh* just like the men's, but wound in a loose turban, often with one white-fringed corner hanging rakishly out.

The older women of the village are the ones, make no mistake, who dance best under the strings of lights rigged across an intersection of two dusty village streets. They are the ones who throw heart and soul into every wedding celebration, and who lead the *dubkeh* in serried circles. Hand in hand, elbows bent, forearm to forearm, they never put a foot amiss, never throw out of kilter the equal pressure of woman's body against woman's body in the curved and circling wall of movement. From among the crowd a woman will suddenly shrill a verse of wedding song with a nasal gusto, which in that place and moment is right, and lovely. When Sahr takes her turn she sets her sisters' names into the timeless formula with its allusions to 'sweet princesses'; in other verses her brothers' names appear. She is answered by another's high-pitched, tuneless song that hovers around similar notes; then comes the refrain from the other women looking on.

The only men actively engaged in all this are the tabla player and Uncle Ahmed's son, Waliid, who walks back and forth inside the circle, the flute never leaving his lips. The music is almost continuous, and the two of them play for the same amount of time as for the men's dances, and with as much spirit. The men, in their *dubkeh*, are never so close as the women. They clasp only each other's shoulders and their torsos do not touch. Their movements are freer and more individual, or seem so because of all the energy let loose, with heavy downbeats of the tabla to accompany the stamping and jumping. But that clasp is strong — no one lets go — and all do the same intricate steps that they have been learning from childhood, at wedding after wedding. Now and then a man breaks free to dance in the middle of the circle for a short while. Only the three or four best dancers take their turn one at a time in that central place for all to admire.

Those are the weddings of the northern villages.

Tonight it is not the flute, but the bagpipe that is playing with the tabla here. Most of these singing women are seated, and I know there will not be the kind of dancing enjoyed in the village.

But wait. As I am thinking these thoughts, people are getting up and I see that a room is being cleared in the house. Some women are already moving inside, and although Sahr stays in the courtyard, she urges me to go with the others. '*Raqsi*, Mishaal!' she says, pointing. 'Dance!'

Shareen is inviting me into the room, where a latest-

27

model stereo-cassette-radio is playing. Several women are dancing, the younger ones demure in dress and behaviour, the nine- and ten-year-olds utterly unselfconscious in their joy-frilled tulle. So are the mature women, in their close-fitting wedding frocks. It is Shareen's aunt who comes to me now, swinging her hips and motioning me with her hands into the group of dancers. I guess she is probably in her fifties, as must be many of the others who are joining us. I am swept up by the rhythm and the uninhibited body movements of the women.

At the edge of the room stands Shareen's grandmother, looking with pleasure on us dancers as the aunt motions me to imitate another movement. How is it that this family I don't know can pay me so much attention in the midst of their wedding? We met for the first time only a few days ago. I'm embarrassed to think of how miserably I behaved on that evening. I probably would not be here now, enjoying this celebration, if Omar hadn't insisted.

I do not bear physical discomfort well, and the sore throat that had started up two weeks earlier, shortly after my arrival, had become a searing pain on the day I met the wedding family.

We had taken an afternoon drive with a friend of Omar, and with the coming of evening I had been expecting us to drive straight home, when suddenly we stopped in front of a house. I pleaded in vain for us to go back, then offered to remain waiting in the car, but the visit had long been arranged, Omar said, and there was nothing that could be done about it. We went inside. The pain of my throat was at its worst in the middle of that visit. I said hardly a word to anyone, but sat morosely with my head

28

and neck wrapped in a thick scarf, and frowning like an old hag. That it was nothing more than 'irritation caused by the change of air and season,' as a local doctor informed me, was of no help to me. I tried to listen to the conversation in a language still largely foreign to me in spite of earlier efforts to learn it, and I leaned forward with my arms folded across my lap, clenching and unclenching my fists.

They wanted to know about me, about the professor's wife they had heard of and not seen until now. They asked questions — the son, the mother, the daughter and the aunt — discreet questions in turn, at spaced intervals in the conversation. Yes, this is she, he said in answer. And their disbelief ran to hide itself in further talk, deflected and as gentle as they could make it. When they learned of my state and could better understand my appearance and behaviour, the daughter — that was Shareen — brought pain-killers and weak tea with lemon juice. The calming effect after a short while coincided with the entrance of the grandmother into the room. Surely she was a cure!

She greeted us individually, so that each of us felt singled out for special attention. Though thin and of small build, she had more presence than anyone else in the room, and her eyes were more full of life. Two long plaits, bright with the henna dye (always an orange colour on the white hair of the elderly), were draped in front over each shoulder. They appeared from under a scarf that was tied behind in a way I had not seen before, black and tight-fitting like a skullcap.

Space was made for her in the middle of the long couch and she began to tell jokes and stories. After a small portion of some anecdote, everyone laughed or chuckled, and she stopped to chuckle with them and look about at all her listeners, inviting response, even from me, as if certain I had understood *something* of her words. She turned all the way to one side and then to the other, soliciting individual comments, mostly affirmations of something she had said. Then, satisfied, she moved on.

At one point Omar retold one of her jokes in English for me. It was the only one he translated, and was about a man who beat his wife once in his sleep … and twice after he woke up and realised what he had done …

What was this?

I laughed politely with the others while my mind scurried to sort out what had happened. Then the pained smile that had previously been sitting on my lips like a transfer, reflecting that other physical pain, made a fleeting return.

A moment's social discomfort always passes. And leaves its mark. Later, in remembering, came the onslaught of questions. Was the joke intended for me? Did she specifically ask him to translate it or did he choose to, on the spur of the moment? How pointed was it? A warning in the guise of humour? I could have asked Omar about it afterwards, but didn't, and don't quite know why not. It's never easy to understand things we seem to do instinctively. Did I believe that questioning him was beneath me? Was I feeling unprepared for what my demand for explanations might bring up? For whatever reason, I acted as if nothing had happened, and I wonder now if he could have explained it satisfactorily.

I have been tempted since that night to worry the joke into a parable of some sort; at the time I resisted easily enough, with the light and laughing mood the old woman created around her. But it surely was a parable. A parable for women, from men. For wives, from husbands. A parable dressed as a joke, told by an old woman, mediated by a husband. I've a feeling that this joke will remain unexplained. I've a feeling that my visit will be like the previous times. Whatever happens to me here, my understanding of it will be incomplete. Jokes, stories, events, decisions — like so many things in this part of the world — remain open-ended, intertwined like the encircled and encircling chambers of the thousand and one tales.

The laughter and lightness of that evening had been gentle and sociable. At this wedding celebration tonight it is fuller and freer, having plenty of festive excuse. A trilling crescendo bursts in on me. Yes! I am here, and this is now. I hip-thrust and shoulder-shimmy among the crowd of women, adjusting my movements to the dancers nearest me. After a while my eyes meet those of the grandmother. She responds immediately to my smile of recognition, approving and encouraging.

Past: Colours and Patterns

My parents' marriage grew out of a wartime romance.

My mother's French was impeccable. She had worked at it because she loved the language, although she was Australian-born. That was how she came to meet my father, who was serving on a Free French Forces ship that was docked in Sydney for some time during the war. She was twenty years old when they married, and he was twenty-two. He went away on his ship and she waited for the war to end.

In 1945 she took the first passenger liner that left for Europe. It was held up in Port Said and she saw plenty of Cairo, which she loved in spite of her impatience to be with my father. It was her first trip away. She joined him when he came off the ship in Marseilles. His father went there to meet him too, but saw them together from a distance and discreetly came home again, leaving them to find their own way back. They lived with his family, and also in England for a while, and then, after two years of postwar rations in Europe, they were expecting their first child. It was time to return to Australia. I grew in my mother's womb during the return voyage.

'Froggie,' the other nursery school children unimaginatively called me at around the age of four. Having a French father was not the best situation for an Australian child in the early 1950s so soon after the war. It was almost as difficult as for German or Italian immigrants. I spoke a little French then — well enough for a child of my age — but was teased for it unmercifully, so that I soon refused to utter another word of the language. Was this bilingual confusion yet another reason for my disconnectedness, or an excuse?

I was an evil child. Intelligent, but wilful in refusing to be part of the world around me. That is the way my early primary school teacher, a nun, represented me to others, and to myself. The story of these women of God and their young charges has become a cliché, lost all its power to shock. And the blame is unfair to the nuns who taught me later, who were gifted, caring teachers. But when you're six and seven years old … For two years I was taught that my other-worldliness was naughty and I must lose it.

So when she found me swinging from a branch of the tree in the schoolyard (I was Tarzan), and when she caught me galloping through the school grounds (the Lone Ranger), she admonished me for my 'unladylike behaviour' and many little girls' eyes stared at me in my shame, absorbing another lesson through my example. I tried for a while to conform, but my inner world refused to dissipate. With the guilt, I dared not reveal myself. We always do in the end, in some roundabout way that increases our vulnerability since we don't have the control. Many saw my dreaminess and disconnectedness as a form of stupidity. Now, not having imbibed the subtle social arts with my mother's milk, I am caught between one extreme and the other, between silence and shouting, between muteness and talking too much, pushing myself at people in inappropriate ways.

I am still plagued by the thought that it is selfish to live in one's own world, to dream and dream. The indulgence of it. Where is community? Where charity? Why, God, did you make me this way? Why did I, like my grandfather, sit on the edge of my bed in the mornings staring into space between each article of clothing I put on?

It was my mother who told me I resembled my grandfather. I still carry the niggling image from my childhood of her standing at the kitchen sink, having stopped whatever she was doing there to turn to me with a meaning look of mixed concern and indulgence. I was no more than seven or eight years old at the time, and have no recollection of what I must have said or done to elicit her reaction.

'I can just imagine you in a few years' time, Michèle, as a young woman, saying to me: "But Mummy, I love him and he loves me, and he has such beautiful fair hair and you should see his lovely blue eyes!" '

Later, when my romantic sentimentalism gave me grief, she blamed the dreamer in me and made reference to her impractical, hypersensitive father. When I did something creative she spoke of my gift of intuition, the poetic visionary that sprang from the Irish in me, again from my grandfather.

By pure coincidence the first boy I loved, the one who accompanied me on my Pacific Island trip, was fair with blue-green eyes, and of Irish background like many Australians. But I was already impatient to go beyond the known world. My romanticism was leaning towards everything other, towards the dark and mysterious.

I have often wondered whether the wanderer in me was connected to the dreamer, or whether it was more to do with my mixed family background. My grandmother's parents were from Tuscany, and there was a 'soupçon' of German on my father's side of the family, since a great grandparent had come from Alsace Lorraine. Coming from a variegated tree surely has something to do with seeking difference.

But my dreaming can't have been easy for my family either. What does a mother do with a child who is always staring at the grass or the sky? A child who consistently loses the money she is sent to the shops with after school, or who, if she makes it there, returns without some items she was meant to buy? If I could not find a place in my inner world for the things I happened upon, outside, then they were nothing to me. I was barely able to acknowledge their existence. When I did find myself drawn to them, I thought I was making them part of me, but it was they that carried me along some wormhole of the mind and took me into themselves.

There was the little tree, for instance, that grew about halfway between home and the local shopping centre. I had no idea what kind it was, only that I felt attached to it, fond of its small tapered leaves and especially its branches, which tended to grow not quite up, but something between vertical and horizontal. There were other trees every few yards along the road, but this was the only one of its kind in the area. It was young, you could tell by its size and the slenderness of its trunk, yet it had a wise old look about it in the wrinkles of the limbs and the way they bent and twisted. It wasn't in a particularly romantic setting, quite the opposite, being on the verge between the footpath and the busy main road. The traffic went fast along there, made plenty of noise and didn't let up most of the day. But I liked the way the tree asserted itself, small and young and alone and lovely against that incongruous rush of steel and rubber. I often stopped on my way just to look at it, and used to imagine it with bright-coloured gems growing like fruit in among the dark leaves. Its sight took me far from the present. Aladdin's treasure came to mind, as if it had grown on a tree like this before he found it. It wasn't until many years later that I learnt it was an olive tree.

I did love the bush. With my mother and sister I spent many school holidays on the property of family friends near Coolah, on the other side of the Blue Mountains. Our father worked hard in a factory, and could not afford to join us. As I grew older, the bush and the beach remained the only places where I could lose the sense of not fitting in, a sense of foreignness in my own country. Even the friends I made at school were mostly children who had just arrived from some other part of the world — it didn't matter where — children who spoke little or no English. Most of them, once adjusted, went off to make their own friends, but not Kam Lau Yuan.

Yuan was from Canton, by way of Hong Kong. She taught me to count to ten in Cantonese with the right intonations, and to use chopsticks. Most of all, I was grateful for the understanding she showed towards my other-worldliness.

I admired understanding. It was one of the 'seven gifts of the Holy Ghost', so we'd learnt in convent school. My favourite of the seven. I felt I could grow in it. Surely I could by experiencing the wider world, finding out the lay of lands and hearts.

I was eighteen, my sister fourteen, when our father died. It was at the end of my first year at university. His voice was what I missed most. And his accent. An absence I wasn't expecting. That sound contained everything else about him, or so it seemed in the sudden rushes of recall. Then, too, beyond the immediate grief, it felt strange and different to find ourselves three women in our little family with no males. My father had been a quiet and simple man, without connections, and still, losing him was like dropping off the edge of the world.

If we did not make our mark in the way that men understand, if we felt we were no longer present, on their planet, we soon came to understand we did exist and had to find ways to continue doing so.

I threw myself into my studies. For the next three years I was steeped in French Literature, especially the great nineteenth-century Romantics, and was bursting with exotic desire, like Flaubert's poor young Emma Bovary with whom I blushed to identify. Nerval's *Voyage en Orient* should have suited me well. We read it in the last year of our courses, or the other students did. I was impatient with the text, and never finished it. By that time, having made my Pacific Island trip, I was no longer content to travel in my head, or anyone else's.

I live in Perth now. The harbour-blue waters of my childhood have given way to the Indian Ocean's translucent aqua. But I did not travel east to west. I went in the opposite direction, and all's in the journey.

Going to France to see my father's family, I made another sea voyage, this time in an Italian passenger liner. The Suez Canal was closed then, so we took the longer route via the Americas, stopping in several well-known ports of call: Fiji, Pago Pago, Acapulco, Cristobal, Kingston ... The voyage lasted a month. A month of water, brightness and colour. All that was needed was a shipboard romance. And there he was, the ship's entertainment officer. An older man (I was twenty-one then), he seemed made to order; delightful, energetic, a good singer and ... 'foreign'. I fell in love, or into infatuation. The ship's multicultural community offered up all the pleasures of exotic difference. I saw it as a microcosm and a foretaste of what I would find in Europe, where I finally arrived keener to learn Italian than to improve my French.

I promised my mother I would return after a year. I did not. I was gone for many years, three of them spent in France, visiting other European countries whenever possible. My life between Sydney and Perth has been painted, stained and rinsed in many colours, but not, after that second ship voyage, the blues and greens of the sea. A palette of places, mostly land-locked.

The first was Amiens: a dreary, monotone grey, like an old canvas challenging me to create my own colours. There I took up my first post giving English conversation classes in French schools. This northern French city is made of fog and dark rain; even the small amount of snow, hardly distinguishable from the heavy clouds of the winter sky, appears dirty on the slate roofs of the houses. I was there for a year. But I often escaped by train to stay with my grandparents further south.

Sens: a storybook town. A haven set in a pastoral landscape of undulating crop and forest greens, punctuated by the stony tawns and browns of castles and cathedrals, towns and villages: Fontainebleau, Troyes, Joigny, Auxerre, Avallon. Nearby was Vézelay with its beautiful abbey, famed as the departure point of Richard the Lionheart's great crusade.

And there was Paris. After Amiens I lived there for two

years. Paris was all I wanted it to be, and more, but what I most loved was to visit the *Cité universitaire*, the international student residence district on the outskirts of the city. Its huge park contained several buildings scattered about, each representing a different country of the world. Penny, an Australian friend who lived at the *Maison Franco-Britannique*, invited me many times to attend concerts and performances there. We made friends with a group of Indians, and for days after seeing Rita Devi with her troupe at the *Maison d'Inde*, I tried to imitate her steps and gestures.

There were other cities and countries too, each with its own mix of colours. My favourite was Florence. I never lost my love of things Italian. But soon it wasn't enough to be a tourist. I had to live for some time in many of those places. To be the other, or as close as you can come: this was the way to know the world, to be alive. Adventure. *'Aventure.' 'Ad ventura.'* Something that comes towards you. Or you come suddenly upon it. Something extraordinary. The white stag or doe speaking to the knight in the Arthurian magic forest, or a fairy woman carrying him away so he is not seen for years. A happening far from the everyday. But *'aventure'* should be courted, is almost impossible to encounter if you stay too long in any one place, letting in familiarity. And I was destined to encounter the world. Had grown up with only this in mind.

Then came North America.

'I won't see you again,' my grandmother told me. I was standing with her and my aunt on the nearly empty open-air platform of the small Sens railway station. 'It's the same as when your father left for Australia with your mother. He came back from the war only to go away again, and I knew then, when we said goodbye in this very same place, that he would never return.'

True, my father hadn't come back. His death from cancer had come suddenly, just when our parents were beginning to think they might soon be able to afford a trip to France for us all.

Now I had been accepted into a graduate studies program in French Literature at a United States university. To me it was another country, another way of seeing the world. I had every intention of returning. Of course I would see my family again.

'Nonsense,' my aunt reassured my grandmother before I could answer, 'she'll be back.'

'I'll come back with a husband,' I joked, '… and little ones too.' But Mémé insisted. 'I know this is the last time your grandfather and I will see you,' she told me '… *la dernière fois.*' She had to raise her soft voice for the last few words as the Paris express came speeding through the station. It sent air whooshing back into our faces. There was the terrible noise of its rush, on and on. And the sudden silence. 'But of course I'll be back,' my answer echoed weakly in the ensuing stillness. When my own train came in, I climbed aboard and turned in the door of the carriage. 'Only a few years at most,' I promised them. The train pulled out. 'We wish you all the happiness Michèle,' my aunt called after me.

But Mémé had been right. I did not make it back. My grandparents died before I saw my father's country again.

On the day I flew out of Paris and stepped into the arrival hall of Kennedy airport, I was twenty-three years old. Although I would be studying in the Midwest, I couldn't imagine landing anywhere in the US but in its most famous city. I didn't see the Statue of Liberty over the wingtip as Gigi did. It was night. But then there were the lights of all those tall buildings, and there were enough epic and romantic narratives containing landings over the New York City lights for this arrival to satisfy me. After a few days, which was all I could afford, I headed west.

I was a keen student, a delighted child eager to learn new things. It didn't bother me to hear of students who spent the best years of their lives studying for a higher degree. I had a Masters from France. I had not been held up in my studies before. Why should I take a long time now? Clearly those other students whose stories were bandied about had problems. Besides, if it did take longer than I expected, that would be so for everyone in the courses with me. Most of us would surely manage. Waiting in the wings to take up my role, I remained unconcerned ... until time began forcing its claims.

There were many students in my situation. Camouflaged by the trees of its beautiful campus, our big Midwestern university, reluctant to give up its lucratively adopted children, proved to be an old Cronus to us all. We were snapped up, masticated, swallowed down, digested. We did all come out of there, finally: rounded, pat, well-formed intellectuals. But before my thesis was completed, I had to take a full-time job. I found one working from 3.00pm till midnight at the university library, with Sundays and Mondays off.

Already I had spent too long in a place I did not care for. My dark-spreading despondency was blocking out life's vital messages. I could accept by then that my time

41

in the States had not turned out to be the adventure I thought it would be, but surely it need not have been the ghostly half-life I had been leading for over a decade in the Midwest. I simply did not belong in that part of the world and felt it acutely. I didn't know where I belonged, only that it wasn't there. It all became slowly, insidiously, more than I could bear. I began to flag.

Then the Arabs swept through.

They came out of the East, disguised as students. Men without women. At first there had been only a few small raiding parties, but these had become ever bigger, till there were hordes. Their arrival caused havoc on the campus. In the Middle Eastern Studies programs, beginner Arabic courses would be filled to overflowing in their first few weeks as American women rushed to learn the difficult language of their new boyfriends. By the second semester, classes were reduced to a third of their size when relationship problems took their toll. There were Persians too, especially after the revolution in Iran, but they did not have the wildness of the Arabs. Before long I became one of the many casualties, surely wrapped in the innocent victim's soft-rose delight, and silently stolen away.

My library job had held up my studies. When I returned to full-time work on my thesis, I moved into the university's international residence centre. But what was all the hard work leading to? A shaky university post after more hard work looking for it? At best a settled life in some leafy campus town. Secure. Suburban. Where was difference? At this point my 'aventure' had to be ... could only be ... Omar.

Present: At Mu'tah

The drive home from Shareen's house in Karak to Omar's apartment on the campus of Mu'tah University seems long. I'm tired now. It's late, and dark, and there's not much to see. At last the three of us are set down in the parking area. We say our farewells and follow the narrow stone path through the lavender garden. We are no sooner inside than Sahr wishes us goodnight and goes to Samira's place next door where she will spend the night.

The apartments are all the same in this section of the campus: ground-level and not large, with one bedroom, a living room, a kitchen and a bathroom. The bedroom is hardly small, though, and if there is not much space to walk that is because it is almost entirely taken up by the king-sized bed. Not fancy or luxurious. Very simple. Even austere with its rectangular headboard of light wood. But huge. And why shouldn't it take up all the space? If you are not dressing, which you must always do quickly, then you are *in* the bed, made for only two things: sleeping and lovemaking. No one goes into the bedroom during the day, except to clean it. In my Australian home, I read in bed. Not here. There is only one dim light, which can be dimmed even further, in the centre of the ceiling, none at the head of the bed. At home I pamper myself on a weekend morning by taking tea and toast back to bed with a book for an hour. In this apartment, as in Omar's family house (though they have no beds there, but floor mattresses laid out each night), only someone who is deathly ill would eat 'in bed'.

Here, as in the village, a man may sleep in occasionally, perhaps after a long and tiring trip, or a long night of lovemaking, or a late night of card playing with his friends. But a woman is always up with the sun. It would not occur to her to lie in. Why should she? There are no responsibilities to evade. There are only things that can be accomplished in the here and now, things like cooking, cleaning, sewing. There may be a few unchangeable circumstances that she cannot afford to reflect on for long, then the immediacy of her work gives her some sense of control, at least over each day.

Early every morning, just after Omar has gone to his office, Sahr taps on the back door and I get up and let her in. She will have already made Samira's bed and tidied up her bedroom and kitchen for her. The kitchens, too, are of a comfortable size, to accommodate all the cooking that goes on. As we begin our day together by making breakfast, our *khofái* — scuffs for wearing outside, or in kitchens and bathrooms — clack about on the tiled floor. Omar wears soft leather ones. I do not hear him making breakfast for himself before he leaves.

Nearly all day Sahr is busy, washing dishes or clothes, dusting, cleaning. Omar likes to keep the apartment immaculate. When living there alone he will do all this himself, not setting aside any special time for it, but cleaning and dusting as he goes. Even in front of visitors he will bend down to the living room carpet to pick up tiny pieces of fluff that no one else can see. But when Sahr comes she works almost as hard as she does in the village.

I help out, washing a few clothes, a few dishes, making the perennial tea for ourselves or for guests, but I always run out of things to do.

In the afternoon Sahr stops for a rest. Before long she is playing a cassette of the latest Egyptian or Lebanese singer, and we dance. Then we visit some of the many friends she has made so quickly, usually the wives of administrative officials from families in the north, like herself. They smile at her colloquial language (which they themselves are careful not to be so liberal with), even laugh openly, telling me in English about the funny words she uses, asking if I know the difference. I laugh with them, nodding my familiarity with a word in the village dialect or learning a new one. She joins in the laughter, not the least discomfited. Most of them know that Sahr does not read or write, but they are glad of her company and seem to take a special pride in knowing her.

And they always tease her about marriage. In the village too. Especially in the village. I am sure they haven't let up, back there in Kufr Soum. When is your wedding Sahr? What! A big nose? Old 'Sheikh' Mohammed in the grocer's? Now, Sahr, don't make fun of your future husband!

I asked her about marriage myself once, not long after I first met her. We were returning to Kufr Soum from a visit to the doctor in the neighbouring town. She had made a joke of his advice to find an eligible bachelor.

'Why not marry Dr Nabil himself, Sahr?' I asked her, half seriously, 'he's not married.'

But my Arabic hadn't graduated beyond single words and names. I couldn't manage a sentence, much less a question. '*Enti ... zowaj ... Dr Nabil ...*' (You ... husband ... Dr Nabil) was all I could muster. She doubled up with laughter, as if I had added to the store of jokes on the topic.

'*Shou?! Dr Nabil?! Fakrak kwáïss illi Mishaal?*' She always pronounces my name with the long Arabic *alif*.

'*Bitakhdhi Dr Nabil lo ma khatbati Omar?*'

Sahr shot deliberate, meaningful looks at me as she spoke, which increasingly took on an air of mischief, reminding me of the looks Omar sometimes gave me.

'*La. Enti, Sahr. Enti.*' (No. You, Sahr. You.)

Her high-pitched response was full of humour.

'*Qasdak ana? lama tuqoum naqat Salah!*' But after a while she became more serious. And just as I was wanting to understand her, the words came in rapid volleys.

'*Dr Nabil rajul tayeb. Hou ishajani azzowaj mishaan sahati. Kul wahed laazim yakoun endou rafiik. Wa hou baraf ana ba:malhaash.*'

'*La.* Stop. You're talking too fast. I'm not understanding anything you're saying. Again? *Kaman?*'

'*Qsdah tayeb. Wa lakim nahou baraf ani mish rayiiha atzowaj hada msh wa ummi mariida. Okhti bitaqdar tatzowaj al mouhim :andi aadiir baali:ala ummi ...*'

She was astonishingly patient with my pleadings to repeat slowly. My own frustration at missing the details, the small weights and the auras of each word and phrase, exceeded her uneasiness at having to repeat herself on a sensitive subject. She even seemed happy to talk to me about it, although I lost a lot of what she said. Through variations on her theme, and with the help of gestures and facial expression, we managed back and forth, so that finally I understood the gist of all that language; the role of her mother's illness in her life choices. This wasn't what I'd been led to believe. Omar himself had told me that at twenty-eight years old, Sahr was beyond marriage. At least beyond a good and worthy marriage. That, he said, was the way most of the village saw her now. She had simply been overlooked. But after that early conversation, I always felt the choice had been hers to stay at home with their mother. It wasn't until much later that Omar told me something else that bore this out.

Never to marry ... though sought out for wedding celebrations even as far from home as here in Karak. But Sahr will not be going to the final wedding ceremony in two days. Omar and I are the official guests, and there will only be room for the two of us in a colleague's car.

We are always dependent on someone to bring us and take us anywhere outside Mu'tah. Omar never seems to worry about it. He accepts all invitations, no matter how far the location, as if certain that transport will be found. When we last visited the wedding family, it was Muammar who took us. Tonight it was a different person, and in two days it will be someone else again.

Omar does not beg or plead for anything. His simple confidence that when they are with him, his friends are in good company, provides him of its own accord with whatever he needs from them. But he does worry about how to fulfil his obligations. Reciprocation is everything.

Is it because of a lifetime of need and responsibility to his family that he invariably welcomes all visitors as long-lost friends? Knock on the apartment door at any time of the day or night, and you will not know the moment's silent thoughtfulness with which he readies himself for another human being. Certainly you will never hear the occasional words muttered when he is especially put out: 'Couss ummak!' (Your mother's cunt!) as he goes to the door scowling at yet another invasion of his privacy, whoever you are. Then he opens it, and registers that it is you, and his smile could not be warmer, his eyes more shot with real delight as he repeats the word of welcome, slowly and quickly, in high tones and low: '*Ahléyn! Ahle-e-e-e-eyyn, áhlen áhlen áhlen, fooot, ahleeeyn, áhlen!*' Isn't it everyone's duty to receive a visitor hospitably?

In spite of this modulated repetition, there is total conviction in the depth and steadiness of Omar's voice, in the calm that always underlies the vitality of his welcome. He is not theatrically unreserved or exuberant. There are no extravagant gestures, he is sparing of gestures. Perhaps he will bend his tall thin body or his long neck very slightly, almost imperceptibly, towards you, or barely move his head slowly back and forth once or twice; that is the most he has a taste for. The delight is all in his smile and eyes. This is not a mask. It is a real switch in his mood. The greeting does not need any formal completion, its understood second part — *wa sáhlen* (and be at ease) — is immediately put into practice as he indicates a place on the couch, plumping the cushions before you sit down, placing bowls of nuts or fruit on the coffee table in front of you, glad of his good fortune that it is you who have come to see him. It is not just anyone after all, but really you, whoever you may be.

So it was when I would knock on the door of his room in the American student residence centre. Whether he was expecting me or not, when he opened that door I felt that no one but me existed for him. Only when I made my first trip here did I see how he greeted all his visitors.

That was seven years ago. This wedding visit is my fourth trip, my second in the five years since our own marriage.

Jordan is the first country of the Middle East that I saw. And it remains the only one. My initial visit was short, to meet Omar's family and come to know the world he lives in. He had already returned here and prepared his home for my arrival. There was no question of my staying at the time. I had many things to take care of in the US where I had lived for some years, and there was my own family to see in Australia, but we agreed that I would come back later with the intention of remaining.

It was towards the end of that second stay, many months later, that we were married. A quiet formality, without celebration of any kind. Soon afterwards we both went away again, this time to the UK, where Omar continued with his studies in English. But I am moving ahead of myself. It need only be said here that there were two more trips to Jordan for me after that, both from Australia. Four altogether then, and this is the fourth.

It feels strange to be attending wedding celebrations with him now that we live apart. Why, if we are husband and wife, do I not stay here? Or why, if we are not together, do I keep returning? This country, so exotic, yet so familiar in its foreignness, is my second home. I fly to it, and when the physical journeys are not possible I fly to it in thought. Escape? Yes, and my dreaming is not so very different from Omar's evading. In this we are well matched. We evade and escape to and from each other. But there is more to me, as to him, a something more that enables us, and is part of our dreaming. I wonder what we might have achieved together, and sometimes I ask myself if it has not already been achieved. In recent years, we have spent more time far apart. Time expands the geographical distance between us, stretching even the dream thin now.

But come with me back a way. In two days we will return for the wedding. Those celebrations can wait. They last for days, and you will not miss anything.

Past: Beginnings

Omar.

Omar Haatem Al-Khaled Al-Eihab.

He lives up to that lordly, lengthy name. Like other Arab names it stretches back past his father, his grandfather, his great-grandfather, until individuals are sifted out, and the whole comes to rest on a final grand patronymic bequeathed to the entire clan by some illustrious ancestor.

It is not his real name. I wrote and asked him how he wanted to be called, and these are the choices he sent back to me. Omar, Haatem, Khaled and Eihab. I have put them all together in the order of preference he told me, so that the new name has exactly as many parts as his own, the same long string making the same grand rhetorical impression on an unaccustomed ear. It is his choice, and its rhythmic weightiness tells more about him, speaks more truly than his own name.

I believe he was not himself the first time I met him. I think he must have been ill. He was sitting across from me at one of the long tables in the enormous dining hall of the graduate student residence centre, on the campus of that big Midwestern university where we were both students. It was a large group at lunch that day, mostly engaged in talk, but he said nothing. He was staring down at the table, disdainfully it seemed, when a fellow student introduced me, and he looked up, breathed out 'hello' with a nod, and stared down again.

The plate in front of him was barely touched, yet there were crumbs and scraps of food scattered around it, as if he had taken a bite from this and a bite from that, laying them down wherever his hand came to rest. Although he was looking down, he held his head high, above an unusually long neck. It gave the impression of a knob on the end of a pole, but a knob that was not much wider than the circumference of the pole itself and little more than an extension of it. The effect was accentuated by a tendency to tuck his chin into his neck. In every other respect he appeared perfectly proportioned, if taller, slimmer, and longer limbed than most of his fellow Arab students. I learnt later that a nickname they had for him, used affectionately, was 'The Giraffe'.

He pushed the plate back from him with a voiced sigh. 'Ooohhhh.' Then the crumbs and scraps scattered about the space where the plate had been were more noticeable. We were in the smoking section of the dining hall, and he leant back and lit up a cigarette. He smoked sulkily, answering the questions of a compatriot student next to him with short mumbled complaints in Arabic, which the other could not hear and asked him to repeat. He did so, raising the volume only a little and breathing out as if the effort of repeating himself were taking all the air from his lungs. This was accompanied with brusque dismissive gestures. His face looked worn. The fine structure of his nose and cheeks was overshadowed by the great dark circles around his eyes.

It was weeks before I saw Omar again, and I hardly recognised him. We were passing on opposite sides of the lobby and he called out a greeting. His eyes, face, gestures, all seemed to join in the generous smile he gave me. 'Well, hello, you still exist then?' I teased. About to enter the elevator he answered, 'I went away.' Later I learnt from his friends that he had gone home. Simply booked himself onto a plane without telling anyone. He nearly lost his scholarship, but then his government offered not to cancel it on condition that he return for the stipulated period of his studies and see it through.

The graduate student residence centre housed students from all over the world. It was also one of the largest campus residences, with twelve floors and four wings on each floor, two for men and two for women. Many of the Americans who stayed there enjoyed meeting students from different countries, and for the foreigners there was an element of protection about the place; it was a shock absorber and a buffer zone between their own world and the one they had just entered. They were less likely to come across people who told them, as so many did outside, how privileged they must feel to have the opportunity to study in the greatest country on earth. The centre also had a reputation for fun and the good life. Parties and celebrations of all kinds were held nearly every week, usually in the huge converted dining hall.

It happened on average every two or three years. Just one isolated event, or a spate of them. And in most cases it was a student from far away. After the lovely young African woman did it — that was just before I arrived — she became the subject of hushed conversations for a long time. I can't remember if she jumped like the others or swallowed poison. Apparently a lot of people had known her, though few of them well, as it turned out.

But they knew she'd been homesick. They knew because she had said something to someone about the way people didn't care for each other, about the terrible food, the tiny rooms where students locked themselves in at night. How could one lock oneself away from the warmth and company of others, especially at night? I was told that she had seemed to be unable to express the fullness of her own reactions. There was a sense when she spoke, and when she would no longer speak, of indefinable, unarticulable surprise and horror. At first she asked if this was the way people really lived in this country that had so much power in the world. Then she repeated over and over that it could not be, that no one could live this way. After that she fell silent, and finally said without words what she had been unable to communicate in language, said it through her body discovered in death. I was told that most people who had met her found her beautiful. A person with soul, they said. In every way a beautiful person.

Omar did not tell his family he was coming home. He took rides and public transport from the capital all the way to the north, all the way to his village where his appearance was a complete surprise. His family was not happy with his return, especially his father. They went to work on him in turns, persuading, threatening and cajoling, and within three weeks he was booked on another plane back to the United States. To make sure he went through with it they took him to the airport. Father, brothers, sisters, cousins, friends, even neighbours, made the long bus journey to Queen Alia Airport, and practically had to push him onto the plane.

Not long after returning, he met Heidi, fair-skinned, with short blond hair and an open and trusting manner. In her refreshing, almost naive effusiveness, she told me that she was strongly drawn to Omar. 'He's so attractive. Of all the men here he's the one I'd most like to know.' 'I agree with you,' I said, thinking of how different he looked now. 'Go for it.' And she did. By the next summer they were engaged. By the next year, after I'd gone away thinking not to come back, it was all over between them. When I did return, my thesis still unfinished, she was gone from the scene, her father having threatened Omar. Never come near my daughter again, he had said, and Omar told me: 'I wished and cursed him to have a cancer.' For a long time after she left, Omar kept travelling to her home city in a neighbouring state and driving up and down her street, past her family home. Later he learnt she had joined the navy.

For several weeks at the beginning of that year he would sit and stand about in the lobby and other parts of the building moaning. Once or twice he cried, oblivious of all the people milling past. The Americans and most other Western students thought he was out of his mind. 'What a goofball!' said one young female 'jock' as she passed him going into the elevator. His Arab student friends were more understanding and tried to cheer him, but he would not be cheered.

It started out as sympathy. Then we were going out with a group of student friends. Soon after, he began making snacks in his room for just the two of us, flatbread with *za:'ter* — a fragrant mixture of sesame seeds and a herb like wild thyme — which he sprinkled into a small dish where we pressed our pieces of bread smeared lightly with olive oil. Or he made *hummus*, or *mtebel*, the eggplant dip best known in the West by its Egyptian name, *baba ghanoush*. Then he was cooking us whole meals, using a small primus camp stove, prohibited in student residences. He prepared the meals so carefully and quickly, and got on so well with the students in neighbouring rooms, that the stove was never reported. When we had eaten, he talked to me of his village home.

'... the vine is strong, and old, and beside the vine is the pomegranate. Two very beautiful trees. I know you would love these trees. They are at the side of the house, near the door of the kitchen. The space is small, not like the front where visitors come. And quiet, just for the family, see? And there is very much shade. Ohhh ... it is very good to sit there drinking the tea with mint. Not sitting like you. What is it when you sit on your heels like this? ...'

'Squatting?'

'Yes, squatting, see? ... and drinking the tea from a glass and smoking a cigarette and talking with my mother, or my brother, or my cousins who live next to us. ... Ohhh, it is good ...' And he paused, his mind transported by memory, and mine by his words.

Omar moved imperceptibly between personal recollection, history and poetry. The garden. The house. The village. Each plant, room, street, had its own story, which he knew intimately. These he wove into the grander events of the past, joining them together; a battle lost or won by a caliph, great feats of rulers and warriors, incidents from the Prophet's life.

During hours of pure enchantment I heard of how his sisters made dowali from the leaves of the grapevine;

then — almost within the same breath — of how Salah Ad-Diin and his followers took over the Crusader castles and built even more impressive ones, and about the glorious views from the ramparts of those castles: Karak, Ajlun ...

And there were the poems in Arabic: incantatory gifts plaited with glimpses of their translation.

When a poem came it was not deliberate, but something he slipped into with ease, like the stories; a part of the natural sequence. None of the poems were his own. He loved and admired the classical Arabic poets who glorified and mythologised the Arab past, and who now belonged to that myth and glory. Telling some event from the history he would break off ... 'Ooh! Wait now. There is a hunting poem about this. What was it? Yes, this is it, I think ...' He brought his hand forward, thumb against the up-curved fingers as if about to make an offering of something small and delicate. His hand rose and fell with his voice, lightly punctuating the rhyming accents. Hand and voice followed the steps and strides of the syllables up and up to the middle of a line where some internal rhyme hung in breathless pause, anticipating the descent that would join it to its mate.

Qad aghtadi wa l-laylu fi maswáddihi
Oft I go forth in the early morning when the night is still black

wardun yuráqqi l-tayra fi munquáddihi
a dark bay colour sending the birds flying as it breaks up

Once begun he was in another world, lost in the poem, his own complete absorption drawing me into the circle. There were famous individual lines and couplets that came up as if of their own accord, like that of Antar Ibn Shadaad. The hero speaks of his last memory before his own death in battle, addressing his loved one:

Haqad thakartuki wa alsiiyouf nawaahilou mini
I thought of you as the swords pierced me

wa biyd al hind taqtor min dammi
and the spears dripped with my blood.

The first time Omar touched me fell into its rhyming place among these offerings. Our lovemaking seemed to me an extension of his pouring out of the heart, a sharing of his homesickness, so that he filled me with his own love of country.

Those student rooms were small and bare, with just a bed, a desk, a small wardrobe and a chest of drawers, but his was brightened and transformed by the large cushions on the bed, the plants on the windowsill and the colourful pictures, posters and photos on the walls. From the beginning my eye was constantly drawn to a particular photo of one of his sisters, taken not long before she was married.

Aisha. I found her beautiful, the photo fascinating. She was wearing a long velvet garment in deep, rich blue with intricate gold embroidery down the front and around the hem and cuffs. The ends of a long scarf in a similar-coloured silky material were hung loosely around her neck and behind her shoulders. Its edges about her face were also embroidered in gold, offsetting her eyes lined with *ko<u>h</u>l*. She was standing by a potted palm tree with an elbow up against its trunk, the hand at her temple. The other hand was at her hip in an attitude of confidence and assertiveness matched by her large and generous smile. When I first saw the photo, I thought it had been taken in her home and represented Aisha as she dressed and looked every day. In fact she had gone to a photographer in the city, Omar told me later, and dressed up in one of the studio's Bedouin costumes.

The bookshelves in Omar's room were filled with books on linguistics and literature, especially medieval romances, which he was studying at the time, and collections of poetry. Among the potted plants on the windowsill was a miniature Norfolk pine that Omar tended regularly, talking to it as he turned the earth at its base with an old pencil.

The wall posters were mostly of wild horses and other animals in mountains, forest or desert. He said that he loved rugged natural scenes, loved the wilderness, and we soon began to take long drives together to the lakes, parks and forests around the state.

Omar did not talk often about Heidi, less and less with time, but he described one occasion that made it clear they had been a couple in love, in the fullest romantic sense. He was waiting to catch a bus across the street from the residence centre when he heard her voice in the distance. He had left her in his room on the twelfth floor, and he looked up to see her waving goodbye. Wanting to catch his attention she was leaning out of the window, calling his name with unabashed joy and waving frantically. It was not only Omar who began to look anxious. At the bus stop every head was turned up in amazement at how far out her body was projected, her waist visible well above the window sash. He begged her to go back inside, calling and signing with his own frantic gestures. She did, after that acknowledgement.

I could tell that Omar revered the memory of this incident as a precious moment between them, something inviolate. He described it with a faithfulness that brought to life Heidi's unassailably trusting spirit, the same that I had seen in her. Did it finally leave her, when she left him? But this residue of love was part of what drew me to him. This and his smile, his long fine-boned limbs, his slender fingers, the meaning he seemed to pour into every small thing he did, and the care he showed to his friends.

There was an uncertainty all the same, a tentativeness about those early days when I could not tell how strongly my feelings were reciprocated. But it did not last. Omar's assurances came quickly then, if not directly.

I used to talk in passing with a young Arab woman who lived in the student residence, on my floor. She was very religious and wore the veil all the time. In appearance and manner I suppose she matched the broad Western image of the Arab Muslim woman: submissive and hidden away, floating at the edge of action, with eyes downcast. And yet, if her behaviour was subdued, there was no timidity about her, but a will that moved with her like an aura. She was not tall but she seemed so upstanding. Her downward look could devastate when she chose. Her moral and religious conviction appeared genuine, but not the only cause of her self-assurance. She was studying linguistics and the relationship of language to culture. I remember her once telling me about an assignment she was working on, a study of Western and Middle Eastern understandings of 'honesty'. Her point was that there are no differences. Only those we construct for and about each other. I thought of how dishonesty is one of the first things we accuse others of, when their different ways come under our suspicion.

One day she invited me to take tea with her, and after a while began to talk about Omar. She said he was 'a good man'. A little later she added that he was from a highly respected family and the Prime Minister of Jordan was his 'uncle'.

Was I impressed by this information? Well, yes, though I knew that 'uncle' does not have to refer to the immediate family. As it turned out, the Prime Minister shared a distant ancestor with Omar, who was from a relatively poor and forgotten branch of the family. But I also thought Omar had asked her to talk to me, to put his 'case' forward. I could accept that he did not come to me directly, as I knew well enough by then that this is the way things are done in his part of the world. Delicate matters are handled through an intermediary. I drank the tea and smiled and chatted with her, taking in new things with my ears, with my mind, with my pores.

North to Kufr Soum

Wedding: The Feast

The celebration and dancing has lasted for two whole days, and now this is the day of the wedding itself, the ceremony that finalises. It will begin with feasting here at Shareen's home, and then, in the afternoon, her brother will be married in the small Orthodox church a few streets away. Omar and I have come with a party of official guests in their car. Things look very different by day. People are more subdued, more serious.

We are gathered together in the same room where we had been dancing. All furniture has been removed; there are only hard chairs lining the walls. Even the wall decorations have vanished, including a small, framed picture I had seen hanging over the sofa on my first visit. It was the portrait photograph of a bearded patriarch of the Eastern Orthodox Church. I had asked Omar yesterday if we would be attending the marriage rites. Were we going to the church, and would the couple be exchanging ribboned garlands? (I had seen this once as a child in Sydney, at the wedding of some Greek friends.) 'Is that what they do?' he asked in return. He didn't know, having never attended a Christian wedding. He wasn't even sure if he should go.

Now I am among the women again, chatting quietly as

we wait for the *mensef*. The generations are more mixed than in that little group I sat with two nights ago. We throw heartening glances towards Shareen and the other women of the house as they pass. They are speeding up their movements on the way to and from the kitchen, or wherever the cooking is done today — possibly beyond the back of the house, somewhere outside.

People go from room to room greeting each other. A few dandle babies on their laps or give soft-spoken instructions to a child.

'*La, habiibti, msh al 'aan. B:ad schwaiy.*' (No dear, not now. Wait a while.)

Someone stops at the doorway to say that the men out under the marquee have received their *mensef*. Knowing smiles are exchanged all round, and there are a few bold chuckles from the three corpulent, grey-haired ladies in the far corner. It will be our turn now.

In a while some light, round tables are brought in. We wait until we are invited to bring our chairs around them. A little longer still, and the huge platters of rice and meat appear, just as another and another are carried past us into adjoining rooms. I note with relief that our tray has not been honoured with the sheep's head, which takes pride of place on top of the mound. Nor did I see it on those other trays that went by. Many heads would have gone to the men's tent. I picture the special guests being exhorted, and politely refusing a few times, then finally accepting, to eat the main delicacy — the eyes — which they must be enjoying now.

We are given spoons while extra hot yoghurt broth is ladled from a large pot over the rice that is strewn liberally with almonds and pine nuts. Our platter nearly takes up the entire table, and each of us eats from that part that is most directly in front of her. These other women guests I don't know make sure to look after me well, piling some of the most succulent pieces of slow-cooked mutton, as tender as lamb, on the mound of rice before me. We all eat with relish.

I have tasted *mensef* in our village many times. No tables there. Everyone sits on the floor. The men form a patty of the sticky rice when they scoop it up in one hand, without spilling a grain. I am constantly amazed at the way the long white shirt, or *jalabiyeh*, that many men wear when visiting is as free of food stains at the end of such a meal as when they first sat down to it. Children learn this grace with food at such an early age that it hardly seems a skill at all. Until you try it.

I smile to myself at the thought of the scraps and crumbs I always left after a meal in Kufr Soum. Even breakfast was difficult, especially when I first arrived. I managed the bread and the olives well enough, and the egg and the *za:'ter*, but not the yogurt. I didn't really learn how not to spill the yoghurt until the breakfast when Omar's father joined us for the first time.

Bilaal and Randa, Omar's teenage brother and sister, had been showing me how to dip my bread in the *laban*, the thin, liquid yoghurt that I now prefer in the mornings. I tried to use the flat bread in the same way, and we laughed together as I spilled a few drops. Omar's father, Haatem, or Abu Omar as everyone calls him, had just entered the room and sat down. He tore off a piece of the round flat bread and gave a brief murmur and a broad smile. He gestured to me to watch as he bent the bread into a scoop shape for dipping. Without pressing he repeated this action in the following days, and I imitated. At first I repeated the gestures with a Visigothic impatience in the belief that I could learn to eat with my fingers in one or two tries. When it did not come so easily,

I began to concentrate on my movements and, after some weeks, it was not so much the grace of the movements that came more naturally, but the very care and attention.

Thinking of Abu Omar I am struck by another recollection. As Omar's fiancée, I had made my 'entry' into the village of Kufr Soum several days earlier, greeted by the family and a host of curious relatives, friends and neighbours. But on the day of my arrival, Omar's father was not there.

The Wadi Mujib
— and Setting Out

Jordan.

From south to north the land changes shape. From the hard, flat deserts and the high central plateau it turns into a succession of ever-steeper hills until you reach the snow-capped mountains of Syria and Lebanon. In Jordan they are still only hills, and between them run deep valleys or wadies, the imprint of primeval rivers long disappeared. Carved with these oblong craters, the land appears crevassed and desolate in spite of its vegetation. If you saw it from a plane, you would find none of those softly rippling folds that we expect of 'hills', but only a moonscape below you.

With no easy sloping in and out of these wadies, where the wilderness still commands, where men go hunting and jackals, or sometimes a hyena, can be heard at night, the sparse villages are built at the tops of the hills. Their outlying houses overlook precipices whose depths range from a few feet to a few hundred. The earth drops suddenly away, and you can look across from one side to another as across a vast crack produced by an earthquake.

But the wadies of these northern hills are thought to be

gentle, and 'as nothing' compared with the great wadies of the south.

It was early summer when I came to this country for my first six-week visit. I found Amman airport intimidating. Its personnel were almost all in soldiers' uniforms, and their manner appeared stiff and disdainfully polite.

'Your tourist visa is for two months. After one month you must report to a police station.'

I felt cold, although it was the first week in June. It was barely daylight and only a small knot of people waited to greet the travellers, Omar among them. I wanted to hug him, but there had been a last telephone call from him before I left the States, and with it a reminder.

'When you get off the plane, do not expect to hug and kiss. It is not accepted here. Do not be disappointed. I tell you this now so you will know that nothing is wrong. But dear, you know how it is here. No one can change these things. Oohh, I will be very happy to see you. I cannot wait.'

He did look quietly, deeply happy. Relieved too, to find me there ready and willing to make my life with him.

His colleague, Haroun, was waiting for us in a big old Mercedes. From the airport we drove south towards Karak, and to Mu'tah University. But we took the longer route, especially to show me the Wadi Mujib.

In the late afternoon we seemed to come upon it suddenly. The road descended and climbed more and more steeply, winding all the while around a rock face. We stopped at a lookout.

There was not a blade of grass nor a sign of anything that grows, but only a wall of solid rock facing us, like the one our road had been carved out of. It rose straight up before us, its sheerness more giddying than cliffs at sea. Nothing to watch below.

The rock was a pale blend of pink and ochre. Even the short iron railing, only sign of human intervention, had been painted with care to match it exactly, so that the same colour met you wherever you looked. The depthless monochrome was relieved only by the blue of the sky, which grew deeper and richer with the growing dusk. The sun's last rays of mingled pink and gold were reflected off the hard granite in a uniform and deceptively soft glow. On this backdrop of two unvariegated tones the full pearl of the moon seemed more stark than bright. Now the contrast was dramatic, grandiose. The wadi appeared larger than life, yet silent and still. I was not surprised to be told that over the years many vehicles had skidded on the narrow winding road and careened off the edge. None of their passengers had lived. Only a week earlier a bus full of schoolchildren and their teachers had plunged to the bottom not far from where we were, with all lives lost. They came, Omar told me, from the nearby village of Dhi'ban. 'It means *Two Wolves,*' he said as he indicated the direction of the town.

Repetition of rock. Sameness. I sensed myself floating, as in a void, then hurtling, diminishing away from myself. I turned back towards the men and the car, glad of their nearness and the road under my feet.

And already Omar and Haroun were telling me how very different are the hills and wadies of the north, with their dark, fertile soil, their trees and shrubs, crops and orchards, and their bustling life. Only the Jordan Valley was better than his region, Omar said. The northern parts where he was from were 'the fruitful, the flowing, the generous'.

Mu'tah University, about halfway between Amman and Aqaba, was physically unlike any other university I had seen. It had been established first and foremost as a military college, and still resembled soldiers' barracks and training grounds. It was also isolated. The surrounds consisted of flat desert, with the nearest large town, Karak, several kilometres away. Then, too, the campus was enclosed by a high wall topped with barbed wire. Approaching the entrance, we had to stop and identify ourselves to the sentry at the guardbox. Even within, wire fences separated the different sections. Although it was divided into a military and a civil wing, I soon discovered that there was no part where you could not hear the shouts of soldiers at training.

There were hardly any trees about. This was the third university to be established in Jordan after Amman and Yarmouk, and it was comparatively new. Most of the buildings were recent, and others were still being constructed. Rock, concrete, dust and rubble dominated. I was grateful for the pretty lavender garden at the front of the low apartment buildings where Omar lived. Several different kinds and shades of lavender grew to various heights. They were spread over a wide area, and through them, as through a maze, narrow paths of tiles and paving stones led to the raised front patio of each residence. These we followed to Omar's front door after Haroun drove off to his own apartment in another part of the campus.

Once inside, we turned to each other, together at last after months of separation. Omar was all gladness, and looking into the fine-structured face I knew and loved, I felt once again the warmth of the smile that his whole being took part in. I believed I was looking into the future, where we would create our own small haven, gentle and balming like the sweet scents and pastel colours of the lavender garden. That was the way I saw our life together. But only two days later, Haroun was driving north and offered to take us. Two days. And a world. The rest of that first visit would be spent at Omar's family home. We would not find ourselves alone together again for a long time.

Unlike the Wadi Mujib, the deserts we crossed to reach the northern hills presented no contrasting colours. Mocking the exotic picture-postcard deserts of yellow dunes against a blue sky, they spread hard and flat on all sides of us, a pale neutral grey like the paleness of the midday sky. Land and sky would have seemed completely melded but for a faint line of mountains so distant that the horizon resembled the low peaks and points of Arabic writing.

Every so often I saw the black tents of the Bedou at some distance from the road, or a flock of sheep with one or two shepherds. Travelling north we skirted the major cities, including Amman. We drove most of the day, and after descending the central plateau we began again to climb. As we approached Jerash, site of the old Roman city, Omar and Haroun became eager to point out the new vegetation, and our new altitude. We were in the mountains now, they proudly repeated, where everything that grows is taller, thicker, greener: 'See the trees!'

On one side of us the land sloped up from the road, so that I could easily see the rocks, stones and low bushes scattered here and there in the dry grass. Every so often there went by two or three small and scraggly pines huddled together as if lost, none of them standing much higher than a tall man. Almost anywhere had to be greener than the deserts we had passed through. But this was not the green of the American university town, for one, where we had met, with its campus of beautiful woods and the great national or state forests nearby. And it was not the green of that pretty region of France where I had stayed with my father's family. As for mountains, I had been to North Carolina, taken many trips into the Smokies and along the gorgeous Blueridge Parkway. So now in the car I turned from the scenes we were passing to the faces of Omar and Haroun, hoping their expressions, if not their voices, might offer a hint of irony. They were both gazing intently, Haroun at the road, Omar at the landscape.

As if in contradiction, I felt glad with a vague sense of the familiar, of being closer to something I had been missing. The reason did not come to me immediately, only a floating nostalgic attachment that I could not have explained. At the time I laughed inwardly at the two men's boyish excitement in showing me their 'lush' land. It was much later that the size of the vegetation and its parched and scattered look brought to mind the Australian bush that I had not seen for many years. The early fondness my sister and I had developed for its dry timber and scrub country meant that I would have those recollections to draw upon.

Omar, like me, had loved the American forests, but knew how to read his country in its own terms. I might come to do the same after a while. My first impression, though, was of a skeletal world, leached of colour.

We passed the occasional cypress or other conifer sporting a bolder green. And we drove through towns where the walls of houses spilled over with the deep pinks and purples of the non-native but much loved bougainvillea, called popularly in Arabic *majnouneh* (crazy one). It drew the eye away from the hypnotic sameness of rock and road and masonry. Later, in the wadi, I would learn to tell the course of small streams, temporarily run dry, by following the direction of the wild, pink-flowering oleander shrubs. But at that point, with so many years spent in the temperate northern hemisphere, I was yearning for deep, cool green. It is the colour of the Afterlife, according to the *Qur'aan*, of Paradise with its smooth and sloping lawns and shady trees beside fresh-flowing streams. It is also the colour of the couches on which recline the beautiful *hoori*, spirit women waiting to greet the believers. And it is the colour of their eyes. A green that the country I saw seemed constantly to thirst for, even in winter. As for summer, a dry wind blowing from the eastern deserts left the landscape at some remove from the real world, behind a dusty screen. If I could only wipe my hands across that space before my eyes the luminosity of living green might reveal itself.

There is one tree whose slim and delicate leaves retain their sheen, although it does not grow tall or give a lot of shade. The pomegranate is little known to Westerners except through Greek mythology. In Jordan the groups of villages that lie towards the northern borders — Al-Rafiid, Kufr Soum, Youbla, Saham — are famous for their pomegranates, which can grow as big as large grapefruit. It is not unusual to find one or two such trees by the wall of the meanest house. Most homes have three or four in their gardens at different stages of growth, together with several olive trees. Outside the villages, and even in parts of the wadi, pomegranate orchards alternate with olive groves.

When I first came to Omar's home, its garden had two fully-grown pomegranates, a younger one and a sapling. The bell-shaped, orange-coloured blossoms were already swelling at the base and giving way to round, tight green knobs that by the end of the summer would attain the size of fat apples with a thick, buff-coloured skin as tough as a shell. A smooth and shiny skin, just beginning to blush.

Arrival

It was under the mingled dim and bright green of the olive and the pomegranate, side by side in the small courtyard, that Omar's mother was standing when our big car, dusty from the journey, pulled up by a low rock wall separating the house from the street. I had been nervous about meeting his mother. Omar kept reassuring me that I would love his family, but I knew that the beginning, at least, would be difficult, if only because I would be surrounded by so many strangers. And I was nagged by the thought that his mother was the one who mattered most, the one I would have to get along with and might find impossible to please. I moved towards the house with Omar, followed by scores of eyes as several groups of children, who had turned up from all over the village it seemed, stood gazing intently from the street.

I heard Omar's quietly spoken words, meant just for me: 'She is there, see. My mother is there.'

At first I saw no one. Was I looking about for one of those hefty matrons whose strong voice would let me know that she was fully in her own element, on her own ground? Or at least for someone whose person would command the space around her that her body might not fill? Or was it the sprinkled light and shade of the trees that caused me to miss her standing there? Only when our little group moved closer did I become aware that the dark, brittle stick figure was a person, a small woman in a long black velveteen *shrsh* that seemed too heavy for her thin frame to hold up. And still I was unsure, until Omar, after speaking to her briefly, told me, 'This is my mother.' In that first embrace I felt overwhelmed by her frailty, not wanting to press too hard against her cheek or cause her to lose balance. I had few words to offer, my Arabic was nil. And so I put all into my smile, and it was not in response, but simultaneously, that her own smile gathered quickly in warmth of feeling what she could not muster in physical strength.

The greetings and questions to her son came tremulously, none of them longer than she had single breath for, and hovering in pitch so that she sounded elderly, although she was not old at all, as I later discovered, certainly not past her fifties. Her fine-structured face, surrounded by the :*assaaba*, was sunken and pinched, her hands thin and bony, and the *shrsh* fairly hung on her small shoulders, weighing her down. Yet she stood very straight, and seemed to regain in this, and in the colourful scarf that a hidden comb brought to a point at the top of her head, something of the height and presence that must have been wrung from her by illness.

As we moved towards the entrance of the house I recognised Omar's third sister, Aisha, from the photo I had seen in his room in the States. She was dressed differently now in her everyday wear — a *dish-dásha* — with a small headscarf tied tightly at the back of her neck. She had a baby in her arms, and she looked heftier. It was her smile I knew instantly, the same broad smile as in the photo, flashing at me as I approached the doorway where she stood. Her rapid and voluble questions to Omar,

75

delivered in a deep but high-spirited tone, were interspersed with the word 'Welcome!' addressed to me in a strong accent and repeated many times.

From the short entrance passage I was immediately ushered into the front room where family and neighbours were already pouring in behind us to see the new arrival. The walls had clearly been freshly painted a pale cream colour — there was even a lingering smell of paint — and a pretty oriental rug, larger than a prayer rug, was hanging on one of them. Two of the other walls had large windows, one looking onto the front garden, the other onto the side courtyard.

There was no furniture of any kind. Omar would obtain a large wardrobe from the city the very next day, and set it up against the windowless inner wall. But on my arrival the room was completely bare except for a big oriental carpet on the tiled floor and some shallow mattresses around the edges. The women were bringing in more of these as I entered, until all the walls were lined with them.

In this room Omar now introduced me to Sahr, who was unmarried and lived at home looking after their mother. She had been indoors when I came and was wearing no head covering, so that I could see the thick waves of her black hair even though it was neatly drawn back from her lovely high-boned cheeks. She was wearing a bright blue *dish-dásha* with a big flower embroidered in a paler blue down the front. From the way Omar spoke to her, evidently asking as many questions as he was answering, I could tell that Sahr, as oldest sister, was in charge of the house. Her manner was not as high-spirited as Aisha's, but more composed. Her smile, too, was quieter, though her eyes were full of expression as she welcomed me in Arabic. As they exchanged news, she moved her head slightly back and forth, serious and attentive when he spoke to her, smiling and approving when she directed her gaze at me. A couple of times I heard her say '*hilwi*' (pretty), a word that was repeated by some of the other women gathering around us.

Becoming aware of the presence of a young man close by, I looked up at him with a smile which he instantly returned. As we were introduced, I detected in his greeting the more passive and deferent manner of the younger brother. Bilaal was nineteen years old, and struck me as gentle and good-natured, an initial impression that was to remain.

'But where is Randa?' I asked. I had learnt the names of family members before beginning the trip, and I knew that Omar's brother Saleh, the second son, was away, but that Randa, the youngest member of the family, was living at home. At seventeen she would soon be in her final year of high school, and according to Omar, of all his brothers and sisters Randa spoke the best English. 'She is coming,' said Omar. 'She was out visiting. The neighbours have gone to tell her we are here.' As he spoke I realised that a little boy with curly brown hair was looking up at him and asking the same question over and over, each time louder and more insistent. Omar answered quickly, then with a murmur of fuller recognition he turned the child towards me.

'Nasser. This is Nasser, Michèle. Do you know which one he is?'

I thought quickly through my list of parents' and children's names.

'Na:aameh's son?'

'Yes, right.'

Omar smiled at me. Then he turned to Nasser, '*Weyn omak?*' (Where's your mother?)

A ripple of exclamations and laughter accompanied a pretty woman with a full face and equally well-rounded figure into the centre of our group. It was Na:aameh, Omar's second sister and mother of the boy. She had come from her own house a few streets away as soon as word reached her of our arrival, and had been standing back among the wider circle of people patiently waiting to welcome us. She tried good-humouredly to say a few words in English, then apologised for not speaking it well. She managed to convey to me that she had studied it in school, but that since she had been married there were no opportunities to practise. Then she introduced me to her four-year-old daughter, Manar, who gazed at me with big eyes.

The room was now full of excited people all asking questions or waiting their turn to greet me. I had met four of Omar's six brothers and sisters, but the mixture of relatives and neighbours who now gathered round were mostly older women I did not know. They were dressed in black, some with the men's red-and-white-checked *kefiiyeh* wound about their heads. A few had tattoos of tiny blue-green dots or other more intricate patterns on their weathered cheeks or chins.

One of these matrons invited me to sit at the far end of the room, on the middle mattress along the wall. She gave me four plump cushions like thick pillows, two for my back and two for my elbow. At first I kept jumping up from this position to greet more people, until some of the women who had sat down beside me pressed me on the arms and nodded their heads in ways that translated their Arabic assurances that I could remain seated.

At this point our luggage was brought in, and as the gifts were handed out, everyone around us commented on them, appraising their worth, upon which my own would at least in part be judged. Omar had already asked me during the drive from the airport whether I had brought the wine, the book, the flower seeds, the film for his camera, the shoes for his mother. Having managed to obtain only two of these items, I had registered his disappointment. This was the custom. Every visitor, as well as every local person coming home from a journey, must be laden with gifts for as many family members as possible.

Sitting among them I felt myself judged in two different ways simultaneously, one material and the other moral. The gift giving seemed to be the occasion for evaluating my practical worth, but my manner and behaviour also came under the scrutiny of these older women, who nonetheless treated me with special respect as a visitor and as the oldest son's wife-to-be.

Their skill was in putting me at ease while they took my measure. I was made to feel welcome, even important, like a foreign queen holding court with them. They encouraged me to lean back regally, resting among the cushions on one arm, passing out gifts with the other, surrounded by spectators. Or I looked on from this pillowy dais as Omar, squatting beside the cases, handed out the gifts with further greetings, all of which brought thanks and praise. Now I understood fully, and in a new way, the greeting that was used so often. *Áhlen wa sáhlen.* For me the expression would come to identify and represent Arab culture. Nor was the day done. It was still only midafternoon, and the rituals of welcome were far from over.

There was a small commotion at the front door, and the group opened up again to reveal a girl in her late teens flushed with excitement. The contrast with all the other women stood out immediately. She wore jeans. A long white T-shirt hanging past the hips was imprinted with the face of a chic young woman wearing sunglasses and a coquettishly loose scarf. But the teenager herself had already removed whatever head covering she had been wearing over her single long plait.

'Randa!' I said as soon as I saw her, and she beamed. Then she drew in her breath for a moment and, with a voice full of animation, announced in accented but very clear English: 'Michèle! I am verrry happy to see you!' Omar was called out to other visitors, and we began to chat, the little circle of people nearest us staring and listening hard, asking Randa what we were saying, and obviously pleased to see how well we were communicating. Randa had brought her next-door cousin in with her, and now introduced us. Temaam was roughly the same age as Randa, and although they were both slim, Temaam was thinner, with fine, sharp features. She was wearing a more traditional *dish-dásha*, but the next day I noticed that Temaam was dressed in the Western teenage style with jeans and a T-shirt, and it was Randa who wore a black *dish-dásha* with white and silver embroidery.

After the gift giving there was a stir in the passageway and the women seated around me were getting up. Sahr said to me, 'Mishaal, come.' Randa added, 'Michèle, now there are many people. Come with us.' I was led into another room further inside and not quite as large as the first. It was so crowded that for a while we were pressed up against each other. Somehow space was finally made for everyone on the mattresses that were being spread about as we entered. Everything appeared suddenly less formal, more relaxed. There was much more talk and laughter and there were many children about. Here I was introduced to at least as many people again. Aisha, who had followed us in still holding her baby girl, let go with

80

one hand for a moment to take the arm of a large, stalwart-looking woman standing sternly in front of me. 'Mishaal,' Aisha said nodding at her, 'Umm Mohammed. Sisterr fatherr Omarr.'

I did a quick backwards calculation. Ah! Omar's father's sister. I had no sooner given the greeting, *'Marhabah'* than Na:aameh came up from the other side of the room with a chuckle and yet another hefty woman in tow.

'Again, again. Sisterr fatherr Omarr. Umm Mahmoud. Sisterr two. *La.* Sisterr second.'

The introductions continued in this fashion for another giddying ten minutes or so. Not until I had met everyone and we were all settled down drinking tea, the sipping from the glasses around me accompanied by audible intakes of breath, did I realise that there were only women and children with us.

'Where is Omar?'

It was Randa who answered me.

'Omar is with the men. They are in another room.'

I had no time to react or respond, because at this point the fun and mischief really began. Randa took my arm with affection and a teasing look.

'Michèle, who is this?'

She pointed to the little girl I had met earlier, and who had sidled up to me on the mattress, staring shyly before giving in to the temptation to stroke my hair.

'Manar.'

I exchanged a smile with Manar's mother, Na:ameh, who then pointed to the lusty-looking baby in her arms.

'Wa mann hatha, Mishaal?' (And who is this, Michèle?)

'Your son, but you'll have to remind me of his name.'

Aisha asked, 'Name? *Shou* name? Ah! Name. *Ism.'*

And several voices answered at once, *'Ism Mu'áwiya.'*

81

Then the game became earnest. The question *'Mann?'* was put to me several times while everyone clamoured for their turn to ask me about someone else. My answers brought exclamations of delight. But soon I began to flag, becoming hesitant, and when I gave up they repeated the name and the relationship. Still, in spite of my 'misses', the women seemed suitably impressed, that first afternoon.

In the evening Sahr and Randa threw buckets of water over the concrete terrace, and after drying it with great sweeps of a long-handled rubber wiper, they laid mattresses along the front wall of the house. There we all sat, facing the garden with its large lemon tree and two olive trees. Nearer to us, at the edge of the terrace, was spread a wide patch of abundant mint whose leaves Randa picked for the evening pot of tea.

It was there that Omar's mother was able to join us again and take part in the conversation. Rihaab had not participated much after our first meeting, but she had been present. I had caught glimpses of her now and again at the edges of the rooms, never staying where the press of visitors was tightest. She suffered from a heart disease, and had been to the hospital frequently over the preceding months, though her health had been ailing for twenty-five years. She had refused an operation at an earlier stage, and now it was too late to help her surgically. Food, or the act of ingesting, caused her terrible pain, which she suffered at a lower level of intensity practically all the time. I cannot say if she was genuinely feeling better than usual that night or was making a valiant effort for my sake, but once most of the guests had gone she seemed to enjoy having her family gathered about her.

Over time I learnt that it was more respectful to address the older people as 'Mother of' or 'Father of', followed by the name of the oldest son. Although I always addressed Omar's father, Haatem, as Abu Omar, by the time the difference was explained to me we had all got used to my addressing Rihaab by her own name instead of Umm Omar, and she never seemed to mind.

In the course of that first evening's conversation I heard the word '*mustáshfa*' many times, and wondered what it meant.

Before we went to bed, my head reeling with new names and faces, Omar told me that the room we were in, the same where I had 'received' the family and neighbours earlier that day, was a later extension to the original house.

'… this one and also the room on the other side of the entrance are added.'

'It's lovely, and it's been freshly painted too, hasn't it?'

'Yes, I helped with this painting at the weekends when I came home from Mu'tah. But my father did most of this work in the week, to prepare this room for you. He is more than sixty years old, and I told him not to do this. I told him to wait until I came, but he would not listen.'

'I have yet to meet your father. I thought he would be here today.'

Omar called to the gathering outside, and in the exchange that followed I heard the word '*mustáshfa*' come up again, one of the first Arabic words I learnt in the village. I asked him what it meant.

'Hospital.' He paused. 'I also, I thought he would be here. But he is in hospital in Irbid. It is usually my mother who goes to hospital, but this time it was my father. He had a heart attack two days ago.'

Thread of Being

Irbid, one of the oldest living cities in Jordan, is sixteen kilometres from Kufr Soum. Several times a day three small buses wind through the narrow streets of our village, picking up people outside their very houses. Then they set off on the real journey, passing through other villages and several outer city districts, before arriving at one of the big Irbid bus stations.

I did not see much of the city on my first trip there, which was entirely taken up with our visit to the hospital. Even then, from the windows of the bus and the taxi that tooted their way through busy streets backed by busier souks, Irbid struck me as little more than an overgrown village. At the hospital we waited for a long time outside the building whose doors remained closed to visitors. A throng of people who appeared to come from other small towns and villages in the region (you could tell from the black embroidered dresses and the peaked or turbaned head coverings of the older women), stood or sat on the front steps and paced the small courtyard. I thought they must not have understood there were set visiting times, or like us they had come only when the buses could bring them.

They questioned and cajoled all those who looked like

members of the medical staff coming in and out of the building. I was no less amazed at the patience of those responding than at the persistence of the questioners. Even Sahr kept waylaying and pestering. But Omar himself, having made some initial enquiries, moved away from the crowd towards a low stone wall against which he alternately leaned and squatted, resigned to waiting. He did not try to hold back Sahr. Perhaps he knew that she was becoming anxious for the sake of their mother, for Rihaab had come with us, though I did not realise how unusual this was. But then none of us who formed the little knot by the wall, Na:aameh included, could know that Rihaab would be making no more trips into the city except to be taken many times herself to hospital. Now Rihaab leaned against the wall, letting out a soft moan and a few words of complaint, and then falling silent again. Na:aameh, too, waited quietly with us. She had been a nurse before she was married, and was probably aware of the futility of Sahr's constant comings and goings.

The doors still did not open, and as there was nowhere to rest and the long wait had become too tiring for Rihaab, Sahr took her home. The rest of us waited nearly an hour longer. The building itself was old and badly in need of maintenance work, its outer walls chipped and worn. As we finally mounted a flight of stairs and negotiated a few dark corridors, all in a state of disrepair, I thought to myself that I would not like to fall ill in this city and have to be brought here. But when we entered the room where Omar's father was located I found it surprisingly light, with clean linen on its four beds and a much brighter aspect.

Abu Omar was propped up and still surrounded by doctors and medical attendants who, when they saw us, left us with him. Now he became aware of my presence and greeted me with more energy than I would have expected from an ill person, the formality of the words *'Áhlen wa sáhlen'* offset by the warmth of his smile. Unlike Omar's mother, Abu Omar was one of those in whom illness did not show readily. His physique appeared strong, and although he was balding, he had taken care to rejuvenate himself with darkened hair and moustache. The lines of age were further repelled by his fullness of face, which I thought I recognised in Na:aameh as she stood there at his bedside, and by an expression of restrained joviality which she also seemed to share.

After another week Abu Omar came home, and for several days the house was once again filled with people, this time come to pay their respects and congratulate him on his recovery.

'This is what is bad among the Arabs,' Omar told me in the midst of all the visiting. 'A man is ill and goes to hospital only to be made sick again when he returns home because he must greet this unending stream of visitors for many days. What to do? These are the customs. You cannot change it.'

He often spoke to me like that, prefacing some critical statement with the words 'this is bad ...' or 'this is what is wrong ...' But in the case of other customs, the ones he condoned or accepted, his attachment ran deep and was never spoken. It was as if he knew I would be drawn to them intuitively, as if my being with him in the village, in good faith, was enough to start me on the path of a similar attachment.

And so began the weighing of my one hand with belonging, to counterbalance any load of isolation or aversion that might accrue in the other.

Abu Omar did not die of all the attention that summer. He seemed to enjoy it.

It was just the opposite for poor Rihaab. When she was ill, too many visitors exhausted her, and when she was in pain she would retreat increasingly into herself, sitting in a corner of some room moaning quietly over and over. Seeing Omar's mother like this, I often felt embarrassed to be young with a healthy body. It took me some time to get used to this situation and to learn to live with the abiding sense of helplessness. She wanted no one too close to her in the worst moments, but it was just as necessary to know that her daughters, especially Sahr, were there to do for her whatever was needed. If she became insistent with them, which happened rarely for someone in her condition, I thought I saw in this an effort to keep at bay the creeping 'immunity' of those around her, as if she sensed that the years and years of her growing incapacitation and helplessness might lead them to an ultimate forgetfulness of her presence.

I was convinced this had already begun to happen to its men. It was not that they did not care, but living among them I had a sense of their not knowing how to use their energies in a situation they could not change. In fact Omar himself, when faced with the crises in Rihaab's illness, would sometimes berate her for them, even becoming angry.

'There should be no hospitals,' he once told me as he was only just beginning to calm down after one of her bouts when she had been rushed off to the hospital in a neighbour's car. 'The sick should be shot, all together at once!' And he made a gesture half of frustration and half of discarding rubbish. She responded to these tirades, and so did her daughters, by saying very little, just letting them pass. It seemed they knew his reaction welled up from his own helplessness, otherwise why did he still, unbid, bring home her favourite fruits from the markets in Irbid and go out of his way to obtain anything she wished? Years earlier they had wanted to do whatever was needed to make her better, as Omar's brother, Saleh, later explained to me, but now it was out of their hands.

I imagined the father and sons in their need to fight down, overcome the situation, to act *upon* it, as in battle. Unable to have the decisive impact that as men they were most used to, each had chosen his own way around this defeat. Omar hated hospitals and to be around the sick, repeating often that the best cure was to kill the lot of them. Abu Omar had long ago wiped his hands of it, resigning himself to the role of responsible head of the household without compensation. There was little love lost between the couple, they had married so young. He had worked most of his life as a policeman and now received a meagre government pension, but she had been a village girl with no education, and could not read or write. She was simple, Omar told me, not stupid, no, but simple. He repeated to me what she had said to him once when he was a boy, during a long dry summer: 'If only we had rain, son. Water is so precious. Do you know, I believe that if there were no water on earth nothing would live?' With the years Omar's parents had less and less to do with each other, though they lived in the same house. The rift was only aggravated by Rihaab's long illness.

When Saleh returned from the Gulf I found his manner towards his mother not much different from Omar's. He was married and lived in his own house a few streets away, and he visited nearly every day, but both he and the younger Bilaal seemed to me to be as much at a loss as Omar around their mother's suffering. They often behaved as if she were not there at all, whereas the daughters were always doing, if only small things in the way of momentary alleviation and comfort.

Early Days — and a Tent

I soon found that the press of people around Abu Omar on his return from hospital was only a stronger form of everyday communal closeness. Space, it seemed, exists only as something to be shared. For me, this closeness became at once the most endearing and the most difficult aspect of village life. A tangle of joy and torment. I fell into dilemma, loving and admiring it one moment, loathing it the next, all the while knowing that without it, more than anything else that distinguished them for me, these people would not be who they are.

Except when dressing, or in the outhouse, or the little bathroom off from the kitchen, I was surrounded by people. Even in these places, if I spent too long I soon heard my name called. From the moment of waking until I went to bed — no, to sleep, because sometimes several of us slept in the same room — I could not be alone. On the few days when I tried to write letters home or make an entry in my diary, sometimes closing the door in an attempt to ensure privacy, I was constantly interrupted. Only Omar understood this need and let me be, keeping everyone away, and at these times I was lucky to have a whole hour to myself. But once he began his summer teaching at Mu'tah, Omar himself was away most of the week. He came home for two or three days, arriving on Thursday (like a Saturday in Western countries) or, if he could, on Wednesday evening, and usually leaving again around noon on Friday.

It might have been from a well-meaning desire to keep me distracted that when Omar was not there the family made sure I had people around me. Neighbours and relatives were always visiting and it would have been impolite for them not to stop and engage me in conversation. I soon recognised that I had always carried with me a sense of owning the space immediately surrounding my person. It moved with me as an intimate possession, like clothes or jewellery. In those early days in the village it fast evaporated. My understanding of walls and doors, and of the width and breadth of places inside and out, became mixed and confused. I sensed that aloneness was discouraged, perceived as an aberration by the more traditional villagers, like an illness, or a shameful luxury. A number of times when I had retired to my room, one of those turbaned older women entered soon afterwards and asked: '*Enti mariiḏa? Mariiḏa? ta:abaana?*' Was I not well? Or was I tired? Or she would unreel a longer string of Arabic questions in which I was completely lost.

Once when I had shut myself in and was absorbed in writing, the door was thrown open without knocking and there stood before me the wife of a man known in the village for his religious observance, one of those men who attended the mosque every Friday. He also refused at all times to shake hands with women for reasons of impurity. There weren't many like him in the village, but a few. The woman was in black with her face surrounded by a wimple such as Rihaab often wore. She asked me if I had come into the room to pray. She knew I was not a Muslim,

91

and I wondered from the tone of the question if she thought I ought to be. I said no, and she gave me to understand that she had come here to pray herself, the rest of the house being full of visitors. I listened and recognised the strains of conversation in other rooms.

I got up to leave, but she turned to Mecca simultaneously, so that I became an obstacle in direct line between her and God. With one arm she majestically waved me aside. Going to join the family and guests I reminded myself that after all, this room was not mine, although it was where I kept all my belongings, and I practically lived here. Still, I marvelled at the imperiousness with which she had swept into the room, and swept me out.

Then there were the others, kinder, who simply could not understand that something as strange and frightening as being alone could be desirable to anyone. And why did I spend so long writing, they seemed to wonder, when everyone knows that living comes first in any sane person? They clicked their tongues in pity to see me in this state. Wholeheartedly commiserating, they tried to make me laugh, stay with them, come out of that room — sad little space in which I was the only being.

At these times I remembered Diyaa, a student from upper Egypt, who had lived on the same floor as Omar at the university in the States. He used to tell us without the least hint of embarrassment that he could not sleep at night because he did not like being alone in the dark. Hardly any of us, even the international students, understood him. He was not a young student; he had left a wife and children behind to come and obtain an advanced degree in his field of study. We saw him as a man from a male-dominated culture, 'macho' in the fullest sense. How could such a person react in that way? And, furthermore, admit it? More strange to us, his countrymen did not seem to have any difficulty with this. They stayed up with him, all equally loathe to go and lock themselves in for the night in those little rooms with their bed and desk. No need to rush into the moment of turning that key, if it could be put off. Those were the moments when they felt homesick, as I did now, stifled, almost gasping for breath among these voluminous women.

At other times it was the children who constantly came in asking me questions I only half understood and wanting to chatter and play. I gave in to them as often as not. Charming little Amira, Saleh's daughter, not yet two years old, already showed a strong will and boundless energy. She had no shyness and could win the adults over to whatever she wanted. She was certainly Omar's favourite niece and he spoilt her as much as her parents did. Everyone was amused whenever she approached one of us with her hand out demanding a '*shling*'. This was a relic word from the days when Trans-Jordan was a British mandate, and it referred to a coin of fifty fils, since there are twenty in a dinar. She wanted it to buy an ice-cream at the local shop. The first time I saw her holding out her hand like this I was surprised at the way Omar encouraged her, nodding and turning her towards someone as he said in Arabic, 'Go on, ask Baba for a *shling*.'

He laughed and sent her with a prod in the direction of the person named.

'Ask Uncle Aziz. That's right. Now ask Michèle. Yes, go on, go on.'

She looked hesitantly up at him and around at the

expectant group, a smile growing on her face, then chose her moment and ran to the person, her great wide eyes holding theirs as she repeated her request, hand upturned and waiting: 'Shling? Shling?' When the shling was produced she turned to us all, holding it up with glee, reflecting the delight and approbation of everyone around her. Although this scene was repeated many times, Amira was rarely as interested in the ice-cream or wafer that her shling could buy as in the effect produced in others by her success in obtaining the coin.

I can imagine children back in the days of the British mandate asking the soldiers or other 'personnel' for a shilling, and I see Omar as a boy doing the same with tourists in Jerusalem where he grew up while his father was stationed there. I don't know if that is what he did, but I do know, or so he told me, that he was the leader of a gang of Arab boys who fought and played in the city streets and threw rival Arab gang members — and once a Jewish boy — into the sewers.

Na:aameh's daughter, four-year-old Manar, was a much quieter child than Amira. She had taken a liking to me from the beginning and loved to be close to me. She was especially fascinated by my fine straight hair, unusual enough in this village to make people stare and talk about it. Not content with looking, Manar would play with my hair whenever I visited Na:aameh, bringing brushes, combs and pins to experiment with. I think she would have been content to fiddle with it for hours on end if permitted, but her mother, always considerate and praising my patience, intervened, and Manar stopped as soon as she was told, displaying no resentment. She then contented herself with talking to me.

Na:aameh brought up her children, including the boys, to be helpful and observant, bringing to visitors, unasked, whatever they were capable of carrying. Sometimes Manar tried to pass around to guests a full tray of tea too heavy for her. Then she spilt it and was scolded. But she bore no grudges and would be in just as good spirits within moments.

Although Manar was the oldest child in the new generation, Omar affected hardly to notice her, often lavishing affection on Amira in front of her. When I mentioned this to him he explained that Manar was his sister's daughter and therefore not of the family.

'She belongs to her father's people, but Amira is from us.'

While this explanation partly accounted for his behaviour towards the two girls, I also wondered if he valued Amira's wily intelligence and natural temerity over Manar's more gentle and conforming spirit. Yet this in no way affected his relationship with his sister whom he frequently praised for her own gentle nature and her patience and good humour. Nor did the apparent favouritism have any detrimental effect on the girls' relations with each other. In fact, as time went by they became very close, as if making up for the imbalance of attention and neglect by seeking out each other's company. I was reminded of the closeness between Randa and her cousin Temaam, Uncle Ahmed's daughter, who lived next door, and who had come in with Randa when we greeted each other the first day.

Like many cousins, Randa and Temaam were best of friends and confidants. They wore each other's clothes and jewellery, went everywhere together, holding hands and talking excitedly. In the house I saw them frequently clutch each other's arms during conversation, laughing and giggling. Their effusiveness was contagious and made the whole house feel young and full of life, except when Omar or Abu Omar returned home to find the radio-cassette playing. Omar did not insist like his father that it be turned off. Invariably he performed this act himself, without a word. And without a word of protest everyone quietly resumed their business. Temaam would suddenly not be there any more, and Sahr would be giving quiet orders to Randa to make tea while she herself finished washing the floor. As for me, I would find myself sitting with whatever women happened to be there, perhaps helping them to pick the limp leaves off the long stalks of *mlokhiiyeh* that lay waiting in a great bundle on the floor. (It is an edible hemp-like plant that makes a glutinous soup or stew.) We adjusted our behaviour with ease. Even I did, after a time. But that adjustment necessitated a complete reversal, especially if we had all been dancing to a lively tune.

By 'all' I mean those younger family members who were in the house at the time, and this usually included Bilaal. I often caught sight of him in the mornings combing back his dark wet hair to look cool and slick as he gazed into the broken piece of an old mirror that he shared with his sisters — and sometimes fought over — to give a final check to his appearance before going out into the street. Most days he came back soon afterwards with olives or eggs or falafel for our breakfast, then left again to join the young men of the village, younger siblings like himself who had little to do since leaving high school.

Bilaal sometimes came home later in the day and hung about the house, and then it was he, as often as not, who turned on the radio-cassette. If Sahr wanted to concentrate on her household chores without the noise, she made straight for the room he was in, armed with her mop and bucket of water, and set to vigorously cleaning the floor around him, insisting he move from this end to that, and scolding him all the while. When she referred to her mother's illness and expressed it as Rihaab's wish not to be disturbed, Bilaal turned off the cassette, but Sahr did not always bother with reasons. She rushed in and harangued him shrilly as she made for the switch or the volume control, and then he was not so acquiescent. He argued, raising his voice with hers, and as soon as her back was turned, he switched the music on again, bringing her screaming back, prodding at him with her wet mop or brandishing one of her *khofái* ready to throw. It was expertly aimed. On these occasions the argument would end in a hitting and wrestling match. With so many years behind her of stacking heavy mattresses, kneading dough and beating carpets, Sahr was strong. I could see it in her forearms and wrists and the thick heels of her hands. But then Bilaal was in the full burst of young manhood, and they made a fairly even match. Still, Sahr inevitably had the upper hand; it was not her physique, but the shrill scolding voice she adopted for such occasions, that sent Bilaal storming out of the house.

Like Randa, Bilaal was especially close to one of his cousins next door, Temaam's brother Waliid, the same who played the flute at weddings. When the older men were out of the house, Bilaal and his cousins took over the guestroom, lounging on the mattresses, telling jokes and stories, Bilaal's or Waliid's head in the other's lap. The room was often full of young men. Waliid's brothers joined him there and other relatives came from further away. The many sons of Abu Ómar's cousin, for example, who lived at the other end of the village, were close to this family, and visited almost daily. On some days Temaam and one or two of her sisters came by to see Randa and we would all be crowded into the smaller guestroom, with its pretty carpet of pale beige and bright blue colours that gave back the sunlight pouring in the two large windows. There we talked and laughed and sipped tea, the boys mischievously telling me the nicknames for their relatives and other village people.

'Mishaal, Mishaal, who is this?'

'That's your cousin Fariis.'

'No, no, it is Meesterr <u>H</u>out (Whale).' And a burst of laughter followed.

'Mishaal, who this?'

Now it was Fariis speaking, indicating Bilaal in return, and before I could say, he answered for me.

'Name <u>H</u>imaar (Donkey). Say, Mishaal: <u>H</u>imaar.'

They carried on for a long time like this, and months later, when I had returned to stay, we spent many winter days in this manner, gathered around the house's only kerosene stove, where my socks hung to dry and frequently got scorched as I forgot them in the general merriment. Each one pointed to another, making me repeat in Arabic: 'Mr Whale', 'Donkey', 'Fatty', 'Bear', 'Daddy Chatterbox', and all vied for a more comical epithet for their name caller than the one given to them. On those days I enlarged my vocabulary tremendously.

Omar had developed a close friendship with another man at Mu'tah.

Tall like Omar, but fairer skinned, Munir was bald-headed, though only in his early thirties. A light goatee compensated for this, and managed to intellectualise him without appearing pretentious. His quiet manner, traditional and reserved, while it matched the strong structure of his face, seemed to emanate from a natural calm and gentleness. He turned out to be, over time, one of Omar's most loyal friends.

One Thursday, Omar and I were invited to visit Munir with another friend who would take us in his car. Munir was living out in the countryside, Omar told me, where his family had a piece of land.

'They live in a tent there until they can go to their new home in the town. It's camping, yes? ... when you live in a tent?'

'Camping? Yes.'

'Yes. They are camping, see, because their house in the town is not yet built.'

It seemed we didn't have to drive so very far to find ourselves in an area of total wilderness. When we arrived along a dirt track, there was a black tent pitched before us that looked for all the world like the tents I had seen in the distance travelling along the highways.

Not far from the tent some stakes had been driven into the ground and branches spread over the top to provide a little shade and shelter for a hen and her chickens. Several pretty goats with long silky ears were wandering about, and a calf was tethered to the thick stem of a nearby sturdy bush, his head deep inside a sack of grain.

We did not go into the tent. Instead, mattresses covered with brightly patterned materials were laid on the ground some way from the entrance, and we were all invited to sit there. Nearby a teapot was hanging over an open fire where two older women looked up and welcomed us. Both wore the long black *shrsh*, and the *silik* or red-checked *kefiiyeh* wound around their heads. One of them was Munir's mother, and he went up to her, teasing and joking in Arabic as she brought the pot over to us. We sat nearly all afternoon on the mattresses in the shade of a small oak tree, chatting and sipping tea. I thought we were the only ones there, and it was not until some time later that Munir's young wife, who was inside the tent all the while, greeted us once briefly from its entrance. Was it explained to me later that she was pregnant and not feeling well? Maybe. I can't recall.

The little goats were tame, and one of them stayed comfortably in my lap while I stroked her head and long soft ears that framed her slim face like tresses. After a while we were each offered a glass of goat's milk that tasted strong to me and fizzed on the tongue.

When it was nearly time to go, Omar told me in a hushed voice to look up. Everyone was gazing towards some bushes where, white against the scrubby background, an Arabian horse was grazing. Suddenly aware, he raised his head and stared back at us. I got up and began walking with Munir and Omar in his direction. We were still some distance from him when he trotted away.

When we left, Omar repeated to me quietly, 'You understand, yes? They are living in this tent because they are building the house in town and it is not yet ready.'

'Yes, that's right,' I replied. 'They're just camping.'

I don't know if it was Omar, out of respect for his friend, or Munir himself who wanted to make sure I did not assume he was Bedouin, but Omar's repeated references to these temporary living arrangements communicated an anxiety that I might perceive Munir and his family as tribal and 'primitive'. I could understand their concern, although I would not have made such judgements when I was so new to the country. Besides, I would have found it far stranger if Munir and his family, knowing about the Bedouin ways of living, had not taken advantage of them under the circumstances.

I have happy memories of that afternoon, but later I

recalled the concern over my impressions of the tent scene with a sense of irony. This was after I had begun to teach at Yarmouk University, where suited and bespectacled colleagues often made a point of telling me with pride that they were of Bedouin descent.

Wall

Wedding: End of the Feast

The ceremony in the church has still to take place, but the midday feast at Shareen's is now over, *mensef* eaten, platter removed. Glasses are brought with steel decanters of cool water. Tea will come soon.

I go into the courtyard and stroll about in the shade of the vine where we sat two nights ago. By day the colours are brighter, the contrasts stronger. They remind me of other contrasts, of the strange way opposites come together for me in this country, without melding or blending. No compromise. All I most love and least like about this world constantly appears at one and the same moment it seems, so that I can hardly tell them apart. Or they follow on so quickly one from another that the impression is the same. Things about Omar himself, things about his sisters, about the family, the neighbours, the daily life, are interwoven to the degree of not being themselves if I try to separate them, which I can't do anyway. I can't. Anger and caring, pleasure and embarrassment, affection and suffocation, generosity and secrecy, these and other things all seem perversely paired.

Perhaps Western society appears the same way to many Middle Easterners. I know that they find very strange, for example, our extravagant care for animals as family pets while human beings go poverty-stricken and homeless in our cities. Or it could be that a quickness to recognise such contradictions is integral to all perceptions of cultural difference. Looking in from the outside, seeing what the insider cannot. But looking back, I recall that these contrasts were not all outside me. Even now I see them as reflecting battles going on within myself. Here are the exotic pleasures of this wedding feast and the hearty, happy wishes for the bride and groom. Although I found sheer enjoyment in all this two nights ago and can participate today, it is not my reason for my trip here, and the reality of my own situation has begun to make inroads on the festive feeling; I'm surprised it did not happen sooner, and can only put this down to my initial pleasure in finding myself once again among the many things and people I love and miss. Now the sour foams up through the sweet, and I find myself reflecting increasingly, I who am one half of a marriage that is quietly coming to grief.

Over by the wall and the entrance, I look up and down the street. A little way off to my left is the large tent where the men have been regaled, Omar among them. It is noisier. Moving away I stare abstractedly at the paving and the shrubs.

Once I leave here this world will recede again. It will become *that* world. For all its meaning, with time it will fade, resembling half-erased writing, or snatches of words murmured in far rooms. And then I'm the one who must snatch, surreptitiously, a thought here, an image there, glimpses to put together again. I will try to write them down, these images and vignettes and telling moments, but I wonder how they will hold together without crowding into a dense mass, how I can maintain their 'hereness', 'nowness', their simple transparency, so that each is a window onto the next. Difficult in Australia, where I float endlessly in and out of dream and reflection. But if for me, in this country, action claims rights over contemplation, so then does living over writing. Here each present moment has always been what I wanted: sipping mint-flavoured tea under the olive tree, joining in a wedding *dubkeh*, climbing with Omar along the edges of the wadi — each point in time fully lived, sufficing, as it happens.

How strange that my awareness of this difference, itself a form of reflection, now wafts and rocks me, wafts me into the past.

A Bath

Kufr Soum. A garden like this one, only bigger. Sunset evenings under Uncle Ibrahim's fruit trees, and the bath I took on my first visit there. We walked up to his house with two of Omar's cousins, Rashiid and Sobhiiyah, and their first-born son, Móntesir, a pretty baby only a few months old. I carried him part of the way.

Ibrahim, one of Omar's favourite uncles — and the youngest of his father's brothers — lived with his wife, Hind, on the outskirts of the village. The climb didn't seem at all steep. You hardly knew the road inclined. Then when you turned off on a well-trodden track, the ground rose more sharply and you stepped with just a little more exertion. But once there you came into a sense of height and space, and of the world falling away before you.

The greetings were followed by a long chat and a hearty meal, in which everything was laid on 'extra' for Omar's sake. After a hot afternoon indoors, we came outside to sip our tea in the garden that Ibrahim and Hind tended equally. We admired the many different fruit trees widely set about us like a sparse orchard. Then we looked beyond. Reclining low on the ground, on straw mats laid over the plowed soil, we could see far into the distance on many sides, the village having dropped out of sight under the rise. Our lungs opened up, glad of so much space.

The broadest part of the wadi stretched ahead, and on its opposite side were other worlds. Separate and far, yet of the neighbourhood. To the right rose the Jebel Sheikh, the snow-capped Syrian mountain with its guard of smaller mountains gathered tightly around it, and to the left, more hazy and less contrasted against the sky, the much contested Jolaan (Golan) Heights. Other worlds, but worlds within the compass of the eye, and so part of ours as we poured from the teapot that Hind had set beside us on the straw mat, poured and talked about that peach tree Ibrahim had planted years ago, just over there, and the three apricot trees Hind had put in along here last spring, and the way this other one had been grafted recently by both of them working together ...

We stayed on in the garden until dusk, and at sunset Hind brought out a platter full of huge pomegranates taken from their own trees the previous autumn, and so well stored that they might have been picked the day before. I had not eaten pomegranate, or even seen the inside of this fruit, and was amazed at the depth of redness in those clusters of teardrop seeds, at their glistening translucence, that for me anticipated their acid sweetness. I felt thankful that this first taste experience was made so memorable by the place and the well-matched time of day.

We were still in the garden after the sun had gone down, and as the darkness grew, it was agreed that we would stay overnight. Rashiid and Sobhiiyah were set up in the main room, but Omar and I, probably at Omar's own request, were given a room to ourselves to sleep in. Hind laid down two thick mattresses for us, side by side. Although it was midsummer, I noticed how much cooler it was here at night than in our house in the village.

Hind was fond of Omar. She was also a relative — a second cousin I think — and he felt as much at home in his uncle's house as in his own. He passed his own sense of ease on to me as we nestled down between the blankets for the night. We talked in low voices, relaxed and at peace, Omar telling me where his uncle fitted into the family and how Hind was related. I said how much I loved the garden and the position of the house, and we agreed that it had been a memorably happy afternoon. As we spoke we embraced, and warmed each other with our bodies. The exchange of words gave way little by little to one of kisses and caresses, until we pressed against each other in culmination to a day of contentment.

Nothing stays the same. Two consecutive days may be so different that we wonder if we are in the same place. In the deepest part of the night a heavy sense of the physical began to encroach on my sleep, a familiar dragging discomfort that attached itself to my repose and slid beneath the floating images of the day's garden scene. But it did not wake me, and remained no more than a weighty attendant on my dreams. When I was roused just after dawn by the trickling sensation, and had moved quietly out from under the blankets, I stared down at my inner thighs and wondered in my half-dream state how those sparkling pomegranate seeds could have been dropped there. But the trickle would soon be a flow, and jolted awake by anxiety I wondered how to ask for what I needed, with everyone still asleep.

The early, unexpected bleeding had come once already in Omar's house, but his sisters had been able to provide me with sanitary pads from the local shop, exactly like those purchased in English-speaking countries, even to the brand name. Now I thought Hind may not even keep such things in store. What would she want with them if she has no children. She probably never menstruates. And now where to go? Is there an indoor toilet at least? It's not my own home, not even Omar's.

I looked at Omar, deep in sleep, and deciding not to wake him, I stepped out quietly in search of one of the women. With relief I saw that Sobhiiyah was awake in the next room. She spoke a little English and quickly understood my predicament. Together we found Hind in her ample kitchen, already beginning the day's chores. It was not long before the two women, in their readiness to help me, took the matter of my body and what was happening to it completely out of my hands.

After bustling about searching in different places, Hind managed to come up with a clean piece of cloth and some safety pins that she made clear were ready for my use whenever I wanted them. Then they pointed out the indoor toilet, a small area of taps and tiles in the usual place, behind the concrete steps that led up to the roof. I had indicated that I wanted to wash or shower, if that were possible, and when I returned to the kitchen there were two big pots of water heating on the stove and a round tub like a huge cooking pot in the centre of the floor with steam already rising out of it. Cold water was added to the hot, tested by Hind herself who then invited me to bathe. Neither she nor Sobhiyah made any move to leave. Signalling that she would help me scrub my back, Hind was already helping me out of my light cotton nightgown.

I had just stepped into the tub when Omar's sister, Sahr, appeared as if by magic. She had taken an early morning walk to her uncle's, wanting to arrive while we were still there.

So I take my bath with all three women's help, and under their appraising eyes. Here is Hind scrubbing my back with one of those straw-like matted washers that feel like loofahs, only scratchier. It lathers well, but strips of it come away in your hands as you rub. Sobhiyah is bringing another pot of hot water from the stove, and as she pours it in, Sahr stands chatting, one eye on them, one on me. I know they are judging my body. For its shape. For any marks or blemishes. Or abnormalities. For my reproductive capacities. They smile and bustle and laugh a lot, repeating '*ḥilwi*' several times back and forth, and getting me to laugh with them. Just as well they like me. How would it be if they found me wanting? And would I know the difference? I wonder if reports will be made back to the men in confidence. I'm certain they'll be made to other women. Here is one of those fully engaging moments: I am unsure, must decide how to react.

As I'm unused to this treatment, it is also an experience that can let in distrust. But I don't want to. Only in trust can I come to understand this world — not fully, but as much as possible. Is that why I am letting this happen? My responses are mixed. I feel invaded and embarrassed. But I also feel honoured, like an ancient princess being bathed by her nurse and maids in legendary and biblical scenes. The centre of a lavish painting. The heroine of my own story. Or of a story Omar might have told me in our early days together. I know all the same that these women are in control. This is their home, their familiar ground. The honour they do me as a guest is part of their life, not the chimeric honour preserved for the royalty of tales. And yet I cannot help the thrill of awe before an experience that for me is so new and unfamiliar.

After I had dressed and combed my hair, and reappeared in mixed company, Omar said to me, 'Na:iiman!' This is a special greeting of renewal to those who have bathed and refreshed themselves. When others around him repeated the old expression, I knew it was nothing extraordinary to those who used it, but it felt to me like a blessing.

Today Ibrahim still lives in that house on the hill, but she — well — *she* is someone else now. For Hind had two strikes against her. As well as being childless, she was full of spirit and knew her own mind. When Uncle Ibrahim took a second wife many years ago, there was such discord between the two women that the arrangement could not possibly continue. Hind was strong, and the other woman returned to her own family. More recently, Uncle Ibrahim tried again, this time taking a very submissive and much younger girl. She was a deaf-mute, believed to have few prospects other than as a second wife. Everyone thought him mad. What if the children were to be born with the same disabilities?

The marriage took place when I was living in the village. Feeling strongly for Hind, I decided to boycott the wedding. No one scoffed at me or at the way I threw this word about, not even those few English speakers who understood it. There was simply the perfectly appropriate indifference to a foreigner's opinion of village and family matters. But I was taken one day to a gathering in a home where the young woman was present. I was not told who she was, and came away endeared to her natural and affectionate ways. Her name is Rabiiya:a, meaning Spring. In that marriage she proved much stronger than her silence and submissiveness led to believe. She was pretty, she was lovable, and within a short time she bore two beautiful healthy babies. Hind, on the other hand, had grown older, heftier. Above all, her own strength of will was too much in evidence. This time, after sixteen years of keeping the same house, of creating and tending its beautiful garden, it was she who left.

The Wall

I have come up against a wall, a wall of words, an opaqueness that prevents the people here from carrying their own story. Snatches and fragments handed down by the Western generations before me — all the things, big and small, that people have said about this part of the world, in books, anecdotes, conversation — stack themselves up independently of my wishes.

I am looking for the chink, where I can tap and tap to find my way through, and then from the other side I will turn back towards this place and time, reversing the look of things. Then the wall will be strewn in fragments, and wild herbs and flowers and grasses will grow, like those of the wadi. A garden where the wall had been.

And here, too, is the point where an actual wall appears in my story.

It was my first short visit, and the decision was made within a month of my arrival. One morning I recognised the voices of Sahr and Randa, of Bilaal, of their cousin Waliid and his brothers, all engaged in excited discussion, mingled with the clink and thud of heavy objects colliding and being dropped on the ground. Nearer to the house, Omar's calm voice intervened every once in a while, followed by Abu Omar's with some annoyance in it. A few words were even spoken querulously by Rihaab. It seemed that Omar's parents were arguing with him about something. He answered them briefly, refusing to be drawn into a quarrel, and then called again to the others, directing whatever operation was being carried out in the garden.

I was writing letters, and took advantage of their preoccupation to gain some space and time. The sounds were distracting at first, but they were directed away from me, and I was soon able to treat them as a background to my own tasks. Whatever was going on out there had little to do with me.

Before the morning was over there came a moment when the general hubbub suddenly rose in pitch and centred on a knot of people in the small courtyard by the kitchen door. Voices called me and then Randa entered the room.

'*Aqraba*, Michèle! Come and see!'

Everyone was gathered round a large, rusty old tin that cousin Waliid now cautiously emptied onto the ground. All those around me, for whom such a spectacle should not have been a surprise, gasped at the scorpion that spilled out. It quickly righted itself, then remained stock still. I had seen a scorpion only once, some years before in Greece. It had been a pinkish, almost translucent colour, and quite small, an inch and a half at most. This was huge — four to five inches long — and black. A definite and smooth blackness. Its stinger arched up over its back like a thick stove pipe, and reacted instantly when first Waliid and then Omar touched it with a stick. When all the family and neighbours had gathered round and taken a good long look, comments flying back and forth, Omar smashed it. Randa, picking up another rock, joined in to help dispose of it. I was told it could well have killed anyone it might have stung. She kept hitting it again and again. She and Sahr had often been stung by scorpions, and loathed these creatures, which are more agile than they appear, and can climb walls easily and enter houses. This was one of the many good reasons for washing the floors every day. Before that first visit was over, both sisters were stung again.

Now that I had been drawn outside I noticed that a large section of the low wall around the house and garden had been dismantled. Scorpions love cracks and crevices, and disturbing the rocks had brought this one out. In most of the villages the houses are surrounded by improvised walls like this, as in many country areas all over the world. But some houses belonging to the wealthier villagers had high walls made of concrete bricks, the only entrance an iron gate, solid three-quarters of the way up, the top section of more decorative grill work so you could see who was wanting admittance.

The rock wall, Omar had decided, should be transformed into a high garden wall with just such a gate.

'But I love the rock wall,' I said at lunch. 'Does it have to be pulled down? It's pretty and rustic and …'

'And dangerous,' Omar answered. 'You saw what happened today.'

'Well if you must replace it, why not a low wall just like it. Why the great big high wall you're talking about? Your parents enjoy the greetings of their neighbours going by. They won't be able to see them any more.'

'This is what is bad. My parents sit out there all day with their pots of tea and talk to every donkey passing in the street. A good strong wall should have been built long ago, but I was away and do you think there was anyone here to take care of these things? Now I am back and it is necessary. Yes, a high wall, and made of concrete.'

As if in further evidence of the rock wall's hidden dangers another incident that same afternoon brought the whole street to our house. It began with a loud commotion in the garden where rocks were being moved ever so quickly one after another, to the accompaniment of rapid speech and exclamations and the odd shriek. I had stayed behind to help Sahr and Randa with the dishes and cleaning, but everyone in the house was now going out to see what was happening. I was about to join them when Omar came in. He made straight for the wardrobe in our room where he kept his hunting rifle. Then he told me, 'Stay here. Don't go outside until I tell you.' But a few minutes later he called to me, 'Michèle, come out of the house or you will be shot.'

What? I frowned. Going out by the side door as told, I emerged onto the street where a small crowd was gathering. Omar said, 'Come here behind the wall, the street side. If you stay in the house you may be killed by a bullet through the window.' He must have translated for the others what he'd called out before, because they laughed, confirming that it was something else he was going to shoot at. I was struck by his capacity to play with language, and in English, even in a crisis.

At first the snake kept hiding. Every time a rock was removed it sought refuge in another crack, and was not exposed enough to take aim until the whole village — men, women and children — had been attracted by the cries of those searching for it. Even Uncle Aziz, who lived

117

many streets away, had appeared with some of his children. At last Omar had his chance and fired, in the direction of the house as he had reckoned. The snake was small, but he severed its head with one shot. Uncle Aziz came up to it first, and with a heavy stone beat the head almost to a pulp. I was told this was because the head of a snake can still bite after you have killed it. We gathered round to look at the black skin with its light coin-markings that characterise one of the venomous species. The second possible killer in one day. Omar gathered together a heap of dry brush, on which he then dropped the snake, setting fire to all. I thought he would be hailed as a hero and made much of, but although we all talked about the snake for the rest of the day, he himself behaved as if no less had been expected of him, and so did everyone else. The following day both events had been forgotten.

In late June Omar began his summer teaching at Mu'tah University. The day after he left, his father had a visit from some roads inspectors to check on the placement of the new wall. The low rock wall had marked the limits of the property, or the place where the family thought their property ended, but a more permanent structure could not be built before the plans were checked and verified by official government representatives. These two men wasted no time in letting Abu Omar know that the original wall had been built too far out into the road, which would probably one day have to be widened.

Yes, the wall had taken up public thoroughfare space and no, the problem was not with the neighbours on the other side of the street. It was here. If a new wall was going to be built it would have to be constructed back from the road, closer to the house.

'*Wal romaaneh*?' Sahr asked. (What about the pomegranate tree?)

She was voicing her mother's concerns, Rihaab and Omar having only that spring planted a sapling together to celebrate his return from abroad; it was to match another one, four years old, that they had planted before he left to study in the States.

Her father replied that the young tree would be outside the wall, but the sapling was right in its path. It would have to be transplanted.

Rihaab lamented that the little tree would probably not withstand the move. Even so, I was surprised to find how meek and accepting Omar's parents showed themselves on the matter of the property. Knowing how much the pomegranates meant to Omar and his mother, I held out vague hopes that this new problem might change Omar's mind, but on his return, he proved no less accepting of the situation than his parents. In fact, he hardly reacted at all. And whether they were genuinely sorry to see their property thus shrunk at the edges, or whether they had always known it extended beyond its bounds to start with, no one wasted time mourning the losses. This gave the mind space and energy to move onto things that could be done. It was around that time that Omar said to me, roughly translating an old Arabic proverb, 'He who is constantly looking behind him never moves forward.'

One day when Omar was at home, the contractor came with another man to discuss the building of the wall. It so happened that they turned up when we were about to eat lunch. Abu Omar had gone out for the day, and Rihaab, who rarely ate with us, had retired to one of the back rooms. But the midday meal is always the most substantial, and Sahr had been busy a good part of the morning preparing a soupy chicken and spinach dish that I was particularly fond of.

Now Sahr had just placed the main dish on the floor before Omar and me when the two men arrived. They were immediately ushered in to sit with Omar and share our meal. I was not surprised at their being invited; I knew by then that this is the way business is done in this part of the world. I was hungry and my eyes were already delving into the large steaming bowl and the plate of rice that remained untouched in the centre of the group while Omar and the men made their greetings and settled down. But Sahr did not come back.

'Go, dear. Go into the kitchen with Sahr. Eat your lunch there today. I must discuss business with these men.'

The men were looking abashed, and their embarrassment seemed to increase with the delay of my response.

I hadn't been a particular gender all day until that moment. Even in a mirror I'm not other to myself, but when men see you, they know. Their reminders come in tiny everyday matters of no apparent consequence. I could sense all this on the spur of the moment, but I couldn't think it through to help me respond. So I decided to go along with what was asked of me, and think about it later. I got up with as much dignity as possible and left the men sitting there eating. I had enjoyed being with the women on other occasions. What was so different about this one? At this early stage there was no point in letting the incident get the better of me. And it would not have, if my feeling of offense had not been pushed over the edge by the sight that greeted me in the kitchen.

There was Sahr, half squatting, half crouching over a plate of food in the same position she'd been in for most of the morning preparing it, and there beside her was Randa. Both were slurping up the soup as fast as possible on that cold wet floor, hurrying through their own meal so that they would be ready to appear at the right moment before their brother and his two guests and remove their dishes.

I ate a few mouthfuls, but had lost my appetite, and after some minutes I got up and went to the front room where I usually slept and our belongings were kept. I cannot call it 'my' or even 'our' room. That is simply not the appropriate term. But I shut the door behind me, and flinging myself down on one of the mattresses, for the first time gave vent to the feelings I had hardly been aware of. They had built up insidiously day by day, with every moment that added its straw's weight of foreignness and difference: his sisters always cooking (never Omar himself as he had done in the States, in fact never any of the men); a neighbour getting up to do her household chores only a day after giving birth, complaining guiltily of having produced a baby daughter; Omar coming home and switching off the radio without a word, and all the women scurrying 'for cover' as it seemed at the time. Now images of these passing incidents, each unremarkable enough to have only the subtlest influence, came to me like spits of fine windblown sand.

Sahr and Randa came to the room after the men had gone, and soon Omar joined us. The sisters could not understand what was wrong.

Sahr said she had only been in a hurry; that's why she had been eating in the kitchen so quickly.

121

Randa said, 'Michèle, do you see us do this before today? No. We do not eat in this way. This is not always. This is one time. Special.'

Omar said, 'We always eat together with relatives and neighbours, but when strange men come to a house, the women should not be seen. These men would not understand if you stayed to eat with us. They would be very uncomfortable, and you know that it is my first duty as their host to put them at their ease.'

I protested, 'But why crouched like dogs on the cold floor like that?'

Randa translated what Sahr kept repeating: Why was Mishaal so upset? Doesn't everyone eat quickly sometimes, when in a hurry? Sometimes standing, sometimes squatting, no difference, because otherwise it takes too long and there's many other things to do.

Randa said, 'We do not want to sit with these men. Why to sit with them, Michèle? They talk about business. And I do not enjoy to sit with strange men.'

And Omar, 'Dear, what to do? These are the customs. You cannot change them.'

Then Sahr made some comical remark about the situation. She did it sympathetically, spreading lightness about us. Omar and Randa could not help joining in the laughter. And nor could I.

After only a few days the two men came back with four or five labourers, all Egyptian migrants, who set in place and cemented the concrete bricks. I had not known there were Egyptians in the village because they lived in a street I hardly knew existed, a street that most people tended to avoid. I'm told that more recently the labour force is only half made up of Egyptians, the rest being Iraqi.

The work went on for two to three weeks, with talking and calling back and forth, and the tapping and scraping of tools and the clink of brick upon brick as the wall rose up around the house, formal and formidable.

Before the actual construction began, I tried one more time to persuade Omar to give up this (to my mind) expensive and unnecessary project, but he would not discuss it, except to tell me that he wanted to give the family some privacy and to help care for his parents who were getting on in years. It was time he did a few things for them, he said. My reminder that his parents did not want this new wall had no effect. Building it was something he had always wanted to do, he added; he couldn't have afforded it before, but now he could.

To conclude his volley of rationalisations, he came up with something that he must have thought would surely strike a chord with me. He no doubt believed it would convey the right sense of finality, that I would see its wisdom and nothing more would need to be said. Now he looked me straight in the eye and nodded his head to punctuate the stressed syllables.

'An Englishman's home is his castle,' he delivered.

Going and Returning

The wall was still not completed when it was time for me to leave. I told Omar I would return after two months. I loved the village and the country around, but I didn't know how I would settle in to such a life, only that six weeks was not long enough to tell. Omar assured me that he could help me find a teaching post, and then I would not live all the time in the village, but near my place of work. I agreed.

The two months turned out to be three. The first of these I spent in the States, putting my American affairs in order so I could quit that country for good. For the next two months I visited my family in Perth. My sister had married a man from Perth and my mother had moved there soon after.

For my mother the move had represented a monumental change. She felt lonely and isolated. Then, within only a few years of uprooting herself, she learnt of her terminal illness. That was when she wanted to have her family around her. I felt selfish in placing my choice before her need, but if I stayed in Perth too long I would give up all chance of making my life with Omar. He had shown his trust in me, waiting for me to join him in Jordan the first time, but it was a sensitive and vulnerable trust. If I did not come back soon, he could begin to feel that my own family was reclaiming me, and I might not return at all.

The timing of these major events could not have been worse. I attempted to resolve my dilemma with a compromise, doubling the period I had originally intended to spend there. For the first time I met my brother-in-law and my sister's two little girls. I showed my family the photos I had taken at Omar's. Everyone marveled at his sisters' beauty and at the way their lovely embroidered dresses were not special, but for everyday wear.

Our happy moments could not mask the concerns. My years in the States had not given my family any great anxieties. Now I was on my way to live in the Middle East. 'Such a volatile part of the world,' my mother said, and she deplored the difficult living conditions in the area where I would be. Now there was her own fight with cancer, a three-year battle she was only just entering into.

Within less than a year my mother would be making the trip herself, visiting me in the village, but at the time of my stay in Perth, none of us knew when we would see each other again. In those two months, all of time seemed to be wound into one tight-knotted ball. Then I left.

Jordan. My second stay here — the one during which we were married and which was meant to be permanent — lasted barely nine months. How can I say, then, that from the beginning I loved this place, and still do? Omar's family took a quiet pride in the best they had to offer. The best was rarely anything tangible, since Kufr Soum is one of the poorest villages in the country, but it was no less real.

And yet one thing had changed. Omar seemed to have been sorely put out by my not returning sooner. Why the extra month away should have made so much difference I do not know, but I had the impression that something had gone wrong. I tried to think of all the possible causes of his strong reaction: taunting from his friends and colleagues as he waited for me, agreements made with the university about living arrangements that came unstuck when I did not arrive at the time expected, a doubt and distrust of me that grew in proportion to the time I was away, a realisation of the trouble he drew to himself by bringing a Western woman home, even — though I felt the idea was far-fetched — the arrival of another person on the scene and some temptation that had placed him in a state of dilemma. I did not learn then, or at any time since, which cause or combination of causes weighed in most heavily to bring on his change of attitude. And it seemed that he did manage to put it behind him, but gradually, as if he had to work at it.

On my return in mid-November, the wall was built, with a big iron gate added, painted black. The little pomegranate sapling planted by Omar and his mother did not survive the transplant. It died within a week of being moved, but the young tree that now found itself on the outside of the new wall continued to grow fine and strong.

Catch Me if You Can

At seventeen, and studying for her final high school exams, Randa was under a lot of pressure. But she knew how to exploit it. Although she helped Sahr in the house, she could plead the pressure of study to be let off the most irksome tasks. The distractions at home were many, but she called on her cleverness and strong will to fight them off, so that she still managed to top her class. She called on them for other things too. Randa tended to have her way more often than not.

The subordinate role she knew well. Randa chose her moments, seeming to intuit exactly when to speak up and when to fade into the background, how to ask for things, and who she could argue with. When Omar turned up, or when guests came, she was right there with the teapot and the tray of glasses to pass round, which she did without a word. Later in the conversations she said little, but interjected some acute and pithy observation that perfectly matched the general tone and kept the talk going, so that she was noticed and not noticed, in exactly the right way. She never contradicted Omar or raised her voice to him, but had other, more matter-of-fact tones and relaxed ways to come at him. I couldn't blame her. Why not exercise her intelligence in this way, to win every possible advantage? What else could a teenager full of vitality do with it there in the village? When Omar was away, she voiced and acted out her thoughts and feelings more directly.

The pressure of study may well have encouraged the onset of religious fervour about halfway through the year. She didn't speak of religion often, but when she did, she expressed herself with the passion of the adolescent. For a few months she prayed more regularly and devotedly than anyone else in the family, and during that period she spoke to me often about her religion.

While the opportunities to inform me about Islam were taken whenever they arose, no one in the family or the village proselytised. I had the impression, if anything, that I was gaining cultural knowledge and understanding, not that the religion was being marketed to me. With the Muslims I have known, I have never felt pressured to convert. The closest I came to that situation was when Randa was talking to me one day about Islam in the midst of her school work. The subject came up unexpectedly for both of us, I think, because I recall that she was surrounded by her books and papers. Somewhere in our conversation she took up a pen and a pencil and held them at intersecting angles, in the shape of a cross.

'Michèle, this is verry bad. Do not believe this.'

'You mean the crucifixion? The death of Jesus on the cross?'

'Yes, Michèle. It is not true. Issu did not die in this way. It is a story.'

She then continued with arguments I was already acquainted with: how Issu was good, but Mohammed was the last of the great prophets and Islam therefore the much needed improvement on Christianity, as Christinity had been on Judaism. She was keen to teach me the *shahada* in Arabic, the profession of faith that is all you need to follow Islam: 'There is no God but God and Mohammed is his Prophet.' It will not make a very good Muslim of you without at least the other four basic observances: daily prayer, fasting in the month of Ramadan, giving a fortieth part of your annual wealth in alms, and making the pilgrimage to Mecca. But the *shahada* is the first step. If I felt any pressure on this one occasion, there was such an appeal of freshness and earnestness in her words that in the back of my mind I was already making allowances for that youthful exuberance in Randa that in so many other ways I had come to enjoy.

Sometimes I helped Randa with her English homework. It was no trouble; teaching was what I did for a living, and it put me at ease in a place where so much was unfamiliar. When Omar wasn't there her English was better than anyone's in the family. Between lessons I was assailing her with questions about Arabic. How do you say this? ... and that? The constant demand for translation had a double-edged effect on her. Together with the formal language help it was bound to improve her fluency in English, but it also added another pressure to those of her mother's illness, her other studies, her subordination as youngest daughter and her family's poor resources. She was as patient with me as anyone young and strong-willed and impatient can be.

As the year went on I asked less of her and gave more formal help towards the dreaded *towjiihi*, the end-of-school examinations. But we were both at our happiest together when she told me some Arab history while we were washing dishes or making tea. What I learnt was no more than a fraction, but it opened a crack through which I could see into a wider space.

At other times, through a crack under the bathroom door, she sent tides of dirty water from the kitchen just as I had wiped my feet dry and was putting my *khofái* back on. I had great difficulty washing in the bathroom. There was no running hot water, only the large basin Sahr filled for me with water heated on the stove. It took a long time. This I could tolerate well enough in the heat of the summer, but after I returned, and when winter was coming on, it became far more difficult. By mid-December I found it unbearable. Two nails in the wall served as hooks, and on these I loaded my towel and my clothes and undergarments until they could hold no more. Something was always about to drop off. There was nowhere else to put the clothes without getting them wet in that tiny room, where I dipped the plastic cup first into the basin of hot water and then into the basin of cold, and poured its contents over me.

Randa invariably chose to clean the kitchen floor at this time. I could hear her moving the great rubber wiper, long-handled like a broom, back and forth over the tiles. The water was about to be pushed and pulled by that giant wiper right up to the toilet drain beside me. I hurried to be done. Too late. The first small flood came rolling under the door. I opened and stepped out, rivulets coursing about my feet, just as Randa entered. The first time I delayed her work she called out to me, 'Hurry, Michèle, I must clean the floor and then I must prepare my lessons.' After that she said little or nothing. Just went ahead, and with a few last competent strokes sent the water splashing in.

Sahr felt more than anyone that Randa was exploiting her position. They fought together often over the household chores, sometimes to the point where angry words gave way to wrestling and throwing matches, like the fights Sahr had with Bilaal over the radio. What was thrown was usually one of Sahr's *khofái* that she slid from her foot or grabbed from the pile by the door as she chased Randa out into the courtyard. Round and round the chase went, inside and out. Randa was always just out of reach, and Sahr was soon out of breath but in a greater rage. Seeing herself trapped in her housekeeping role, Sahr vented her frustrations on her two younger siblings, calling them both lazy and irresponsible. Bilaal had not done very well in his exams the previous year, and there were lower expectations of him, but Randa was clever, everyone knew, as they knew that she used that cleverness to her gain. Sahr was not the only family member to become exasperated with Randa's manipulations.

I recall one occasion when Abu Omar began to reprimand Randa for something she had done or not done. It was during my first visit and we were in the room that opens onto the side courtyard. Randa started to speak as the women of a house should not. She was answering back.

At first Abu Omar let himself be drawn in, but an argument was developing as she kept it up, and I could see the moment coming when Haatem would realise that he was caught up in quarreling with his daughter. I held my breath and stepped quietly out into the courtyard.

Within a few moments she came rushing out, her words flying back at him louder and faster than ever, and followed by her father with raised hand. But she turned the drama into a farce by making him chase her twice round the olive tree, and as he came closer she grabbed hold of the trunk, pushing off from it this way and that depending on his movements. He was closing in. Then, clever thing, she made straight for me. My arms were pinned to my sides, and myself to the spot, as she clutched tightly from behind, making quick skipping forays to one side or the other. These she accompanied with little screams interspersed with some astonishingly well-remembered English, given the situation.

'Michèle, Michèle, save me! You must save me!'

And there was Abu Omar, facing his honoured house guest with raised arm. He brought it down slowly, smiling and shaking his head, as if in recognition of the comedy of it all, and the helplessness of being the father of such an unruly young woman. By then Randa had wholly relaxed her grip on me. He said a few words of admonition, and this time she looked down, just apologetic and subdued enough to satisfy him. She was safe now, and the three of us went inside together, our eyes twinkling with the knowledge of what had happened there in the courtyard. Or not happened.

In the old days the rock wall was so low that anyone could have seen from the street what was going on in the courtyard. Now with the new wall, there is privacy.

Village Idiots

Kufr Soum was acknowledged to have two 'madmen' and one simpleton. I didn't learn the names of any of them.

One was a great hulking man with a shaved head. He was not fat. He was even well built, and young, but almost a giant. Occasionally his family let him out to roam the streets of the village. You could find him sitting under an olive tree on one of those unenclosed plots of land between houses. Sitting in his world. Undisturbed. Undisturbing. When I first saw him I thought he seemed gentle, and would have been surprised to learn he could harm anyone. But I was told he could suddenly become violent, and there were times when we all heard him crying out repeatedly from that part of his family's house where they kept him locked away.

Whatever triggered his violence, it was surely not helped by the village children. I found it hard to believe the first time I saw it, and harder to believe the general indifference. I had gone for a walk up the street with Omar. It was afternoon and we were sitting with some neighbours in front of their house. The young man came along the street and went to sit down on the churned up soil of a plot of land opposite, but a group of children were following him, jeering. When they began to throw stones, he protested meekly but did nothing. I called to the children to stop, but they took no notice. I asked Omar to say something to them, and he interrupted his conversation to call out a few words of reproof. They stopped for a moment, looking across at us with confused and doubtful expressions, as if they had not quite understood what Omar was saying. When he returned to his talk they continued as before. All the young man did was to protest quietly again as he fended off the stones with arms bent across his forehead. I got up and went over to the children, but after more vain attempts to stop them, unable to bear the sight, I went back to our house alone.

The other 'madman' was not at all like the first. He was out and about all the time, and he loved to talk. People found the things he said funny, and goaded him into his inane chatter with absurd questions. When they laughed, he laughed too. They called him 'The Clown'. He was completely harmless, more of a nuisance if he latched on to you, but most of the time he was teased and asked to repeat his latest comical pronouncements. He always obliged. Omar was among those who baited him and then moved off when tired of the performance.

He was not spared by the children either. They taunted him, and sometimes threw stones too. Once I was sorry to see Saleh's daughter, Amira, among them, putting as much energy into the fling of her arm, and as much hostility into her words, as she had on an earlier occasion when I had seen her beating a scorpion with her *khofái*, over and over. At that time it had made sense when everyone encouraged her. On this occasion I wondered what her mother, Nawal, would have done if she were there. Would she have said anything to Amira, or let her be?

But most of the time the children just followed 'the clown' down the street, calling names and chanting rhymes at him. Or asking questions to set him going, as the adults did.

It sometimes happened that in the middle of the day a gentle and soft-spoken man came by our house, and if he saw the family gathered together chatting and relaxing, he moved towards us tentatively with a greeting, at which point he was invited to join us. If it was a mealtime Omar always made sure to offer him a serving of whatever we were eating.

The first few times he came Omar said to me after he left, 'Poor man. He is simple and cannot do much for himself. He is an orphan, see. His parents died, both, when he was a baby.'

The family were kind to him whenever he turned up, especially Omar, and also Saleh, who was with us often. The two brothers heaped his plate with food, gave him tea or coffee, talked to him, but I thought he never left without paying a small price. They exacted it from him in the form of a mild teasing which had them chuckling over him while he ate and answered their questions between mouthfuls, smiling bemusedly at their reactions to his words.

He still came after the wall went up. But he stood outside more hesitantly, and only entered the courtyard if the gate was left open and he could clearly see us there by the garden. He also came less often.

It is strange the way walls end up protecting you from the effects of problems they helped to cause. I am just as glad not to have been present in Kufr Soum for last year's events that Omar described in his letters to me.

It appears that a brawl broke out at a wedding, where a number of disaffected young men such as are found in every poor village — younger siblings like Bilaal — had begun to exchange insults, inadvertently at first, then with intent as they became heated at the words of their antagonists. And, as always, the abuse was soon directed at others not present, at whole families that were the target of village resentment at the time. Before long the strife had spread with a ripple effect beyond the place and time of the wedding brawl, and had become a gathering tide of gossip, backbiting and ill feeling, infecting everyone.

Stones were thrown at the windows of a few houses. Men rushed with rifles to the homes of the supposed culprits. Someone's tact and persuasion managed to defuse the situation then, but only days later a gun went off, and this time someone was killed. Soon afterwards a house went up in flames. Bilaal had nothing to do with it, Omar wrote, though he was at the wedding where the initial quarrel took place. I could not imagine Bilaal in the thick of the fighting, but when the entire village is swept up in the hostilities, no one is spared. All the complex politics of simple village life must then have come into full play. The troubles really centred, Omar wrote, around the stranglehold of the most powerful clan. The minor families had had enough. They would show those conceited Al-So-and-Sos.

In the midst of all this, Omar made one of his rare

phone calls to Perth. When I asked after the family and he had given me their news, he told me that the situation in the village had deteriorated, with the powerful family giving back revenge tenfold, as only mean and oppressive people can do. I knew Omar's family was one of the minorities. Even though his grandfather had been greatly respected as a spiritual man, they were a family of outsiders after all, having come from Syria quite recently. Only five generations before. They, too, had resented the power of the big family. 'I am sick of that clan. Ooohhhh, they are terrrible!' His 'ooohhh' came through the phone with a strange whoosh.

I could not understand Omar's vehemence. 'After all Omar, your brother-in-law, Adnan … he's one of them.'

'Mmmm,' he answered in listless confirmation after a moment's silence, and continued with more family news.

Whenever I had tried to draw Omar out on family matters and the relationship of the different family members to the larger clans, he reacted in the same way, telling little or nothing. It had become clear to me early on that he preferred not to let me know, and he had once pointedly told me not to ask so much. I would not understand these things, he said, and they were not my business. I had answered that surely if we were a couple and I had been taken into the family it would benefit me to know these things, that I needed to know them if I wanted to understand the community. But his response to that came in a chastening tone, as if, it seemed to me, he believed that not just I, but we Westerners all, are for ever asking questions, and as if the act of asking were in itself a coarse and crude thing to do. To ask about many things explicitly and requiring clear answers is to resemble the child who points and calls out in public.

Still, admonishing me for my questions could serve

conveniently to shut off the flow of knowledge — and communication — whenever it suited him. Omar did not much like to give of himself, though he could be generous in so many ways: welcoming, cheerful, helpful. The early days in the US were the closest he came to a personal sharing of himself and his feelings, the days when he told me all about his family and country. I know it is widely believed that many men have difficulty with intimacy, and I could have put his noncommittal responses, like this one over the telephone, down to gender, or down to culture. But it is easy to forget the person. Even within his culture, Omar, like all of us, had been shaped by specific conditions that applied only to him. In his warmest moments Omar was not expansive, and there were times when he became all moodiness and brooding, especially away from the public eye, and especially in the mornings, between waking and breakfast. At those times I was no more privileged, as his wife, with communicativeness than any other member of the family.

As for the various forms of family, clan and village embroilment, I would have to learn about those for myself as best I could. He may have had good reason for it, I don't know, but he would tell only what he wanted to, and no more.

So it was that a letter he sent soon after that call informed me that the crux of the problem in the village was the poverty and lack of education. I knew from living in Kufr Soum how hard life had been for Omar's own family. But I learnt from the next letter, about three months later, that 'the uneducated' were burning down 'the houses of the educated' all over the village. Someone had decided that Omar's was one of these and a mob had gathered at the gate with torches. They would have scaled the wall, Omar wrote, but he had foreseen this possibility, and having wrapped the top of the gate and wall all along with electric wire, he waited, ready to throw the switch. They went away.

I have been told that Sahr has since painted the gate and grill work along the wall a pale blue. I will see it soon, when we go to the village after this wedding. Blue is not my favourite colour for house exteriors, but I can imagine the effect — far less forbidding than the black gate had appeared all through the many months that I lived in Kufr Soum.

Rumours and Questions

I don't like the winters in Jordan. I knew the summers were hot here, but I had not expected the winters to be so cold, and my first in the village was difficult. The kerosene stove was the only form of heating, and was carried from room to room, wherever the family wanted to gather. The tiled floors made it worse, as everyone went about barefoot indoors, and there were carpets spread like large rugs in only two of the rooms. I wore socks most of the time, but they invariably got wet from the twice-daily washing of the floor. I'd hang them on the handle of the stove to dry, but they'd be scorched first.

In Amman it snowed, but Irbid and the northern villages hardly ever saw snow. Instead, as if to make up for the dry summers, it rained for several days on and off over a period of a few weeks. It was winter when I obtained a position at Yarmouk University in Irbid, teaching in the Department of Modern Languages. Aware that it would take some time to obtain a campus apartment I was content at first to remain in the village and make the sixteen-kilometre bus trip into the city.

Going to the university became increasingly difficult. There were no problems on the bus, but getting on and off, changing buses in the city, or walking across the campus to reach the Arts Faculty building, became an obstacle course of water and mud. The rain did not come in drizzles, but in great downpours that could last for hours. The streets became rivers of dirty water with no way of crossing other than wading through. The whole exercise might not have been so tiring if I could have lived on the campus or somewhere in the city nearby.

Omar told me he was not permitted to bring his wife to live with him on the military campus at Mu'tah. I wasn't concerned, since to live in the city, near my own place of work, was what I wanted, and to organise it before we signed our marriage contract. It meant I would be living alone instead of with him or the family. This Omar could not accept.

Marriage with a Westerner was hardly all benefits and advantages. In fact it was generally regarded as a regressive step, since the majority of Westerners appeared to lack dignity, manners and a sense of honour, and the independence of Western women is understood as the equivalent of a sexual freedom that translates into sexual impropriety. No matter how 'good' I was, the very fact of our being a couple was already taking him into difficult terrain. The reputation of a man among his peers is very important in Jordan, all the more so when you come from a small village where your family is known. You cannot afford to appear weak.

I was taking the bus into Irbid one day with Nawal, Omar's sister-in-law, wife of Saleh and mother of Amira. Nawal spoke English well, if in a formal and stilted manner. Although she came to the house often, I did not manage to talk to her alone very much because there were always other people there. But on the bus she began to ask me about Omar and what I thought of the family. I felt I had to be wary, since in marrying her, Saleh had made ties with the largest and most powerful clan in the village, and one with whom Omar's own family had not always got along very well. I had also not forgotten the argument I heard with the neighbours across the street soon after I arrived. Randa told me that Nawal was spreading the notion that Omar was a 'bad man' for bringing me, a Western woman, back to the village. By the time of the bus ride Nawal had accepted me, though I always sensed an element of reserve stronger in her than in anyone else in the family. But she was as polite and welcoming whenever we visited her and Saleh at their home as our best hosts in the village had been. On the bus she began to tell me how 'weak' all the males in Omar's family were. Didn't I agree that the women, in the end, appeared stronger? And wasn't Omar, ultimately, the weakest of them all?

At first I was taken aback. Omar saw himself as the acting, if not the titular, head of his family, and used every opportunity to show up his father's own 'foolishness'. It was not so unusual in these village families that an older son should begin to rival his father in the running of affairs; it was even half expected as the fathers grew older, but more filial respect was usually shown than Omar tended to take the trouble with. Certainly no one would have denied that his style was more autocratic than his father's. Omar himself thought of his brother, Saleh, as weak and pussyfooting. True, Saleh seemed less decisive, but also more sensitive to the needs and feelings of those around him, I thought, and wondered if that was why Nawal held this view of the men in Omar's family, generalising from what she observed in her husband.

But she was goading me too, wanting to know how I would react to such a statement. I remember vaguely hoping that from somewhere in my French background I might have some Norman ancestry to call on, the Normans being well known in France for their non-committal responses. During the whole of that sixteen-kilometre bus ride I was carefully engaged in a hedging dialogue, full of *ni oui ni non* answers to her questions, and asking as many in return. What did she mean by 'weak'? In what ways were the men of Omar's family weak? And I really wanted to know, too, whether she meant that he was weak in wanting to marry me or in not standing up to his peers.

Later I thought that she had picked up on that evasiveness in Omar that was so difficult to pinpoint in the midst of the manliness he projected, and she was curious to know if I was aware of it. I suppose she saw his bringing a Western woman back to Jordan as another expression of his evasion of responsibility to his own community, and the projected image of strength as illusion. The women in Omar's family were strong-willed, but then so was Nawal.

Her questions left me wondering about myself as much as about Omar. Was it courage or weakness that led me to follow him to this place? The challenge of broadening my human understanding through love? Or mere foolish exoticism in the headiness of romance? I wasn't sure. And I am one who always wants to be sure. But the confirmation I really wanted, though I could not have put it into words then, was that the two could go together. Now I say it: understanding and romance — or romantic feeling — need not conflict. The one feeds the other. Or what then moves us, gives us the *desire* to understand?

The Sharers

Wedding: Travellers and The Switch

I've been sitting on a bench in the courtyard of Shareen's house, wondering about my comings and goings between this country and that. Omar once said that we shared a love of travel and of seeking out new experiences. We are not the only ones, but what is it that drives so many of us in this way? The reasons could go on forever: adventure, challenge, exoticism, escape — from one's situation, one's very self. All different, yet in some way connected.

I also wonder about the other Western women who have travelled to the Arabic-speaking countries long before me, drawn by ... what? I didn't know much about them when I came here. It was only after I went back to Australia that I began to read some of their books.

They seemed to fall into a class of their own. Other women travelled to other parts of the world, and wrote about their time there, and along with their writings they are highly regarded, respected. Isak Dinesen and her *Out of Africa*, for example. But those who went to the Middle East were perceived more often than not as 'batty', 'potty', eccentric in some way, as if the judgement of the world were already upon them for going there. What woman in her right mind ... ?

Many were criticised, too harshly I think, as pure

romantics, like Isabelle Eberhardt. She was one of those who got around the gender-role problem by adopting male guise. Quite a few were wealthy aristocrats. Lady Jane Digby and Lady Hester Stanhope could afford to indulge in the theatrical make-believe of this exotic-romantic form of Orientalism. Lady Stanhope adopted more than male clothing, becoming 'queen of the Arabs' and slaking her desire for power that could not have been slaked in Britain with its own form of gender restrictions. Some formed relationships with men in the places they stayed in. Several married, like Omar and me. Others maintained a degree of freedom by living apart and allowing only wider social friendships to develop.

A few, like Lady Anne Blunt, joined their European adventurer husbands on their travels. Even learnt Arabic. I have read that her grandson, years later, called her 'tiny and shy, with something of the wistful disposition of a mouse or jerboa.' This was the same woman who rode horses and camels, hunted, ate locusts and stood by her husband in hardship, supporting him through the disastrous journey he insisted on taking into Persia. No, not mousy, and yet I sense in her that pressure to conform — to her class and to the customs of her day. I sense it in the way she allowed her husband to frame her beautiful descriptions and sketches with his pompous editor's preface, as if he gave to her writing, through male patronage, a legitimacy it would otherwise not have had. Thanks to Dervla Murphy, another accomplished traveller, we can read Lady Anne, although her work is more readily available in the bookshops of Singapore than in those of London and New York.

And then there are those who did not write, or who came without privilege of class and allowed these places to leave their mark on them. They are still coming today. Marion, the Scottish woman married to the doctor in Omar's village, and a Russian and a Czech woman too. All three seem happy enough. They are not talking about their experiences here. They are living them. Every day is spent in living. I was not a first in the village, not special, and writing will not make me so. I dreamed of telling the world about life in Kufr Soum, about the privilege and honour I felt in being there, about my own responses to events, which at the time I soaked up passively. I know I do not own the scenes and events I am relating, any more than I own the places where they happened. I wanted them to be part of my world, but they have a life of their own. Writing, telling, will not give me possession. I do not even own those experiences I had thought most personal.

I wonder if the women who wrote about their travels came to feel the same way. I am not these other women, although our motivation could have something in common. How much of what fed them also fed me? drew me here? Omar and I may well have been creating each other according to some deep-implanted programming, a myth of East and West handed down by our own cultures over generations. Drawn across the imaginary divide, enthralled by the mystery of the Other, we perceived the reality through a kaleidoscope of exotic, erotic, romantic colours, and were so sure of what we would find, even if that was mystery, that for a while the reality fitted. Then it grew beyond that mould into a tangle of things we love and things we don't, things expected and things that surprise, affinities where we thought there would be none, gaps in understanding where we were sure to sympathise ... And because we came this far, we continued. Our effort was not futile, though it led us along a way unlike the one we thought we were taking.

For me there is also a challenge. A sense of wanting to balance things, redress things, a sense of keeping fairness in the world. It is a drive to work against prevailing forces rather than with them, to counteract the restless acquisitive energy of modern Western culture. It is also a drive to move beyond my own limits, the limits of my society. The two go together. This is how I become a more complete human being. This is the challenge of my life.

If the difficulties of living with Omar in his country have become insurmountable, does that mean I failed to meet the challenge? I am here to find out where we stand, he and I, though I suspect I know the answer. I cannot bear to think of it now. Surely we will yet find a way and it will not come to that. Not to a complete sheering off in opposite directions, like spheres in the void whose gravities and magnetic forces attract at first and then repel each other the more forcefully.

Could I still come back here to live then, as some of those women did? If I find myself with no choice than to return to my part of the world for good, is there any way I can salvage that challenge, redirect it?

I know one thing: I would not have done this a jot differently.

My thoughts have been interrupted by another wedding guest who joined me for a while on this bench, a woman who speaks a little English. We chatted over a glass of tea served to us out here before her daughter called her indoors. She and her husband are both second cousins of

Shareen's and her brother, and came with their children from Amman a few days ago, lending a hand with the preparations. She said the church ceremony won't be for a while, and once it's taken place everyone will go home. That's just the opposite, we agreed, of the custom in most Western countries, where the reception comes after the service.

Whether Muslim or Christian, the weddings here have in common the many days of celebration. I know that in Kufr Soum, at least, they are a culmination of weeks of preparation, including a party for the women. I don't know if the men hold one too, but there is nothing like being in a group of women together and really letting go.

The first time I attended such a gathering in the village, held for a neighbour across the street, I thought we would spend the entire afternoon sitting talking, but before long someone there among us started to play the tabla, and soon an old woman stood up. She was Umm Shukri, in her seventies, and grandmother of the bride. With encouragement from the singing and the drumbeat, she began to sway her body from side to side. Then she lifted her feet to the rhythm and moved with surprising suppleness, every step deliberate and assured. The drum played faster, and raising slightly with both hands the black velvet material of her *shrsh*, Umm Shukri speeded up her steps, looking down the length of the cigar that hung from her mouth, down the length of her movements, upon all of us and upon the world.

On my first visit, when I had been little more than a week in Kufr Soum, Omar's sisters took me to a cousin's wedding. The women's *dubkeh* had just begun when we arrived. I watched for a while, then Sahr and Aisha took me between them into the circle, clasping me tightly on either side.

The wall of bodies was so solid, and each step so solidly performed as one, that I could sense I would spoil the dance if I did not pick it up quickly. That single stamp with the inside foot, only one compared with the many in the men's dances, came on the offbeat, causing me some difficulty at first. It was clearly the movement that gave the dance its character. After several misses, I had at last just brought my foot down at the right moment when the mother of the groom (who was Omar's father's sister) appeared suddenly inside the circle with a great switch in her hand like a strong sapling stem.

I didn't know where she had got this switch, for there weren't many trees about. Now she was hitting at my legs with it in time to some shrill words I could not understand, but whose message could not have been clearer: get out of the dance. Sahr began remonstrating with her, back and forth, the knot of dispute moving with us as we circled around. Then Sahr broke free to argue more forcefully, and the young woman who had been behind her moved up and took my arm. Aisha nodded to me, and with her beautiful wide smile said, 'Come!'

We continued on, my whole concentration on the dance now. Gradually things quietened down and Sahr rejoined us, and after a while I was keeping up well.

'Good, Mishaal, good!' whispered Sahr in one ear, and 'Verrry good!' said Aisha in the other. Then the young girls dancing nearest me remarked to each other. Words flew back and forth in Arabic amidst the singing, and the older women leading the dance began to steal glances across at me from far on the other side of the circle. A couple of them called out to Sahr, and imitating her they cried 'good' to me, nodding and smiling. Theirs was the approbation required, and now, just as suddenly as before, here was the groom's mother in front of me again as I danced. She had no switch, but a great broad grin that changed to a frown and back again as she apologised and congratulated me in turn.

The Sharers

I am wondering what it would be like to go to a wedding where the man is marrying a second wife. The first wife usually attends, I'm told, even helps to organise it. I'd probably behave strangely at such a wedding, staring at all three lead actors, watching for their reactions and responses to each other. Perhaps that was my real reason for not attending Uncle Ibrahim's wedding. I was afraid I would stare. I'd tell myself it's because I want to understand, but there would be something of the voyeuse in me ... When do we cross the bounds of healthy curiosity associated with meaningful knowledge and experience? When does the love and generosity of being able imaginatively to 'step into others' shoes' and understand something of their condition degenerate into morbid vicarious indulgence?

During my second, longer stay in Kufr Soum, a neighbour used to visit Omar's mother and sisters.

Khola came to the house several times when I was there. Not frequently, but regularly. Early in each visit she hardly spoke, but sat on the shallow floor mattress holding her child in her arms or nursing it at her breast. Her head covering, which she did not remove, framed a full face. Made of the same material as her ample cloak-like dress, it resembled a hood rather than the scarf that most of the other young women wore. She was all in one colour: grey.

After a while, Khola would begin to cry, and was comforted by Sahr and Randa. Her complaints rose up out of her initial silence, and rose in pitch as the tears welled too, at odds with her physically healthy appearance. Then they stopped, peculiarly short. When she spoke, the sisters gave back in chorus: '*La, la, Khola, leysh ...?*' as if patting her with the words, with here and there a click of the tongue as they swept and worked about the room. 'No, no, Khola, why should you think so? ... It's not like that ... You'll be fine, you'll see.' I'm not certain this is what they said. I gathered it from their consoling tones. I was always gathering and inferring, and then wondering if I had guessed wrong.

After a while she began again, but the sets of exchanges were spaced with long pauses in which could be heard nothing but the sounds of the tasks performed.

In those days Khola always entered at the side door and sat in the room nearest the kitchen, never in the front room where guests were received. Sometimes they gave her a glass of tea. Sometimes not. But they did not stop working. Her visits were informal, as with most neighbours, and she took care not to outwear her welcome or my sisters' patience. When the round of plaints, consolations and pauses had recurred two or three times, she became very quiet, only answering softly when spoken to. Then she got up all of a sudden, wished us goodbye, took her child and left.

At first I had the impression that Khola was poor, or

perceived in the community as unimportant, but with each of her visits, I noticed a greater presence about her. Did she initially believe she had a problem which she discovered was not one after all? ... or which, with time, dissipated of its own accord?

The first time I saw Ibtisaam was in our street, when I was walking with Sahr on our way to call on relatives. She said only a few words in passing, but although she was fine-boned and petite, her manner indicated a person at ease with herself, sure of who she was. I met her formally one afternoon when Omar and I visited their house across the street from ours. She and her husband, Majiid, welcomed us like any couple receiving guests.

Later, whenever I came across Ibtisaam, she made a point of greeting me. Her small steps and grace of bearing confirmed my initial impression of poise and inner strength, and her smile told a finesse of spirit well matched to that of her frame. She greeted me with more than mere politeness, by the look in her eye and her warm and unhurried manner. We did not talk for long. She always had plenty to do, and was never seen standing in the street gossiping, but being an English teacher, she was glad to speak with me on the few occasions we met.

Ibtisaam is also religious. Not in any ostentatious way. Like many village women she keeps her religion faithfully but quietly. She did make the *hajj*, however. She was away for several weeks, and when she returned, there was no trumpeting of the fact and none of the pious display that some returned pilgrims liked to indulge in.

It was on an early evening walk. I used to stroll with Omar at sunset along the road in front of our house. Sometimes Omar's brothers or sisters joined us, and sometimes we went together, just the two of us. At the end of the street the paved road gave way to a dirt one that began the descent into the wadi, but you could turn off at any of the adjoining streets or lanes and come home through the village, stopping at the houses of friends or relatives when they called a greeting to you. This evening we were about to take the shorter walk to the end of the street and back, but had no sooner stepped out than we saw Majiid returning from just such a walk. He came straight over to us, and at first I did not notice the two women. Then, as we turned towards his house with him, I saw them there by the gate: fine-built Ibtisaam, and beside her, the taller but younger Khola.

Majiid said to me, 'You know Ibtisaam.'

Her warm smile accompanied her words:, 'How are you Michèle?'

As soon as I answered, Majiid took up again. 'I think you have met Khola, yes?' Khola smiled too, more shyly, and nodded as I said hello. And then, as if to formalise these introductions, Majiid indicated each again in turn, 'This is my wife and this is my wife.'

About to enter through the gate, Ibtisaam and Khola were turned partly towards me, partly towards each other, and for a moment all stood saying nothing, as if in expectation, both women smiling broadly at me now, and with tranquil composure. As I remember it, that composure, more than our motionlessness, fixed the moment and the scene.

I immediately felt the onset of a distorting hyperconsciousness, like boxes within boxes, a sense that I knew that they knew that I now knew. If I had lived a century earlier and met in my travels a man with two wives among a family of Bedou, I would have anticipated difference and simply accepted the fact. And the Bedou, less exposed to Western ways, would not have been expecting to shock. Or had I gone into a modern Arab city where people of all cultures mix, and met, say, a sophisticated lawyer with two wives, we would no doubt have conducted our mixture of business or socialising with all the required urbanity, fully aware of each other's customs, impervious.

The villages strike me as a border zone where difference acts itself out. There, in Kufr Soum, I had the impression that Majiid and the two women, and even Omar, were all waiting for a reaction from me, so that any reaction I might have had was transformed by this anticipation and watchfulness, its immediacy lost. But the crowded moment was, for a moment that stood still, quickly gone. Ibtisaam spoke a few words to Majiid in Arabic, and the two women said goodbye and went behind the gate. Majiid turned back to the middle of the road with us, and we walked to the end of the street, the men chatting, and I in the company of my silences: being entirely taken up with experience, I did not speak and I did not reflect.

I knew that Omar's Uncle Ibrahim, married to Hind, was contemplating a second marriage. No decision had been made yet; the reality was still a long way off. Besides, at that time I had not met the proposed new wife, and Uncle Ibrahim lived on the other side of the village, on the outskirts, over the hill.

Majiid's house was opposite ours. In a few weeks Omar

and I would be signing our own marriage contract.

We had just begun to turn back when Majiid addressed me in English.

'*Ya Mishaal*, what do you say? I have two wives.'

It was unusual for any man there to ask my opinion, and I wavered. It seemed to me that the rituals of courtesy and community in that village, being more than mere form, returned by way of the social circle to offer their own mode of honesty. Where to step between this and the kind of directness that would appear vulgar, blunt and offensive?

'I'm not sure. I don't quite know what to say.'

'In Islam, Mishaal, this is good and lawful, and acceptable to God. Ibtisaam is my wife. I care very much for her, and she cares for me, the same. I have another wife because I had no children.'

The child I had seen Khola nursing was the youngest of three. Neither she nor any child had been at their house that first time I visited Majiid and Ibtisaam with Omar. Khola and the children had been away visiting her own family.

'And Ibtisaam?'

'Yes, of course she wants this. She and Khola will share the children. She will care for them as her own.'

I imagined Ibtisaam with those children of Khola's, scolding and encouraging in her kind-firm way, poised between deep caring and proprietorship, until I remembered that here parents do not own their children, who belong to the family just as adults do. I had myself carried babies in my arms many times, indoors and out of doors, or played with small children while mothers, aunts, cousins went about other chores.

'In the West a man has only one wife, yes? In Islam too, God prefers this. To have more than one it is necessary to treat them equally, and that is impossible. But if a man has no children, this is a good reason. God accepts this.'

Clearly and simply, Majiid explained. Yet his manner was not, I thought, that of one telling a foreigner about customs that remained unquestioned and in which he felt secure. He gave me the impression that his kind of marriage might be viewed in the village as less acceptable now than in the past.

'Ibtisaam and Khola are very happy,' he concluded. 'Believe me, they are as sisters.'

Could he say otherwise? I told him the very concept of two wives was one I could not comprehend. But then here were two real women. We were acquainted, yes, but I did not know the reality of their daily life. As I wondered how they could be happy, I felt myself calling up some centuries-deep European notion of love and happiness in marriage. A notion whose basis in reality was so fragile and distant as to have little relevance. Perhaps it had always been so, and I was only discovering it now. I tried to recall if I had yet heard the Arabic word for 'happiness'. Yes, Randa had recently told me a proverb: 'Patience is the key to happiness'.

During the conversation with Majiid, Omar was content to walk quietly beside us. Afterwards I wanted to discuss the encounter with him, but visitors were arriving and the following weeks were full of comings and goings. We were making plans for our marriage, to be followed by my mother's visit and a trip of our own, one that for many weeks I had been working hard to persuade Omar to make. We would leave Jordan with my mother, visit my family in France and then go on to the UK, where Omar would take up further studies and I, having him back in the Western fold for a while, would help and guide him to a point where he would entertain a broader perception of the world and understand me and my needs as much as I understood his. He would be my sole focus and full-time project, so that when we returned my situation would be much improved.

As to these neighbours, it was to be a long time before I would see them again.

Himaar

I don't think I'll take many photos at this wedding, though I've brought my camera. With each visit the camera is a heavier burden: remembering it, carrying it, taking it to the wrong places, not having it when I want it most, and especially never bringing away the wished-for scenes, only scores of squared-off, flattened-out, coloured images that do not speak to me. Me on a donkey at Umm Qeiss, for instance, with my brother-in-law, Saleh, standing beside.

Himaar. Donkey. There is another photo that a friend took of me years ago, riding a donkey on Ios, up the pale stone path from shore to village. Playing the bohemian Greek-island wanderer, and still so much the tourist. Then, and years later, at Umm Qeiss.

We visited the ruins of the ancient city of Gadara, now called Umm Qeiss, in the early spring, several weeks before our marriage. There's only one photo I like from all those taken on that outing. It is of Saleh's three-year-old daughter, Amira, sitting in the lap of the headless goddess: a great stone woman, presiding over a scattering of columns, some upright, some fallen, her lap so generous and well contoured it might have served as a chair for a priestess. From this larger-than-life-sized seat, all the place around asserts itself, even in ruins. The woman is wholly present, and imposing, in every solid limb and fold of her garment, from her foot on up and up to that epic-telling break, to that fragmented stone neck, above which the surprising void. I am both drawn and challenged to complete her, adding some dignified Hellenic head that may or may not match the original. But here from the lap that is her centre a small girl's laughing eyes and mouth radiate the power of unconscious lifejoy. A little daughter of Islam as yet without language, to speak of, is breathing, gazing out and laughing for, in place of, the pagan woman of stone. These thoughts did not occur to me at the time. I took the photo spontaneously.

Then the boy with the donkey came by.

Was it me who asked them to persuade the boy to stop and let me sit on the donkey? It must have been. The photos were too many and too much alike, as they always are when you think you're doing something special, different. Only, strange ... I keep forgetting ... when I went home and had them developed, Saleh, my brother-in-law, was not in any of them. And yet, I was sure, when I handed Omar the camera his brother was standing right beside the donkey and ... no, that's right ... he refused. This is the memory that wanted to emerge. Off to the edge of the camera frame, Saleh kept laughing, and insisting he would not be in it. No explanations, but I thought at the time he must have meant to let us know he was not going to be taken for the donkey boy, fixed in that relationship to the beast, to its rider, to anyone looking at the photos.

I remember that when I had them developed, I stared at myself trying to look comfortable sitting absurdly astride the animal in my long *dish-dásha*. Then my eyes strayed past this ridiculous image and began to draw, draw in the place where Saleh stood beyond the frame. Whatever his intention, it was not with anger or malice, but good-humouredly, that he stood aside and refused. His laughter, his light-heartedness — these were not in the photo.

Supposing it had not been me on the donkey, or any of the party at Umm Qeiss. It could have been a photo of a local villager, perhaps even of Uncle Ahmed himself riding to his fields of lentils on the slopes leading to the edge of the wadi. A picture you would come across in a travel magazine. I can imagine the caption.

Arab villager with donkey, Jordan.

Trapped in local colour, in the romance of exotic paysage, like the donkey's leg raised in the midst of the trot and the rider's stick held above its haunches, the picture would go nowhere. Even my imagination could not fill in the real place that the real donkey goes to.

Some people have cars, which they use to travel to the cities or from village to village. Cars go where there are roads, but it is the donkey that takes you up and down the steep sides of the wadi, in and out of the olive groves and the pomegranate orchards, and to everyday work among the lentils.

In the West, the donkey is an unconscious icon, evoking biblical scenes, religious nostalgia, the exalted role of the humble fool, and other associations; floating assumptions that evade articulation. But when I think of donkeys in Jordan, it is not an image that comes to mind, not a 'picture' of the animal itself. What I recall is the house in the dead of night.

Lying beside Omar on the thick floor mattress that his sister, Sahr, always prepares for us, I become aware that I have been woken by the early morning call to prayer, which no one else seems to hear. Then, just as the quiet of the night is returning, I am brusquely and thoroughly roused by a series of amplified sobs and hiccoughs, long drawn-out and startlingly loud and near. These resonating sounds halfway between pleading and desperate protest are no sooner ended than taken up again at a greater distance. And so, like dogs barking to each other in the night, five or six donkeys bray in turn about the village before the pre-dawn peace is restored.

Donkeys bray unseen at night, Kufr Soum, Jordan.

Something from the iconic still hangs like an aura over this braying, this depiction of sounds.

Yet donkeys can be recognised by their brays, which change not only with each individual animal, but also according to age and health. Sometimes they cough or sneeze right in the middle of a bray. And sometimes a fulsome, powerful aria unexpectedly peters out in a weak wheeze.

Our preconceptions are so often confirmed. It's true then, donkeys are stubborn, I thought to myself one night. I had been woken by a mixture of sounds: a trotting that stopped and started, and the coaxing and cajoling of a human voice interspersed with muffled grumbles and curses. The man tried stopping and waiting too, because all would go quiet for a while, and I began to think they must have gone. Then the silence was broken by the same noisy repertoire.

But this stubborn donkey had a special trick. The man must have dismounted, and no sooner done so than the trotting sounds began again, increased in speed and moved quickly out of hearing up the street, while the cursing, grumbling voice, left way behind, broke out more loudly outside our house. It passed too, eventually, accompanied by tired and heavy footsteps.

In the morning I was woken by another voice in the street, loud and insistent: 'Bandoora. Bandoora.' (Tomatoes.) The fruit and vegetable vendor was doing his rounds of the village, knowing that the women get up early. Out in the courtyard Bilaal, also awake unusually early, heard me imitate the vendor's cry. He laughed and joked with me over my mimicry, then went and bought a few tomatoes to have with our breakfast.

Omar has told me of a tradition that says: when many village donkeys bray in the middle of the night Satan is passing through. Another form of religious association, then. But this one belongs here, to this place. More telling than the superstition is the representation of the lowly donkey as a creature sensitive to the presence of evil, despite the invoking of his name on those you want to call stupid, foolish or stubborn, as in so many languages. Some years ago, a new imam came to the village. His resonating nasal calls to prayer annoyed many people and were often followed, in the privacy of their houses, by a string of verbal abuse sprinkled with the word _himaar_.

The early morning calls to prayer, when everyone is still sleeping, seem to go unanswered in Omar's house. No one in his family has ever connected the noise of the donkeys at night with responses to the prayer call. For them, the sequence goes unnoticed or is a mere coincidence. For me, this antiphonal connection is mischievously encouraged by my language, and perhaps exploited by the devil who sees me lying awake thinking as he passes over our house. My Anglophonic mind, aware of the Arabic speaker's tendency to pronounce the English 'p' as a 'b', all too easily catches up the pun suggested by 'pray' and 'bray'.

My mind loves these games.

But the space of the mind in which puns are made is not the physical place of the village. *English is **not** spoken here.* In this village Arabic is the only language, and I am a stranger, the *ajnabiiyeh*, the foreigner. This place does not belong to me. What I think of night calls to prayer is no different from what I think of donkeys. It is neither here nor there.

I discover later that of all the people in the house, Abu Omar does respond to the night call. His voice reaches just above a whisper, so as not to disturb the others. He prays quietly at night, audibly by day, though never loudly, and in community at the mosque once a week. I wonder if this is from a conscious desire to emulate the Prophet Mohammed, or because it is built into the religion from Mohammed's example. I am reminded of the verse from the *Qur'aan*: 'Neither speak your prayer aloud, /Nor speak it in a low tone, /But seek a middle course /Between.'

It is not any donkey that is the first to bray. One morning, when I heard the sound so close, it occurred to me that this could only be 'our' donkey, Uncle Ahmed's. This animal had long been the subject of a mild familial discord, because it was between his own house and ours that Uncle Ahmed had built an extra room, not for the sake of his family (eight children have never been considered many in Kufr Soum, and half of them were married and living in the city anyway), but as a shelter and 'home' for the donkey. No wonder I found some of the night braying so loud! He was literally next door. You could only enter there from the outside, and the floor remained earthen, but the side walls were the outer walls of the two houses, later joined by the same cement brick in front and back, and sharing a common roof. The stone huts that many villagers build for their animals are often right beside their own houses, but quite separate. Omar and his father, who is not a farming man but a retired civil servant, were not happy to have the animal so close, right there in the same building, right 'between us'. *We are not animals, to be living with animals.* In fact the donkey was no more 'with us' than if he were in a barn several yards away, but Uncle Ahmed was constantly under pressure to remove him. Steady, even pressure that did not at any time flare up into loud family dispute. If the matter came into anyone's mind when the donkey brayed inside his shelter, it was rarely mentioned and soon forgotten.

The donkey is gone now. I do not know at which point he was taken away. There was no argument, and no change in anyone's behaviour. The parents and children of both families were in and out of each other's houses as always, helping with meal preparation, house cleaning and other chores, or simply relaxing and enjoying each other's company. Clearly something more than the demands of male kinship underpinned the bond between them, something of strong mutual esteem and affection, brother to brother, wife to wife, and cousins to cousins.

No possible caption.

Picnics and the Shepherd Teacher

The important river in the north of Jordan is the Yarmouk, a major source of water. Its course is a narrative of history and geography. Ancient battles of the same name took place nearby. It wanders between countries.

I did not come anywhere near its banks, but saw it in the distance when we were driving somewhere else. It was always pointed out to me, a landmark whose mere sight seemed to heighten some tacit understanding, as if its being there, a silver snake curled through the hills, brought all its viewers to recall the same things together. Not that I could tell what things they were, but I knew about the battles and the stories, and the way Jordanians saw the river as theirs, the sign that they belonged to this part of the world.

And it had been made to serve political ends, either as a border or as a source of tension concerning the growing water shortage. First there is the Arab neighbour, Syria, which shares part of its border with Jordan at the river, and has been building dams there. Then there is a small section of the river that forms another border, looking towards the Sea of Galilee.

It must have been there that I went on a picnic once with Omar and his brother Saleh and a group of their friends including Munir. We travelled in one of those trucks often used for taking fruit and vegetables to the markets, the back and sides girded with railings of different bright colours. We stopped in a high place from which you could see a wadi below and hills on many sides, all far away. The hills were probably higher than we were, but I had the impression of looking down on them. The area immediately around us was like a large park with plenty of small oaks and other trees, more trees than I had seen in any one place together, and it was full of wild red poppies, and flowers and herbs I did not know.

After our meal we sat on a rock overlooking the wadi where the Yarmouk River flowed. The hillside below us was steep, but not too steep for a shepherd to pass along it with a large flock, the hollow clinking of the sheep's bells reverberating up to us and out across the valley. They took a long time to go by, moving at a leisurely pace, and making it hard to believe that just beyond them was the great divide between this and another world, like another planet. Even when you looked up and out beyond the river, you saw the same land stretching and folding away from you, all the same. But if you used binoculars, as I did that day, then there were the barbed wire fences in the distance, a lone building like a large guardhouse and, though too far off for its engine to be heard, a military truck coming along a road.

I loved the picnics, and the wadi. I went several times into the wadi with Omar and with others. There was the time Omar found some giant field mushrooms, and we took one home with us, its top as big as a dinner plate. And the time we brought home many sprigs of wild thyme in which I recognised the aroma of the *za:'ter* I had eaten with him so often. On other days when he was away, I went with his sisters, usually Na:aameh and Aisha and their children, and sometimes Randa too. I don't remember Sahr coming with us, not once. She always stayed at home or visited neighbours. We picked *seleq* and *khobeize* and other greens and herbs along the bottom of the wadi, and then climbed part way up the other side, where we often came across flocks of sheep, their bells tinkling along the hillside, but the shepherds were rarely close enough to greet us. They were usually quite young, but they moved off whenever we appeared, preferring to keep to themselves.

The climb was worth the view it gave us back across the wadi. At one time we found a group of young men who had built a fire and made tea, which they offered to share with us. We chatted a little and learned they were from Yubla, the cheese-making village behind the hill, and were acquainted with people in our own village. It's always like that here. Talk a while with anyone you don't know and a connection will soon be found.

There was also the time in spring when we struck out in a different direction where the wadi sloped more gently, and we found a beautiful almond tree which Randa climbed, throwing down *loz*, almonds in their green casings, for me and the children to pick up. Another day we were on some land that Uncle Ahmed owned at the edge of the wadi where grapevines grew in wild clumps. We gathered the leaves and brought home several bags full. One of my favourite trips was the day Omar and I spent with his friends from the village of Al-Rafiid. They were a family of brothers dear to Omar and with whom he often hunted.

There was not much hunting this time. A fire was built

by the stream's bed not far from one of its sources in the hillside, and we were enjoying our picnic lunch of lamb chops with bread and fruit when a shepherd came by with his flock, and stopped to talk with us. Most of the shepherds were in their teens or early twenties, but this was an older man, of much darker skin colour than most of the people in Jordan, and clearly very poor, his scant and worn clothes covered in dust. He talked and laughed, and joked with Omar and his friends. At one point Omar turned to me and said, 'See this shepherd, he is a teacher.' The man nodded and laughed. I couldn't be sure if he had told Omar this or it was the other way round. 'He is a teacher,' Omar repeated, and then indicated the sheep that had gathered trustingly round us, 'and these are his pupils.' Then everyone laughed.

The shepherd stayed to drink some tea, but refused the food we offered him. I had brought my camera with me, unusually, on that occasion, and after tea we took some photos. If they were developed I did not see them. Somewhere along the way the film was lost, so that I now have only the memory. The shepherd would not be photographed, but he was willing to let Omar take a shot of me standing with his staff among the sheep. I felt that I must surely look like a shepherdess, because that day I was wearing the traditional black *dish-dásha* with red belt and red-bordered sleeves. Black and red. Rain clouds and blood — fertility colours that young Bedouin women used to wear soon after marriage. I think that was the last time I wore it.

Grandma

Omar's grandmother usually lived with Uncle Adel, an older brother of Abu Omar. But she also spent weeks or months with Ibrahim and Hind, walking alone all the way up to their house and arriving unannounced.

On odd occasions she stopped with us. I say 'odd' because although Grandma came by often enough during the day, she rarely stayed overnight, and never for more than a few nights at a time. I gathered that Haatem was not her favourite son, but Omar was a much-loved grandson, partly because of the many ways in which he reminded her of his grandfather, long dead, who had a reputation as a good man.

There was no knowing how she decided who she would stay with. I had the impression there were no reasons other than the way she felt about her sons and the whim of the moment. Her face was tattooed, and wrinkled and weathered-looking like the faces of all the old women. But her mind was sharp. In the same red-checked, turbaned *silik*, she came in, sat down, stayed a while and listened to all the news and gossip, and then went off again. Most of the time no one took much notice of her. But that only made it easier for her to pick up what was going on in every household.

Even in the past Grandma had been the one who kept an eye on everybody. She was there when anything important happened. And she was there the day that baby Omar climbed onto the roof of the house and made his way to the edge just when Rihaab wasn't looking. The small boy cast his eyes at the beloved garden below and prepared to follow with his body, engaging the world with his eager smile that Rihaab didn't see. But looking up at the right moment, Grandma knew at once and was there in the right spot. She caught him, and from her own moral perch berated the less observant eyes of the mother, her inexperience, her carelessness. Grandma saw to it that the story of how she saved the life of the child made the rounds of the village, but while friends and neighbours marvelled, they watched through the years and noted how her scolding and belittling added to Rihaab's burden.

Sharp-eyed and shrewd, even today in all her crumpled age, Grandma moves from son to son, taking only the clothes on her back, but gathering up the news and gossip. She lets all of us know, subtly and not so subtly, just where she thinks we each stand and what we are worth to the family.

'How much are you earning in this job of yours, dear, at the university?'

I could tell she was asking me something, mumbling away as old people do. Was she too old to recognise that I didn't speak her language, that I couldn't understand her? But sitting there beside me, having all day if need be, with a patient insistence she repeated her question over and over, touching my arm or picking at my clothes, until finally I had to ask others around me what she was saying. They didn't know either, they hadn't been taking much notice of her. It was at Uncle Adel's, while I was visiting there, that she first did this, after paying me several compliments in simple words that I could comprehend.

'*Enti kwáisseh,*' (you are nice) … and she looked at me with that sideways movement of the head — not a nod, but a small emphatic gesture that came exactly with the first syllable of the important word, *kwáisseh.*

But what was she saying now?

One of the other women of the house turned to her.

'*Shou bidditch, Jiddeh?… Na:am …*' (What do you want, Grandma? … Yes …)

Then to me: 'Ah! She wants to know what you receive *bil jaama:eh* … at the university … how much money each month for your teaching.'

'My salary?'

'Yes. Salary.'

I couldn't remember the exact amount but told her a round figure in dinars. Then Grandma began calculating and commenting aloud, comparing it with this one's and that one's pay, and making sure that all those present heard as she repeated the figures. After which she patted my arm and looked at me again.

'*Enti kwáisseh.*'

Aaliah and Aliaa'

Not all of Omar's uncles were his grandmother's children. His grandfather had been content to live with his first wife for many years, though he had no sons with her, only daughters. Then one day, taking a rest from working in his fields, and hidden from the road by a hillock or a rock, he overheard two neighbours talking about him as they passed. 'He works so hard,' they said, 'and what a pity! All this for his nephews!' On the spot he made the decision, and was soon married again, and by this marriage he had a daughter and two sons. This, at least, is the story the family tells. But he must have enjoyed having more than one wife, since it was not long before he married a third woman, Omar's grandmother, who gave him five sons and two daughters. Now Grandma is the only one still living.

Uncle Aziz was one of her children — a full brother to Abu Omar. He was also one of Omar's favourite uncles. He knew a little English, but sometimes I had difficulty understanding the few words and expressions he loved to show off, antiquated phrases from the days when he had been in the army. Uncle Aziz was always jolly, and didn't mind if it took me a while to work out what he was saying. He derived the greatest pleasure from talking about the 'hubbly bubbly', a term he repeated as often as possible and accompanied with comic gestures that made clear he was referring to the hookah.

He was thin like Omar and although Omar's father was the closest to him in age, there seemed to be many years between them, even though Aziz seemed more energetic. And he must have married relatively late in life. His pleasant, plump wife appeared to be some years younger, and the oldest child was only about eleven.

Whenever we went to call on Uncle Aziz we would be spied in advance coming along the road by his two youngest daughters who went everywhere together. They were about seven and eight years old, still young enough to play outside the house, and so close in age and appearance as almost to be twins. It was they who came up to Omar and me on our first visit and each took me by the hand, leading the way past the backs of other houses along the edge of the wadi where you could slip on the loose gravel and simply fall off. They kept turning their faces up to me, smiling shyly, but overcoming their timidity enough to pull me along when my footing was unsure, or stare at me more boldly when they thought I wasn't looking their way.

At first I had some difficulty telling them apart; even their light brown hair was roughly the same pageboy length. Then it was their names that gave me trouble; I could not pronounce them in a way that distinguished one from the other. Their parents had followed a common Arab custom of calling their children by matching or rhyming names. Not only could I not produce the Arabic sounds that made the difference, but I actually *heard* no difference. I would ask them to repeat their names one after another, and they always obliged, though with quizzical looks and smiles and the occasional giggle. They found it peculiar and amusing that I should not hear the differences so obvious to them, but they were always patient with me. To me our little dialogue would sound something like this as I went from one to the other:

'*Shou ismik?*' (What's your name?)

'Alia.'

'*Kaman?*' (Again?)

'Alia.'

'*Wa enti?*' (And you?)

'Alia.'

'*Kaman?*'

'Alia.'

'*Wa enti, kaman?*'

'Alia.'

'*Wa kaman?*'

'Alia.'

Theatre of the absurd!

When I began to shake my head in frustration, they simply took over with their own questions about English. I had the impression that apart from their keen desire to learn, they were also compensating for my difficulties with their names, as if righting the balance between us of knowledge and ignorance. They began by asking me how to count, and would go over the numbers in English just as slowly and carefully as they had previously repeated their names, but with far more success than I had. Then I asked about numbers in Arabic, and they taught me. In conversation with adults I had already been told a few numbers in passing, but it was from these two girls that I first learnt to count in Arabic. They were good teachers and good pupils, throwing themselves as eagerly into correcting my pronunciation as into reproducing the English sounds.

Their older brother and sister were a little more

reserved and self-conscious. At ten and eleven years they were past the stage of barrages of innocent questions. The sister also went off frequently to help her mother in the kitchen, but there were moments when both she and her brother stole envious glances at the forthright intimacy that their younger sisters had developed with me.

I was at roughly the same stage of learning the Arabic alphabet as Aaliah and Aliaa' had reached. When I taught them the game of 'Hangman' using Arabic words and letters, they improved their spelling while I learnt many new words.

Sometimes when they came with their parents on a visit to our place, if Amira and Manar happened to be there, all the girls joined in telling me stories. Their uncomplicated vocabulary and expressions, and their graphic ways of explaining words I didn't know made their stories easy to follow. From these sessions with the children I learnt much about the language and its background that I might have otherwise missed, like the traditional way of beginning a children's or folktale: 'Marra fi wahed ...' (Once upon a time there was a ...). In fact, my clearest lessons in Arabic pronunciation and all that I have retained best about the language came from these children.

Uncle Abdullah and Aunt Khadija

It seemed that the word *mustáshfa* (hospital) was on the lips of young and old much of the time. On one occasion Omar took me to see his oldest uncle whose wife was in hospital. Under normal circumstances they came to the house regularly, but not since Aunt Khadija's illness which, as they were very poor, added much to their burden of age.

Uncle Abdullah and Aunt Khadija lived at the 'edge' of town in a more literal sense than I could have imagined, at the narrow end of one arm of the wadi, where the village, mostly flat, took on a terraced look. On the other side of the road were houses backed by a few more streets and buildings in descending order. Behind these the land became too steep to build upon, but on our side the entrances to people's homes actually led into the rock.

Omar had said nothing to me about the oldest couple in his family living in what was essentially a cave. It was the size of a large bedroom, but it looked quite comfortable, with bright mattresses and rugs about on the earthen floor. I thought, too, that it must be cool in the height of the summer. Uncle Abdullah did not seem to notice what he lacked. Was this because here there was no shame attached to making your home in the rock face, as the ancient Nabataeans had done? Or simply because this couple bore their age and condition with a grace I found remarkable, and that appeared to keep their spirits young?

Omar asked me if I had a 'green note' (one Jordanian dinar). I gave him a couple which he then added to some of his own. He went to hand them over as is the custom when family members are ill, but Uncle Abdullah refused to accept them. He requested us instead to visit Aunt Khadija in hospital in Irbid. We could give them to her there if we insisted.

It wasn't long before they were visiting again. Aunt Khadija, more or less recovered, sometimes came on her own and sat in the sunny part of the courtyard. She wore the traditional *shrsh* and *silik*, and the pipe in her mouth stood out against the blue-green patterns that almost completely covered her chin.

I grew particularly fond of this couple, noting how well they took care of each other. I was also struck by the dignity in the way others treated them as well as in their own behaviour. Well into my second stay, Omar and I visited their daughter in Ramtha, near the border with Syria, where she had married and had her own family. There I felt the same empathy. The children were accomplished, and highly creative. One was an artist who had already had some of his work exhibited. Though not poverty-stricken like the old couple, they could hardly be called wealthy, but in this country they did not have to be. They were liked and respected for who they were, and for their manner with others. I felt the close connection between these young people's abilities and their charm, unpretentiousness and optimism, all of which, I was convinced, must have been passed down from their grandparents.

$\mathcal{K}oh\underline{l}$

I did not bring my *koh̲l* with me to Jordan this time. I'm afraid of losing it. I left it back in Perth, in its small glass phial that must have been used at first for medicines. Probably Rihaab's.

I still haven't learnt how to apply *koh̲l* without spilling more than I manage to put on. Some goes into my eyes as I move the tiny wooden applicator between closed lids. I'm afraid of using it up, and rationalise that this is another reason for wearing it only on special occasions, three or four times a year. Lose it or use it. Sooner or later one or the other must happen. One day the *koh̲l* will be all that will remain from this place and time. I have a few other things back in Perth, a couple of tea glasses and one or two small porcelain cups without handles, dead things. There was a packet of tea, the leaves long and curled to give a strong flavour. Now it is used up. The *za:'ter* I bought yesterday to take back with me next week, that aromatic mixture of sesame seeds and a dried wild thyme, will be gone within a few months at the most. The *koh̲l* will be the only living thing I'll have left. Although it is made of stone, it moves. Its level drops imperceptibly with each use, and on the last occasion I noticed with surprise that the glass phial was only half full. It lives, my *kohl*, in its scattered flight over my upper cheeks, in its movement of hourglass sand, and in the sprinkled memories that gleam from its depth.

The day I obtained the *kohl*, I accompanied Omar and Uncle Aziz, father of Aaliah and Aliaa', into Irbid. After they had finished their business we visited an out-of-the-way neighbourhood with several shops that sold antiques and unusual objects, and one of these we entered. There were some fascinating things in there: brass coffeepots and houkahs, and items whose purpose I couldn't begin to guess. It was the kind of place I would have taken for a curio shop, the sort you can read about in nineteenth-century French novels. But the salesman was not the wise and mysterious old merchant of those settings. He was young, full of energy, eager to sell us something, and clearly good at what he saw as his line of business. Omar and Aziz were determined not to be drawn in, affecting the desultory interest of the half-hearted customer. I played along and followed their example, picking up an object or two and asking a question about this or that. In a sense we weren't really role-playing at all, since we had little money even between the three of us, and knew that 'window-shopping' was all we could afford.

It was Omar who called me over to the counter where the young man was showing him a black stone that glittered and gleamed a silver brighter than coal under light. They told me that this is where *kohl* for the eyes comes from. It looked as if it would not be crushed easily, but when I took it in my hand, I could tell by running my fingers over its surface that it might be reduced to a fine dust. Omar asked if I would like to have it, as he was sure his mother knew how to prepare it. I loved the idea of making it from the beginning, of watching the transformation of a stone into a soft dark powder. Already the shop assistant was explaining what to do, his knowledge and keenness making themselves felt well before Omar translated his words. 'It needs a brass container and something to crush it with,' Omar explained. The young man wanted to sell us a small brass mortar and pestle, but Omar was sure his mother had these. I thought of Rihaab's illness, and wondered aloud if she would be strong enough to make the stone into *kohl*. 'My sisters know, and if they don't she will show them, and you can learn too. Yes? Would you like to learn to make it?' I needed no convincing, and we left with the stone in a small paper bag.

A few days later I heard a rhythmic tapping and clinking in the house, and followed the sound to the room just off the kitchen, where Rihaab was sitting with a mortar and pestle almost identical to those we had seen in the shop. We had shown her the stone on our return from Irbid and she had said immediately that she knew what to do, but I did not expect to see her working at it so soon. With Sahr's help she had found the mortar and pestle in the deep, back part of the house, the cool dark room with the earthen floor where most of us rarely went. Its two outer walls were not of cement brick like the rest of the house, but of stone, and its only 'window' was a small opening where one stone had been removed. You took a steep step down to enter there, after parting a curtain drawn across the doorless entrance, and as your eyes adjusted to the shadows you could just make out far at the back the large bins where the flour, sugar and rice were kept. This was the room where scorpions came in easily, and Sahr had been stung more than once while rummaging among those stores in the dark. On the right was the old oven where she sometimes baked bread. On the left were shelves piled up with old suitcases, blankets, clothes and odd objects belonging to the women.

In the brighter room now, and at Rihaab's command, Sahr was pouring with great care tiny single drops of water from a cup into the mortar. Then the pounding began again. They invited me to join them, and the three of us took turns. The stone had already been reduced to what looked like coarse crumbs, but when I was working at it there appeared to be little change. Na:aameh came by later and told me it would take many days of pounding, for an hour or two each day, and that the amount of water added was the secret to a good fine powder, as too much too soon could ruin it. Rihaab wanted to work at the powder as much as she could, but when she felt too weak we took on the habit of passing the work back and forth among us. Whenever the other housework was done and we sat together around a pot of tea, the mortar was produced. Then anyone who came by would be recruited to the task — neighbours, relatives, sometimes even visitors — and they never seemed to mind. We became absorbed in the *koḥl* crushing in a way that reminded me of the many other women's group activities, except that here the men took part too. When Omar was home for the weekend, he too sat with us and pounded. All through the week, every time his brothers Saleh or Bilaal came into the room, whether to stay or to pass through, they stopped and took up the pestle for a while. Even when caught by surprise at first, they did it with a good grace, having no option, since their mother asked them. It did not occur to them to refuse what Rihaab asked. When Uncle Ahmed's sons came by it was the same; whether their sister Temaam was with them or not, they joined in. And there were the cousins from Abu Kariim's place. Strong young men who chatted and joked as they sat pounding, some offering only a few token strokes with the pestle, others lending themselves to the task more earnestly.

At the end of a week, the stone had been transformed into a smooth sooty dust that held together when pressed, and shone like black silk. Rihaab said it would still not be ready for a few more days. We all kept pounding, and each day she added another drop or two of water. The sound had changed too; the hollow clinks as the pestle hit the brass sides, soon muffled by the powder, gave way to light thumps like the soft beating of wings, or of the heart in a smooth round place. My eyes would be blessed, said Rihaab, and the *kohl* precious, with all these dear ones taking part in its preparation.

You

Wedding: To the Bride's House

It is the hottest part of the afternoon. Since the wedding feast, long done, tea and coffee have been served more than once, and I have come in from the garden. Now the tabla is playing, yet again, somewhere outside.

The women around me begin to stir, and make their way out of the house, joined by others from adjacent rooms. Scattered groups are heading up the street, among them the crones who were on the bench. They chant as they go out into the road. Others pass them, but they walk at their own pace, contented, singing all the way. They haven't missed a beat of the tabla, which is now far up ahead, and they can be heard all up and down the street shrilling out the traditional wedding songs to its rhythm.

I see Shareen and her young friends a little way before me, and join them.

'Where are we going?'

'We go to the bride's house. And after, to the church.'

We climb the street, turn into another and another, now descending steeply, turning again, and here is a crowd of women on the outer steps of a house, calling out and trilling to music that comes from deep within. The press is terrible, and tighter as we ascend, so that we also progress more slowly. Inside there is a passageway to negotiate. Looking ahead I have glimpses of a room which must be the centre of activity. There is a small group standing at its entrance, probably family members, letting in a number of people at a time.

I stand for a long while by a small window along this passage. It has an ornamental iron grating, and reminds me of something, but I can't recall what. I know I have seen the identical design before, or a similar one. Where? It won't come to me. I distract myself peering out at the street, not that there is much to see there. Someone tells me that the church is in that direction. Is that where I will meet up with Omar again?

And when we meet how will it be? We came here together in the morning, as a married couple attending a wedding. A whole day gone by in celebration and festivities, and I am still with the women. I am now so lacking in confidence, in us and in myself, that it does not occur to me to ask myself how I feel about him. My own feelings and behaviour will depend on his, will come in the form of responses and reactions only. Will he greet me with that look of admiration and contentment I have seen before, when I first came here ... when I had faith? We both had faith. We believed in each other when we embarked on this life together, and in our own ability to live up to that belief. The longest look or the smallest exchange of glances was a homecoming of the gaze. Now, I wait and stare out through this ornamental window.

Where are you Omar? I would like to be with you now, after all this time, the months stretching into years. But then why, after so long? What binds me to you?

Protection

Of physical things it is your slimness of body I love most. It is a tapering body; tapering feet, hands, fingers. The absence of chest hair matches perfectly this sinuous length.

Take Muammar, your friend who took us to the wedding family that night. He is of much more solid build. He is tall like you, but thickset, with a sinewy wide neck attaching his rounder head to a torso that I could not help seeing as bovine. A Taurus, in appearance at least, where you are lithe, as expected of the mountain goat of Capricorn, your birth sign. He has a moustache, too, like so many of your countrymen. You do not. It seems that all the absent facial hair is concentrated in the tapering sweep of your lashes.

So often you used to stand with your flat chest and midriff thrust out in front of you, sure of yourself, and vulnerable: the cocky man, the little boy trying to look strong. While you seemed ignorant of the contradictory effect of this stance, you also seemed, to me at least, to be vaguely aware of giving yourself away, without knowing quite why. It told me something about the men from your world, something far from the dark and threatening images of you that my world has been so keen to conjure up. Here was a transparency, which the powerful in my world refuse to see, putting on their opaque eyes.

Twice you wept real tears in my presence, once because of a professional setback and the thought that you might never achieve, and the second time when I was leaving you. It was supposed to be temporary, but it was as if you knew that the months would run into years. Yours were tears of grief, and welled up from the foreknowledge of losses still to come. I knew because I sensed the same grief for myself, and that you were crying for both of us.

In the village one morning, long before, we were dressing to go into the city. You had been rubbing hand cream into your hands and arms, and before it had been quite absorbed you rubbed your hands over your neck and chest. At last you put on your shirt and pants, so that your sisters, who were dressed, could come into the room again to brush and pin up their hair and apply their make-up. In the midst of this you said to me, 'Just look at this nose. See how straight it is. Have you ever seen a better nose? Of course not.'

And then, before I could answer, you went straight to the next piece of business of the day, speaking of something we had to do, somewhere we had to be. The bus would be along soon.

I smiled at you and laughed to myself. A rhyme composed itself in my head: 'Nothing more exposed than the nose'.' All sorts of different sayings, beliefs, conventions, superstitions concerning the nose crowded into my mind at once. I remembered words of Rabelais and other writers about noses and the parts of the male anatomy they have been made to represent. I also thought: that's why Cleopatra died defeated. She must have said to someone — Caesar? Antony? — 'Just look at this nose! Have you ever seen a better?' But she was a queen. You were a village boy making good, returned from his overseas studies with honour that belonged to the place as to you, and you never learnt the art of self-protection — beyond the physical.

For me the strutting of your nose in that bald statement resembled the bare, hairless chest thrust forward, bringing the tummy along part way. How different from the concealment your mother sought as she covered your face with a blanket, and your brother's too, when you were babies. It was to ward off the evil eye. The more beautiful a woman's children, the more she must protect them from the envy of others, especially from childless women and those with less beautiful babies. So no one saw you then.

Now showing yourself is not compensation enough. Still the young boy at heart, you must show and tell. It is you who have told me about what your mother used to do. It is from you that I know these things. She was protecting you, but what covers you now?

Time

I romanticised you. In all the Orientalist ways. That was part of the wall. My part. It did not feel like a wall. It was far more soft and subtle — a dream we floated in, oblivious of the world, untouched by it.

We went back in time. Centuries back.

To begin with, we met in a hostile climate. The revolution in Iran had taken place some years before, but I think, looking back, that memories of the 'hostage crisis' and the campus draped with yellow ribbons were still fresh in the minds of many Americans. It made you angry when even the most intelligent and sophisticated students around us, obtaining PhDs in esoteric sciences, referred to 'Middle Eastern society' en bloc as medieval. And they incited my own resentment of their too quick judgements and ready images. Yet in the headiness of love, and the desire to predate these stereotypes, it was to medieval Europe that I turned for my bearings.

Later, much later, you would become my reference, the departure point of knowledge for me, but not in the beginning. In the beginning, hadn't I learnt the rudiments of Old French and discovered in some of its literature the first stirrings of European knowledge about your part of the world? The Middle Ages: a time when, in spite of religion, the differences between our cultures would surely not have been so great as they seemed now.

There was *The Song of Roland*, set in the time of Charlemagne. On rare occasions, in your room, it was me who spoke, and once I told you all about this epic that sings the battle of Roncevaux, mourning the defeat of the French army's rear guard by the Saracens, and the death of Roland, the king's nephew. But did I tell you that the real battle of 778 was not with the Moors, but with the Basques — people who have fought for centuries with the powers on both sides of the Pyrenees in their struggle to maintain their separate identity?

And did I tell you that the epic was composed much later? Around the 1100s, closer to the time of the First Crusade. Suddenly it's a Muslim army, a more relevant enemy at the time of composition, described as formidable, with some of its warriors singled out as no less noble and heroic than those on the French side. Still, there were the crusade propaganda claims that the 'pagan' Saracens worshipped three gods: 'Mahomet', 'Tergavant' and 'Apollin' (Apollo), an attempt to turn the tables on the Muslim accusations against the Christian belief in the Trinity. False representations of the Middle East have a long history.

But love gives courage. I loved you, and like the knight of La Mancha in feminine form, I would go forth to right the imbalance of the world. A Joan for Justice! I had no experience of war and battles, but love would be my weapon, the only one I had. Love is the way for the powerless to resist, to make a difference, at least for individuals, if not in the wider world. It is a means and an end.

Love is in abundance in medieval writing. Not in the epics of course, but in the courtly love poetry and the romances, and in the *chantefables*. I know I didn't tell you about the 13th century *Aucassin and Nicolette*. I'm sure you would enjoy this delightful tale ... then again, perhaps not ... of a young Christian knight and an orphan girl captured from the Saracens and brought up by a neighboring family. They are separated and spend a large part of the story searching and yearning for each other. After many trials and adventures they are reunited, and she is discovered to be of Christian and royal parentage after all. Now love can triumph! Inter-religious marriage would have been impossible. But how charmingly love across the cultures is played out *before* it is annulled by this discovery.

A little self parody. My foil against the deceptions of romantic love, all the while allowing me to indulge it. Like the poem I made for you, Omar, in something vaguely approaching Old French. It had to be a poem, combining the flavour of the old epics and romances. Medieval lyricism was as close as I could imagine to the beautiful foreign sounds and rhythms of the poems I heard from your lips. And poetry is an acceptable language of love for you. I know you admire the glorified Arab past, a past that gave to honour its rightful place, and meaning to every gesture. It was the past of Arabic poetry. It was the world of Sheikh Haatem — the one you told me about — so poor that in order not to betray the ideals of hospitality and generosity he killed his beloved horse, his only remaining companion, and with all graciousness served it up as a feast to some unexpected guests, saving his grief until after they had gone.

I addressed my love poem to the person I thought you were, and the person you seemed to want to be, in that ideal world. And since you did not speak French, I translated it into a vaguely antiquated English. Do you still have this poem, or have you lost it?

195

Chanson cortoise

Biaz doux sire, jeune et cortois,
(Good sweet sire, young and courteous,)
Si proz, gentil, et gran et droit,
(So worthy, gentle, and tall and straight,)
Gent, hardi, et leste a l'amor,
(Graceful, bold and nimble in love,)
Merci a Diu por toz li jors
(Thanks be to God for every day)
Que par Son Vuel te preste a moi!
(That by His Will He lends you to me!)

Tant biax vis avez, et li cors
(So beautiful a face have you, and your body)
Tant par est gent, tant par est fort,
(Is so graceful, is so strong,)
Si que la dame vostre mere
(That the lady your mother)
Molt proz deit sentir, et molt fier,
(Must feel very worthy, and very proud,)
Et, par foi, ele n'a pas tort.
(And, faith, she is not wrong.)
    Ah! Li biax sort!
    (Ah! Such a beautiful fate!)

Molt fiers vos ancestres aussi.
(Very proud your ancestors too.)
Iceulx vos voient de Paradis,
(These see you from Paradise,)
Iceulx qui ont li miens tues
(These who killed mine)
De lors longues espees corbees
(With their long curved swords)
    An les guerres es temps enfuis.
    (In wars of times fled.)

196

Ami, la vostre espee est droite,
(Friend, your sword is straight,)
Et faite por la gaine estroite,
(And made for a tight scabbard,)
Or, oncques concquestes forz cele
(Today, no conquests save that)
Des dames et des dameiseles
(Of ladies and young damsels)
Hui ne s'offrent a l'arme adroite
(Now present themselves to the adroit weapon.)
    Las! Triste esploit!
    (Alas! Sorry state [of arms]!)

Diu sait ben por queles raisons
(God knows well for what reasons)
Jo vos ai pris por compagnon;
(I took you for my companion;)
Vos, seul, deduit et poesie
(You, alone, give me delight)
Me donnez por tote ma vie.
(And poetry for my whole life.)
Cils sont, jo croie, li plus biax dons.
(These are, I think, the most beautiful gifts.)

Portant, une chose m'effroie:
(But yet, one thing makes me affear'd:)
Ami, vos biaz longs cils de soie
(Friend, your beautiful, long silken lashes)
Voilent des ialz li fin regard,
(Veil the look of finesse in your eyes,)
Subtil comme cil Maistre Renard,
(As subtle as that of Master Renard [Fox])
Qui m'oste li gran part ma joie.
(Which steals the greater part of my joy.)
    Malheur a moi!
    (Woe unto me!)

Why did I reverse it like that at the end? That sudden switch to foreboding. What was I afraid of? I believe now that I was mistaken. That look in your eyes was more mischievous than sly. Yours was the shrewdness of the village man, not the truly harmful cunning of the sophisticate. No. It was our sense of what we did not know — of all that we both had yet to learn about living with difference and with generations of mistrust — that stirred and shifted at the bottom of our hearts.

But then, delight and poetry you did give me, in abundance. That is what stays with me now. It was rare in those days for me to be the one to talk. I was the listener. I listened and absorbed your stories as a lover of stories must. I took in the timbre and rhythm of your voice with the very air I breathed.

I could never tell the exact moment when you switched to Arabic. Only after a while did I realise that somewhere your English must have flowed into it. Then I recognised from the cadence of your speech that you had moved into poetry. Or my recognition came from an interruption, a moment when you stopped and shook your head in wonder at the poet's ingenious choice of an expression, placement of a word, or at the way a line had been set out, simple yet condensed. Then you wanted to show me — 'You see? This is what Abu Tammam is doing here' — and found yourself lost for words, rudely wakened to the realisation that translation would not do it, laborious explanation would not enable me to understand as you understood, to chime with one chord to the poet's miracle. You attempted it anyway, trying to condense your own rendering to as few words as possible.

For both of us, the sense of completion came later, in a kiss or a caress, and in the wordless exchanges that followed.

Handkerchief

You must know one thing Omar. I would not exchange my life for anyone's. My wish is that whatever happens between us, you, too, will have no regrets. In coming and living here with you and your family, for whatever time, whatever the reason, I have done what I wanted to do and what had meaning for me.

Even romanticism may be a good enough reason. I would have no care for my life without the inner world it brings. The stories of the *Thousand and One Nights* made their deep impression in my childhood. I loved their magic and mystery. Behind its folk simplicity every story is another wayward voyage, another labyrinthine quest ... and another movement of self-justification and self-completion for the teller. The olive tree of my childhood left its mark. Why should it have affected me to no end? And, if my mother touched on some truth in her reflections, my dreamy Irish grandfather left his influence. All the strands are woven together, and memory itself has a reason as we create our identities — and create the meaning of our experience — partly out of fleeting, nostalgic images from the past.

Once, in that twelfth-floor student's room in America, I was looking at you as you were preparing to go out, and you, dressed in a suit, pulled a handkerchief from your pocket, and a world rushed forward to meet me. It was my grandfather, in my grandmother's apartment, during one of his visits or even, I think, before he went away, because I was a small child. A tall slim Australian of Irish origin, sensitive, my mother told me, poetic and dreamy like me, she said, but also very 'dapper' as I heard him called in those days. There was a way with him of moving and walking, of bending and of handling objects. He took care.

You, from the other side of the world, merged with him. The gesture, and the way you bent forward just a little to do it, were his. Pulling that handkerchief neatly folded from your pocket, with that slight stoop and preoccupied air, you were him. In your movement time was collapsed. And I loved you.

Into the Wadi

There was one day, one amazing day, that seemed to encapsulate everything you meant to me. You did nothing special, nothing out of the ordinary. But I had the impression that both you and your country were offering yourselves to me through the day itself — in the time we spent together and the things we did. A gift to memory. This day holds its place at the very centre of all my recollections.

The first summer visit was drawing to an end. When you told me you would take me hunting with you, and said we would go into the wadi the next morning and spend the day there, I could not picture hunting in the country I had seen. It seemed too dry and scrubby. Where was the forest? And too biblical, a 'wilderness' where the shepherds belonged for sure. What could possibly be hunted there? Sheep? Goats? Donkeys?

You were as good as your word. We left soon after sunrise with a small picnic lunch you had prepared yourself. Into a canvass knapsack you had placed the *khóbuz*, round flat loaves of bread you layered and rolled together, a few tomatoes, several of those sticky green fruit like small cucumbers, plenty of salt for you — you loved salt — and some oranges.

The descent was steep, first along a wide dirt track leading out from the village, the soil mostly a thick rust-coloured clay, and then down through jutting rocks, stones and boulders. We went jumping from one to another here, slipping and sliding there. Plenty of narrower pathways led down gradually, crisscrossing each other along the flanks of the ridges, but they were the sheep tracks, and it would take all day if you followed them. Once at the bottom the going was easy, except for the patches of thistles.

After weeks surrounded by people I could hardly believe that we were alone together, me empty-handed and feeling light and free, you with your rifle and knapsack. We were accompanied only by sounds in this wild place, ripples in the expanse of heat and stillness: insects whirred in the long dry grasses, birds called, and our legs brushed past the shrubs and bushes. The few loud reports from your rifle were lonely and disturbing. Then there was the rushing of a stream up ahead, and before we reached it, the subsiding of our bodies onto darker, softer grasses in a grove of pomegranates. Your long slender fingers brushed over me, the same that had prepared the fruit and bread, the same that had pulled the trigger, would pull it again, would delicately gather up the small bird like a pigeon and place it in another part of the knapsack. I could smell your perfume through it all, the one you rub over your chest and arms every day, smell it here in the wild, mixed in with the earth and rock and grass, and with the herbs growing wildly beside us.

This was after you missed the partridges that flew down at the first shot and scattered through the underbrush on their fast-running legs, knowing better than to fly again.

And it was before you took the pigeon-like bird, dead

on, as it flew. It dropped, giving up the effort of its wings as if overtaken by the heat. The heat I hardly felt until later, just as we came upon the spring, and the deep pool where we bathed.

We found the source. A spout had been made from a large leaf wedged into the rocks at a height roughly level with our shoulders. But the water of the spring was oozing and bubbling from the rock all around, and near the spout a pale green leach was heaving its fat little body ripplingly up the wet surface. We drank and turned back to the pool where we took it in turns to watch and bathe. The pool was surrounded by a crudely built low wall, and after dressing we sat side by side on its cool damp stones that lay just within the shadow of the hill, our backs drying in the summer sun, our feet dangling in the shaded water as we ate. Opposite the source the stream ran limp and shallow away from the pool, losing itself among silt and stones and new young grasses. From among some bushes on the other side a donkey trotted out along a narrow sheep track and quickened his pace as he approached the stream. He had no rider, and no one accompanied him, but you were sure he must belong to one of the shepherd boys whose flute we could hear in the distance. The donkey drank, raised his head, turned and trotted off the way he had come. We gazed after him until he had disappeared in the brush and we could no longer hear his hoofs on the track. Then we looked downstream, our eyes wandering over the bright colours of the oleanders that had found out the way of the water, which we soon followed. After a while you shot the bird. You held it up, beak pointing limply groundward, and allowed its blood to run out and form its own spent pool.

We walked a long way, deep on the floor of the wadi, the hillsides rising high around us. You took aim at more partridges, pulled the trigger once or twice, but they were too quick. Lovingly, you told me about their ways, traditions of another clan. 'These are the customs of the partridge,' you said, and explained how clever she is. So lovingly you spoke of them that I wondered if you had been trying to miss your shots.

Soon we veered away from the stream, into an arm of the wadi that looked as if it led nowhere, if not to another steep climb to the top of some precipice that itself might signal the edge of another village. But it opened out, and after a shepherd with many sheep had passed above us along the slope, the bells and the bah-ing echoing long after he'd gone, we came to another stream where you stopped to wash some of the remaining fruit in the fast-flowing water. It was here that you noticed how the fruit took on a strange smell. You puzzled over this for a while, then said you thought you knew what the cause must be, and we continued upstream until we came on another source where a rudimentary fountain gushed from a hole in a wall. A large group of women and children were gathered at the edge, great piles of sheep's wool beside them. Two of the women kept beating with large wooden mallets a thick layer of wool that was spread in the shallows.

You greeted them, and when they asked where you were from you told them the name of your village. 'But I have taught in M——,' you said, aware that we were nearer to that town. 'Ah, yes, we are from Agraba, and my sister lives in Yubla,' one of them answered, tilting her head at a woman beside her, 'but I have another sister in M—— and her daughter goes to school there.' You laughed and joked with them at leisure before crouching to wash the wool's grease from the cucumbers, upstream of the women and their work. Then you handed out cucumbers to everyone, women and children, and there were still plenty for ourselves. I did not recall that you had brought so many. Your knapsack seemed bottomless as you kept dipping your hand in and bringing out more fruit. We sat for some time chatting with the women and drinking their hot sweet tea from glasses they had brought with them, filled from a pot on an open fire. There was no hurry. The day seemed to stretch on and on, accommodating whatever we wanted to fill it with.

We left them and continued on, away from the stream, no longer on the floor of the wadi, but at a slightly higher level along the slope of the hill. As we walked you pointed out different plants and bushes, naming them and explaining what they were used for. Nothing escaped your eyes, not the tiniest sprig of delicate leaves lost among the courser brush and thistles. It was usually a spice or herb you spied, from which you picked a leaf or two, crushing and rolling it between your fingers before sniffing. 'Smell this,' you said, and one after the other you put these crushed herbs and plants into my hands or under my nose, or rubbed them into my skin. Often you knew what was there without looking, just by the smell in the air. 'Stop, there is wild thyme somewhere here,' you said. Or you named some other plant, and almost immediately you would find it.

I thought we were wandering freely, carelessly, but all along you knew where we were. And where we were going. Towards sunset we began to climb a very steep and rocky hillside that at times seemed almost sheer. You moved on up with grace and ease, quick and sure of foot like the goat that is your sign, while I kept sliding on the gravel and running out of breath. You teased me about it, but offered your hand and showed me ways to climb more easily. When I asked why we had to take such a steep route where there was no track, you said we must arrive at the top before dusk because that is the time of day when the snakes most often come out from their hiding places in the cracks and crevices of rocks. Although I would have liked to be a child again with a child's agility, my body actually enjoyed the exertion and wanted to test itself in this way more often. When we reached the top it was well into dusk and there before us, as I had half expected, were the peripheral streets of a town just like ours. 'We are in Al-Rafiid,' you told me. And so well had you gauged where we would emerge that we did not have to go into the street at all, but simply moved to the front entrance of a house whose back garden we had climbed directly into.

Dear old friends. A whole family of brothers you had known for years, grown up with, gone hunting with, exchanged visits with, and who appeared overjoyed to see you. When you told them where we had been all day, they brought water from their well onto the tiled front porch so we could refresh ourselves. We washed our hands, our faces, our feet, and were given towels to wipe ourselves dry before going in, leaving our shoes at the door. All the generations of their family were there, old men and women, the brothers and their wives, and children of every age. We were spontaneously included for the evening meal, as if we were family or they had been expecting us. There was plenty of cool fresh yoghurt and salad, and other good things with bread and tea. Later we went into a back room to look at the latest of the falcons they kept there which one of the brothers trained for hunting. They showed a lively interest in me that had nothing of mere curiosity, and when the conversation stayed too long on a subject that I could not follow, they changed it and indicated with nods and warm smiles in my direction that I was included in the party, or they asked me something I could answer in my simple Arabic.

Finally an acquaintance visiting a neighbouring house gave us a ride back to Kufr Soum. The car kept winding through the dark, in and out of different roads and villages. We drove for so long I could not believe how far you and I must have walked and climbed that day. A day that was perfect. At the end, before sleeping, came the gathering sense of something that could never be matched. Dare I think it? ... the best day of my life.

Rifle

You love your rifle. Using it, wearing it, caring for it. After every hunting trip you go through the ritual: cleaning, checking, putting away. You take your time. All this cleaning and caring is, of course, part of the obligation of ownership, but it belongs to the pleasure too. You chat quietly with your hunting friends about unimportant things as the cloth-covered rod moves gently along the barrel. It is a caress.

On two occasions you gave me your rifle to carry. One was on our picnic at the reserve overlooking the Yarmouk River. It was winter then. I was wearing a long-sleeved shirt and over it a thick red knitted sweater with a large white and grey koala on the front. And over all that bulk the rifle was slung across my back. It felt strange standing for the photo you took of me, in front of a tree that leaned out over the valley, me with the rifle and behind me, forming the photo's background, the river, and the other side where soldiers came and went in trucks, in uniform, with guns.

The other occasion was on one of our hunting days in the wadi. We returned by a different route, arriving at the other end of the village, where your father's cousin, Abu Kariim, lived. Do you remember? It was my first time there and our visit was unexpected. What must they have thought when you appeared with this stranger, this foreign woman, a rifle slung across her back? You're a favourite with them, and always welcome. They love and understand you, whatever you do. Still, we took them by surprise, coming in the back way, past the numerous hutches full of plump and healthy rabbits of all colours that looked more like fluffy pet bunnies than food. I had always associated rifles with rabbits, and this scene struck me as oddly consistent. The only time I had actually used a rifle was rabbit shooting in Australia. My teacher was so good that on my very first try I shot the rabbit dead with a bullet clean through the head. The next time I only managed to wound the animal, and its neck had to be wrung. I didn't use a rifle again.

At Abu Kariim's you explained to me how some Muslims eat rabbit and some do not. The prophet Mohammed did not state if it was acceptable or forbidden food. When asked about it, he did not answer. I've often imagined to myself how that incident would have taken place. Here is the Prophet making one of his pronouncements about clean and unclean foods. He has dealt with sheep, cattle, pork, cats and dogs, seafood, reptiles ... Someone asks him what other animals may be eaten. The questions become more and more specific. He is patient, answering each in turn. Then another calls out to him: 'And rabbit. Can we eat rabbit?'

It is not the question of the animal itself that makes him hesitate.

It is just that with rabbit the point has been reached where a voice cries out within him: 'Enough!' But he does not say it. Ah! How foolishly the people become carried away with the letter of religion! Don't they know that hypocrisy begins there? Still, patience and gentleness are his hallmark. So he does not rebuke them. He simply leaves the question unanswered, and with mildness — smoothness — moves onto the next order of business.

$Shouts$

You were demanding. No one complained. To you.

The manliness in your physical and mental comportment, in the way you could take control and coax things into functioning order, that same manliness that drew people to you, was always overstepping the bounds. For me at least. Or is that what manliness is?

I wonder sometimes if you knew yourself why you had to build that wall just when you did, how much my presence was connected with this decision. Was my not being able to live in Amman, or Irbid, or even on the campus of Yarmouk University where I taught, really because of the circumstances alone? I could not accept this for much longer, but would have to bring you to understand that you were deceiving yourself as much as me in keeping to these reasons. If your possessiveness had meant that we saw more of each other, I might have found in that some sort of compensation for our living arrangements. Instead, not only did I see little of you for a married couple, but my influence was diminishing daily as that of your peers built up.

You did not take your responsibilities to your family lightly. You shouldered them well. Like a man! No one could fault you in that regard. But your bringing me to the village, well, maybe that was a form of evasion, as Nawal had implied. Evasion through trying to have it both ways — be the responsible oldest son (I don't understand how any oldest son can bear such a burden) and take a piece of the West all to yourself, keep tasting it long after you left, through me. In a world where for centuries conquest and domination seemed to go all one way, here was a means of achieving some small victory in the opposite direction.

And I ... idealistic, romantic, other-worldly to the point of vexation with conformity, unhappy with my culture's power mainly to consume, its refusal to imagine being in the other's place ... I complied. I came, in actuality, to the other's place. Yours. And I found so much of what I looked for, including the beautiful things you had told me about — wadies and castles; olive and pomegranate trees that bear living treasures; also things so normal and natural in your world that you could not measure the chasm between it and mine. Not all negative things. The chasm works both ways. They care deeply, the people of your family, your country, your culture, care for each other in a way that Westerners could not fathom. If we ever had this sense of community we lost it long ago. I slept more soundly every night in your house than in any other place or time, with half my burden of living removed, lifted up into some centre of custody — not a place but a shared space in the collective mind. Even in the daytime cares weighed lightly. These were among the things I loved and that kept me going. I was determined to find a way for us to be together, in spite of the difficulties, and the challenge justified my 'aventure' in coming here.

So when I saw that you would not budge, when I saw that the wall was going up, that we would not live together in the city or on one of our two campuses, that the bond with your friends and peers was more important than the bond with your wife, I began to cast around for ways to make this work and last — this couple that we were. I felt that you needed to go away for a while, back into the international world to find out more about other ways of living. Even as the wall was being completed I sat with you outside the house, in the bright sun, and against the clinking and scraping of the wall-builders' tools, I spoke quietly of your goals and aspirations. After my return it took a good month of this, on and off, at the end of which time you were ready to make enquiries into furthering your studies in the West, this time in the UK. It would be a respite for me, a time for bringing you round, helping you to understand that we could not go on as we were. Then, if you could be persuaded to do things differently on our return, to agree willingly to my not staying all the time in the village ...

You didn't know that for me everything would hinge on the success of that venture — getting you to leave, working on you while we were away, all so that we could still be a couple. I could put up with the disappointments for now, build on the positive side of the life here, so easy to forget when we must live daily with difference, with the loss of our own ways. You didn't know of my hidden agenda. I hardly knew it myself, spurred along as I was by a need and force that remained at the threshold of consciousness. I didn't recognise my underlying control, and I especially didn't know that building on the positive meant increasing my attachment, to you, to your mother and sisters, to all your family. I didn't know that I was making it harder for myself, if the time came that I would have to leave. Why work so patiently through the problems of cultural difference, why develop so much understanding if it will all come to nothing in the end? I was making the act of leaving increasingly difficult.

If I was only half aware of my motivation in persuading you to make those plans to leave, you continued simple and trusting, manly and demanding, commanding, as expected of an oldest son. Because you worked hard, and there was no doubting that you did, you had a right to receive something in return. A form of power. And so you handed out our tasks, and waited for others to wait on you.

I suppose you were not the only one. When you made everyone on the bus wait while you went into the butcher's in that village halfway between Irbid and Kufr Soum, others took advantage and went in too. Other men. It's just that you took longer, and even they became impatient while you chose a whole sheep and had the butcher cut it up, making sure nothing was omitted: head, innards and all.

As soon as you got off the bus you went into the kitchen and handed over three or four bags of warm, fresh flesh to Sahr, who had not been expecting this, not on that day, at that time. She was in the middle of washing the clothes in the old round washing machine she dragged out to use only for heavy loads of laundry. Water and piles of clothes were everywhere on the tiled floor. Now as the bags were emptied onto a large round platter, a strong and steamy smell of offal rose up from it. She said nothing when you came in and stated with offhand authority what you wanted done with it all. She did complain, bitterly, when you had left the room. I tried to help her, but what do I know about cleaning the intestines of a slaughtered animal?

Poor girl! All the menial tasks go to her. And all because she cared for her mother, your mother, too much to finish school. In any case, you told me that girls didn't stay in school long when she was a child. Only ten years between her and Randa, and all the changes that elsewhere occur over generations and generations, have been squeezed into those years, the difference between two siblings. Oh, she can reproduce her letters with a little prodding, and she can write her name, I've seen it. And I know you respect and value the talents she has. Low literacy makes no difference in the shops and markets of Irbid. She can bargain with the best of the souk merchants. I love to see her in action when we go to the city together, though her best bargains are accomplished when I'm not with her. A Westerner in tow tends to stiffen the prices. But the limitations brought by those years of change have turned her into a scold, so that Randa and Bilaal sometimes resent her. It's only a passing resentment, but it adds to her burden.

She was quick and efficient that day, not allowing her annoyance with you to hamper the work: squeezing the sheep intestines from one end to the other between her thumb and forefinger until they were completely emptied, boiling them, soaking them in lemon juice and boiling again. Her arms are thick, and strong enough to break the jaws of the sheep's head, but this time she had to call a neighbour, an older, tougher woman, to help her. Once the meat was handed over, you had no more to do with it. Why did you give her so much work?

But then, it was your celebration, on returning from your studies. Yes, I'm jumping ahead here. This was an incident in my last visit, well after you returned from Scotland. You knew people would visit with their congratulations over the next days. Days and days. They would expect to be fed, and fed well. Regaled. Sahr knew too. We all understood that. Still, you hadn't changed.

The worst time of all with you was during my second stay, a couple of months after I returned. It was a relatively early sign of future problems, well before I began to teach or even to visit Irbid regularly. I had developed a headache and other flu-like symptoms that were treated by the local doctor with tranquilisers. When these made no difference and you decided in mid-January that I should go to Mu'tah with you for a few weeks, in spite of the regulations there, I welcomed the change, believing it would do me good to leave the village for a while and stay with you on the campus. That way I would soon be better, and ready to take up my post.

At first you looked after me well and I recovered. There were some interesting new people to meet among your colleagues and their families, and after a while the wives began to invite me on weekday afternoons when you were teaching. But it soon became clear that you felt increasingly uncomfortable with my presence. I knew you were ill at ease because I was not supposed to be there. We would be married in July, still six months away, and until such time there was the prospective problem of explaining my presence to your superiors. You always introduced me as your wife.

But I sensed that you were bearing with me, with having to share your living quarters with another person. Your routine could not be disrupted. If I had to be physically, bodily there — and at times you didn't mind that at all — you still preferred to find no other signs of my presence. No extra clothes or towels about, where you could see them, not even hanging up to dry, no extra dishes that hadn't been washed, dried and put away, no extra pieces of fluff on the wall-to-wall carpet. In your early thirties, you had become so used to the single life in your home away from home that you could not bear an intimate sharing of your days with anyone for too long.

I soon learnt that you behaved best towards me when we were with your family in the village, or when we had visitors at the Mu'tah apartment, like those army corporals, captains and lieutenants who came in the evenings, always in uniform. Stiffly polite when I offered them tea, they were nonetheless always more at ease when I withdrew.

For me the mounting tension became unbearable when we were alone together there. It was at this time that I sensed how deeply your disappointment at my returning a month late had cut into your faith in us as a couple. I knew that the early period of romance had given way to a new phase of effort and compromise. This would be the time of greatest challenge.

It wasn't that you had given up on us, at least I did not believe so, because in your own way you seemed committed, making meals for us, talking to me about your work and asking what I thought, patiently explaining aspects of Jordanian life, but you found fault with every small thing I did and rarely talked about our relationship. When you felt moved to do so, it was always to say what you were thinking, not to hear out my own concerns. You even became easily annoyed if I wanted to continue a conversation that you decided was done. I began to feel unsure of where even to put myself bodily — in another room? in the same room? on the couch? making tea?

Relief did not come when you were gone. I would

think about ways of trying to communicate with you, feeling that they would fail, and desperately aware that our life as a couple hinged on making them work. But I also felt the desolation of the place. I didn't know the immediate neighbours, and the cold was as penetrating as in the north. Although the apartment was heated, there were times when the whole campus was shrouded in a mist that could only be dispersed by a biting desert wind that blew for days. I don't know how you put up with that yourself. It whistled and moaned through the buildings. It banged the foot-square hinged metal frames that were cut out, like peepholes, in the front and back doors, themselves made of heavy metal. It pierced all outer layers and burst furiously into my very spirit, sweeping away the lavender-garden images of our future together that had first taken root there.

Even with all the doors and windows locked I was unable to keep out the wind's rising, falling, rising lament, or that other sound it often brought with it from the military wing of the campus: the shouts of soldiers at training; strong, sharp and sure one moment, drifting and fading the next.

Beads

I was given two strings of beads, one from your brother-in-law, Adnan, and the other from your cousins, Uncle Kariim's sons. I still have them. One is of clear glass pieces: oblong, and six-sided, threaded onto a pink translucent cord like fishing line, which sends its pastel paleness through the glass prisms making them blush. Three round medallions like small, light coins tinkle at the end of three short fine chains attached at the join. After every eleventh bead is a small metal disk, a separator. Eleven and eleven and eleven. To be read three times.

The other set is more traditional, its beads rounder and a bright opaque blue, fifteen on each side of the join in the silky blue cord. They meet up with thirty yellow beads in the middle. The yellow beads are transparent, and through them the blue cord turns green. It is knotted at the join, then divides into three short cords with a tassel of blue, yellow and silvery metal beads at the end of each. Fifteen twice, and thirty, and fifteen twice. Then the nine beads on the tassels. The combination changes with each string, but always amounts in the end to ninety-nine, the names of Allah, whose one name is engraved onto the first string's tiny medallions. Their tinkling reminds me of a woman's ankle bracelet when she is dancing. But no. That is a blasphemy.

There has to be enough room on the string to move each bead along and count. I touch it and imagine the weight of the larger bead or ball on an abacus. Does everyone always count the names? The Compassionate, the Merciful, the Forgiving: attributes, so we may know the Lord, the Divine One.

I used to sit for hours in the little room among the guests and family that came in and out, sit with one or the other of my strings of beads, watching, observing, unable to speak the language of those around me. But without it, I learnt more quickly the many wordless languages.

The older men are talking and counting, counting and talking. Some of them are fat, in the way of dignity. A few of these, in the way of flesh, never let the beads out of their hands. They seem absorbed in their bodily thereness, as if the fat beads in the plump hands were taking the place of other things they would like to hold, fleshy things, and rounded like beads. But they don't know, and when they see me count my own — which for me is like Patience or Solitaire once the language has become too much and clatters like a gate shutting before me — then they suspect and wonder. She's Christian isn't she? This one's old wife nudges him and jerks her head at me: is she praying? Ah good, she says to me then, you are becoming a Muslim, and nods with approval as I patiently count: one, two, three, Our Father Who is in Heaven, or Al-ḥamdulillah, rab al :allamein (Praise be to God, Lord of the Worlds) — same God, and same prayer, essentially — as everything and everyone and the words rolling off their tongues turn slowly around me.

I have never seen you with beads. They are not the sort of thing you would like. The appearance of piety does not belong to your self-image. Neither does the absent-minded fiddling these men seem to indulge in. God will do what He will do, and no difference will be made by a set of beads. And in the world of men you must show decisiveness, focus, strength. This playing with strings of beads would not become you, who mean what you do and do what you mean, no gesture wasted. You are not one for games, except cards of course. Poker and No Trumps are a serious business. But this, no, this is a weakness.

Your young cousins handle the beads well, those who have them. They are not obsessed or engrossed. It is not, as with the older men, a habit for them, a decadent dependency. They fling the beads as they talk, even throw them down to make a wild gesture or deliver the punch line of a joke, and a few minutes later they pick them up again, offering some quieter, more sedate opinion. But youth is no model for the head of the house, which is what you are when you are here, all your actions designed to make clear to your father that as oldest son you are in charge now. When you are gone he is left in peace, and all resume their daily chores and pastimes as before. You should have a household of your own, like any older, strong, decisive man. That would solve many things.

I am still counting, but growing tired. Tea arrives, and as I thankfully set my beads aside, I think of the ancient worship of stone idols. Suppressed and diminished now. Still held and touched, but as mere symbols of the Unseen. Could it be as a wine is reduced to its sediment?

Forgetting

I remember only peripheries, not centres. In the taxi returning the first time from Amman to Irbid you told me something very important. I knew it by the way you spoke. And it left its mark. You said: 'Forget the past.' A simple statement, which you explained and embellished and fired with meaning beyond itself. The reasons you gave, the words you used, your gestures and all the small things that showed its weight and wisdom, are forgotten.

Now only the scene comes back to me. The taxi is winding its way through the hills with many scraggly pines along the road, and a few cypresses and other trees I don't know, enough greenery on both sides to give shade. It must be the only part of Jordan where you can drive for more than a few minutes in shade. Off in the distance dotted bands of olive groves attempt to geometrise the steep hillsides, or here and there a house totters on the edge of a drop into more deep green.

The man and his wife and their little boy in the back of the taxi are very quiet, the driver silent as they always seem to be, and I begin to feel uncomfortable as your soft low voice continues in what for everyone else is a foreign language. They surely recognise its counselling tone. You are telling me why the past is behind me, and I am here now, and this is my life. What was it you said?

The minor commotion in the back seat comes as a surprise. Father and mother both speak to the driver and he pulls over. We all get out, and the small boy vomits again at the edge of the road. The two of us are off to one side. 'See this family,' you say to me, 'they are Palestinian.' I wonder why you are telling me, and how you can know. I try to look for the signs that would have told you. Is it the veiled mother's embroidered dress covering her stout frame? Is it their accent, or some dialect of Arabic? But they've hardly spoken. Or their general appearance of impoverishment? Are they from one of the camps outside the city — Amman or Irbid?

The driver could well be annoyed, but if so he's not showing it. He is patient with the boy and accepts and dismisses the apologies that both parents make in turn. They offer these not abjectly, but in calm, steady voices, with pauses between, maintaining dignity. The father is using a large handkerchief to wipe the seat, and the driver gives him some tissues. They pour a little water from a bottle the driver keeps with him and wipe again. When we get back in, the smell is still there, and just as I am thinking to myself how quiet the boy has been through the trip, not complaining, though he tried to warn his parents at the last minute, you speak to him. 'You're a good boy,' I hear you say in Arabic. Then you joke with him and make him laugh, and the parents smile.

The smell is soon gone as we drive on, air whooshing in at the windows. You return to our talk, warming again to your theme, weaving conviction into conviction. For a moment I glimpse the world as you see it, a space where the past does not exist. There is only now, I am with you and we are 'walking together as one'.

That was the way you used to say it. But how you showed me that glimpse, that flash, I don't remember. That day, moving through the hills, belongs to the past. Now there is only now, the wider now when I am not here with you in this country, and you are gone.

Bidoun Kaalima

Wedding: Raqsi!

Shareen's brother is absent, like the other men who are with him at his home, dancing and helping him to prepare. Here at the bride's house we have moved along the passage, and now women family members motion us forward into a long wide room, completely bare except for folding metal chairs around the edges and a sofa at the far end. On it, in the very middle, the bride is sitting all in white. I find it unusual for the bride to be sitting. In the northern villages she stands, for hours on end, on a dais or platform of some sort. Once, I remember, it was a table that did not appear too steady, with carpets and other wall hangings behind her.

She never speaks or moves. She is a statue, her plaster smile as stony as her eyes. In some brides the gaze is petrified by nervousness and the excitement of the moment, in some by timidity, in others by submission, or by terror. They are always beautiful. Perfect, with every hair and fold fixed into its preordained position, ready to crack if they stir.

This bride looks more relaxed. It must help to be sitting down. Her mother and other women attending on her hover to one side of the sofa. At the other side is a group of musicians, different from those in the street. Here they are all women. The tabla player is especially good. She is fast. And exultant. Before them, out on the bare floor some women are dancing more or less in a circle, with wild movements, fiercely wild as if to compensate for the bride's immobility. It seems they are defying the constraints of her role by proxy, for her who cannot. The group of us who have just entered take our seats around the room and look on. This dancing … so much energy … forgetfulness of care …

At our own wedding there had been no dancing. We are both older, beyond the age of fresh young weddings, and Omar could not afford the festivities. Marrying a Westerner meant he could circumvent the customs: the house and new furniture that must be prepared for the new couple, the entertainment over many days of feasting, all paid for by the groom's family, and the gold jewellery he must give his wife as surety against future loss. I had not come expecting any of these things. In fact ours could hardly have been called a wedding. It was a marriage, quiet and solemn. It was the act that the Muslim couple performs with all simplicity, in signing a contract before a judge. Not in a place of worship. Not a religious ceremony at all, but a legal procedure with religious overtones. Soon afterwards we left for Scotland, just when I would have been expected to settle down to married life, and to life in this country. There are no photos from that time, but I know that I was not — just as I am not now — stiff and still, like those brides in their stiff tulle.

The dancers invite us to join them a few at a time, as some of their number leave. I am hesitant, but one of them comes towards me. '*Raqsi!*' she encourages, and draws me into the magic circle. Then it is impossible not to let go. We are free, all women together, dancing for each other and especially for *her*. For the bride. Our combined vitality rushes to meet her future, riding hope, expectation, the desire of happiness. I take my turn at the centre of the ring, in partnership only with the joy that dances and sparkles from the eyes and mouths around me.

When I leave there are not many people waiting to be admitted, and I walk back down the nearly empty passage. I rapidly pass the small window looking out onto the street, and it must be this rapidity, the flash as I go by, that allows the window to give up to me what it held back before. That something recognisable that I could not recall. Now it is before me in this glimpse of light through an ornamental grating. Here is the same shape and design as the bars on another window, one I looked out of so often in expectation.

Bidoun Kaalima 1

The close narrow bars of the iron grating crossed the window horizontally, but towards the centre these gave way to decorative scrolls and swirls. Through them I looked onto the garden, and out towards the iron gate with its grillwork painted black. I had heard the crunch of a vehicle, and seeing Sahr and Randa go outside, I knew Omar must have arrived. As he stepped out of his friend's dusty old Mercedes and saw his sisters there, I wondered if he was expecting to find me with them. But his eyes had passed peremptorily over the scene and he was still talking to the men.

I wanted to run out there and hug him, but what he had told me about kissing and embracing before others was true. I saw it in the behaviour of his two married sisters and their husbands who called at the house every day. No touching; no glances or words of affection. Nothing but the attentive way Aisha poured the tea into her husband Moussa's glass or the way Moussa, when it was time to leave, spoke gently to her as he wrapped a blanket around their sleeping baby and carried it into the night hugged to his shoulder.

Omar had got out of the car and was leaning down, chatting to the driver and two other passengers, laughing every so often. With the rise and fall of their voices I wondered at the stillness of mine, and of my body which felt tense and impatient after the days of anxious waiting.

Every week it was the same: the emptiness when he left, the settling down to everyday life with the women — which wasn't so bad in itself, was even pleasurable but for his absence — and then the anticipation. His sisters always seemed to know in advance when he would return.

'Omar come *boukra*, no *shams*, verry verry black, Mishaal.'

If Randa was there she would correct her sister: 'Tomorrow he will come, Michèle, late in the night, in the dark.'

'Yes,' continued Sahr, 'verry night.'

Or Randa would come straight to me and clutch my shoulders with excitement.

'Michèle, Michèle, he is coming tomorrow in the afternoon. He will not teach *el-arba:a*.'

'*El-arba:a*? ... Ah yes, Wednesday.'

'Yes, Wed-e-nes-day Michèle, anotherr day herre with us!'

They all talked about it, his mother rejoicing with them. Yet once he was there the entire family, and no one more than the women, went about their daily routine as if he had not gone away.

It was the winter of my long stay. Omar was well into the academic year at Mu'tah University. The scene on this day was not new, when the car rolled up outside the gate as it had done several times, bringing him home for the weekend.

Omar was still standing chatting with the driver, and I decided to leave the room and stand in the courtyard, near the well, where I could see and hear more without obtruding. His sisters did not speak to him either, but remained by the gate in respectful patience. Something of the men's talk floated across to me. I recognised a few words I had often heard.

'*Fooot.*' Come in.

He was repeating it to those in the car, addressing each by name as he asked them in, and they were giving their excuses. Munir was among them, and some men in army uniform. He pressed.

'*Ahléyn, ahléyn, fooot shrob shai.*' (Welcome, welcome, come in and drink some tea.)

I could tell they were going to agree. His conversation was serious and jocular, and they were enjoying it, ready to yield as so many did to his gentle nudging. The car was started up again and turned slowly onto a dirt strip where tufts of course yellow grass held fast amongst bits of broken rock and pottery, pastel-coloured plastic bags and other odd discarded objects. The ground inside the wall was as neat and clean as it was neglected without.

The talk kept up volubly over the car's engine, and through it he cast the occasional glance back towards the gate, noticing, but taking no notice of his sisters, or of myself standing further back between the well and the front door. By now I understood it was expected of him, just as I understood I could rarely speak my love without entering some forbidden territory. No more could he. Everything, it seemed, was '*bidoun kaalima*', without words, tacit. Without a word he would make love to me that night between the rough wool of the heavy blankets that would cover the two thick mattresses laid down for us side by side. He would make love as on every night we were together, without a word, as surely as the sun would rise the next morning. And without a word, also in the morning, he would give me something he had brought

231

with him. Something from Mu'tah, or from Amman if he'd stopped there. Something he had selected for me. Like the blouse, a few weeks earlier. I had been reading a magazine article on women's regional dress, with photos of colourful weaves or embroiderings from many places in and around Jordan: Ramtha, Bir Sab'a, Salt, Ma'an. On that occasion he brought home a black linen blouse cross-stitched brightly in the Ramallah style. A Palestinian student, who got it from his sister, had given it to Omar for me in exchange for extra English lessons.

There would also be something for his mother. I caught a glimpse of the packet of *loz* he passed to Sahr to take into the kitchen: unripe almonds in their fat velvet-green casings. The week before it had been apricots and the small sweet bananas that his mother loved. Although Rihaab ate less as her illness advanced, she did not give up her favourite foods and always accepted his small gifts, her look replacing any thanks she might have spoken.

If he had brought nothing, then I would take the sixteen-kilometre bus ride with him into Irbid the next day. Walking through the city's souks to the fruit and vegetable markets, he would ask me to pick out what I liked from any of the small shops along the way. That was how I got the sheer white scarf, edged along one side with gold and glass beading. Or we would go with his sisters to one of the many pastry houses where you could sit and eat *kanaafet*: orange-coloured strands of wheat pastry, fine-spun and brittle, encasing melted white cheese and dipped in hot syrup. Metal jugs and cups full of cold water waited on each table to finish the treat. Often I was satisfied with an ice-cream cone sprinkled with pistachios from the vendor at the street corner, but sometimes he bought me something else too, unless I insisted that I wanted nothing more.

Advising me one time, consulting me another, he made me feel I had been privileged with a role I must honour as guardian of his inner life. I would somehow help to keep his integral self together as he went about his business in the wider world.

It was not an articulate thought. Words could destroy, just as words could bring into being. In the village people do not spout 'thank you' and 'I'm sorry' in every direction. These are used only in formal situations. At other times you act out their content. Actions really do speak louder than words. To speak, or even to express strongly in other ways, feelings of gratitude, repentance, love, is base, vulgar, dishonest. You live them, in the things you do for others.

It was not that I could never speak. There were times when women talked for hours; they have their own rituals of visiting and conversation. And no one in the village was as well informed, as skilled in this art, as Sahr. How often had she invited me to accompany her to buy yoghurt from a neighbour or to retrieve a *shrsh* that was being embroidered by someone at the other end of the village, telling me each time that we would not be long? I would go with her in the early afternoon and not return until sunset, my legs numb from sitting with them tucked under me for an hour at this house and two hours at that, and my bladder full to bursting with all the tea and coffee drunk with numerous women. I tried to join in these conversations, and the women always encouraged me, but I flagged when I lost track of what they were saying.

One morning Sahr asked me to join her to take grain to be ground into flour. Watching her pull the sack of grain from the dark back room with the earthen floor, I thought we would surely be quicker this time. She would not want to be carrying it all over the village. I was wrong. First we came upon three women on the side of the street under an olive tree, and Sahr dropped her sack and squatted and chatted for about twenty minutes. Then about halfway to our destination — a house only a few streets away from ours — she became thirsty, and stopped at someone else's home for water, staying for another ten minutes of conversation. Just when we were saying goodbye, the people in the house next door called out from their garden, *'Sahr, kéfal haal?'* (How are you?) I could tell it was a formal greeting, because they didn't say *'Tcheif haalitch?'* — the Kufr Soumi colloquial version of this question. So we went over to them, stepping carefully through a large vegetable plot before settling down to a glass of tea with plenty more talk in their courtyard.

Finally we reached the house where an entire back room was given over to the large metal machine that ground grain into flour. There Sahr chatted with the lady of the house during the milling. And for some time afterwards. We drank coffee. The flour was poured out onto a large round tray that was placed in a plastic bag. Then I understood why Sahr had brought a towel with her. She wrapped it around her head and placed the tray on top, putting one hand up occasionally to balance it as we walked home. This not only made it easier to carry, but also left her other hand free to gesticulate as she stopped and chatted with three more groups of women we passed along the way. On that occasion we ate our lunch, the most important meal of the day, in the late afternoon.

But the women's rituals took second place when Omar returned from the south. We spent his weekend at home with many small and large understandings passing tacitly between us across and around the relatives and neighbours. I was rarely alone with him, even indoors. The contrast with our student days in the States seemed extraordinary. There, too, he had been loved and sought, but in his room the two of us could lock the door against the demands of the world. When he cooked for us on the prohibited primus camp stove, it seemed from the meticulous attention he paid to every small thing — the amount of oil or water, the temperature, the cooking time, the spices and side dishes — that he was preparing those meals for me alone.

A ceremonial feast for a queen. But a feast with all the intimacy of our togetherness in that small space that he marked his own. Communion transformed beyond words.

Bidoun Kaalima 2

Jordan was beautiful in all the ways Omar had told me, but I found myself craving the intimate retreat of the early days, a retreat whose very elusiveness in the village, ironically, heightened our sensibilities one to the other and deepened our bond.

His friends in the car had relented, and were coming in through the gate. I watched at the window again as they crossed the courtyard and came up to the front door. Yet again he must look to his guests. Offer all that is required of the generous host who knows how to put visitors at their ease.

His sisters knew. Already they were brewing coffee for the guests, the bitter, bitter coffee I had grown to enjoy, that distinguished the Arabs from their former Turkish invaders who always added sugar.

As I passed the door to the small guestroom, he invited me to join him there with the men. I was not sure, but his two married sisters had just arrived with their husbands and were going in. Aisha was pregnant and beginning to show it, but she did not hesitate to join the guests. Besides, Moussa was with her. So I entered too, and took my place on one of the mattresses.

Two sips. Three sips. The small china cup without

handles was emptied; I held it out, knowing it would be refilled, smiling to myself at the recollection of how difficult it had once been just swallowing those few drops. The bitterness might make a man of me. This was the first time I asked for more. Two sips. Three sips. I toyed with the possibility of a third serving. Three is the limit, but I had not seen anyone at the house ask for three. I wiggled the empty cup back and forth as I held it out, to indicate I had finished. The coffee pourer took it in silence and, pouring, passed it on to the person next to me, the conversations all around continuing uninterrupted.

The person next to me was cousin Bassiim. At any time of day cousins turned up from the other side of the village, whether Omar was there or not. It was amazing, the comings and goings at this house. In my childhood home in Sydney it had never been like that. People had seldom called in spontaneously. The apartment, in a suburb of gardens and mansions, and with the beach almost on its doorstep, was nonetheless small for a family of four. It had good furniture, especially in the lounge room where we were not permitted to play. Until the age of five, anything I picked up I was told to put down, and I did not play out of doors with the neighbours' children until I was six or seven. Indoors it was dark. Only in the early morning did the sunlight manage to slip from the road down over the terraced rock garden and into the sitting room, where the view of plants and flowers gave the eyes a breathing space. The other rooms looked across at the dark brick walls of the apartment building next door.

Here in this country the sun, like the visiting relatives, came boldly indoors. Outside and inside ran fluidly into each other. The delineation was not between your front door and the outdoors, but between the edge of your property and the world beyond. The brightness of day was part of the inner world, showing its participation in the way it entered your home. To keep healthy, son, let the sun visit your bed and all the places where you eat and live, at least for some time every day. That was what Omar's mother had told him just before he went abroad the first time. Her last advice. And the houses here seemed to let the sunlight in all the time. In the room where we sat, the brightness spirited lacy curtain patterns onto the deeper designs of the pale beige carpet.

I caught the eye of Omar's father sitting beneath the window; he smiled. And there at the entrance was Uncle Ahmed from next door, with one of his sons and two of his daughters, all grown, taking off their *khofái* and stepping in to greet the more formal guests. I loved all the people here. I loved the formality of their manner and the informality of their calls, if only they were not here all day … would go away for a while, just for a little while.

The room kept filling as it always did on the afternoons when Omar came home. More visitors would appear around sunset, when they would all move out to the courtyard and sit against the wall of the house facing the garden. Some would stay on for the light evening meal, tearing off their share of the flattish round loaves of bread, dipping into the dishes of yoghurt or tomato between short sips of air and hot tea from the small glasses set before them. I already knew that by then I would begin to look across at Omar meaningfully, wondering how soon the guests would leave and whether there would be a chance to talk, about anything, before bedding down.

'Dear.'

The English word cut through the Arabic that filled the room around him, though it was no louder.

'Dear, Abu Samir has just reminded me that we are taking the students on a bus trip next weekend, down to Aqaba. I will not come home.'

'Oh …'

'… But the week after next I will come early. I will have an extra day.'

'I see.'

I sighed the words and nodded, the other men's eyes on me for a moment, registering the inability to hide my disappointment. One more day with him, then two weeks of waiting and wanting to touch and share. I did not look up from that pretty carpet.

I told myself I understood. I understood. How many men made a round trip of four hundred and thirty kilometres each week to be with their families? Many, in fact. But few who, like him, had no vehicle. I thought of the time we had waited for him late into the night. Whatever his sisters expected had not come to pass. When he turned up it was long after midnight. The taxi he had taken from Amman to Irbid — another of those old Mercedes that serve as inter-city public transport — had driven into a flock of sheep crossing with their shepherd at a bend in the road. Four of the sheep had been killed and the traffic police called. Omar had had to give evidence and then wait in the open country with the five other passengers, looking for a way to continue his journey. He had arrived long after midnight.

Understanding. I had it in abundance. I looked up from the blue arabesques that my eyes had been tracing in the carpet, tracing carefully, to stem the brimming signs. The young ones jostled and joked with me, the emptiness at my centre girded around with so much warm presence.

A neighbour with his wife and young children was entering through the gate. The little room would not hold them all, especially since, unnoticed by me, his two brothers had also come in. Without a word or a signal, but almost together, the women rose to go into another room deeper within the house and nearer the kitchen. In my first weeks here, on such occasions his sisters used to call me to join them. Once or twice he himself had said, 'Go with the women. Dear, it is better.' Now I instinctively felt the numbers of women fast thinning. It was a feeling with something of panic in it. A feeling of not wanting to be left behind with the men. I would be safe, but uncomfortable. And they would be courteous, but uncomfortable. Oddly, it would soon be boring. They would move on to jokes or card playing. Or to negotiate some tricky men's business. They were always transacting something, if only gossip, which must not be seen to resemble women's talk.

There were too many men here already. If I was the last to leave, they would stop talking and watch me go. No, I must slip from the room now while Randa was passing round the glasses of hot mint tea on a tray. It was the women's hearth I wanted now. Hearthfulness. I waited for the right moment, when the men were deep in conversation. Unnoticed I got up and went to the back room.

Halwa

Rihaab came into the room off the kitchen one afternoon, using her stick, just as Aisha and Moussa were arriving with their children. She was no better or worse than usual, offering up her pain in low intermittent moans or a long drawn-out '*Obaiyeeeah*'.

Tarik, Aisha's oldest son who was five, followed her in, asking for sweets. '*Halwa, halwa*' he kept repeating, looking up at her. She didn't stop or slow her uneven walk, and her moans continued as before. At one point she said something to Sahr who was passing through from the kitchen. Tarik did not give up. He stood still for a moment, looked at me, looked around the room as if searching for something, then back at his grandmother. '*Halwa, halwa.*' I was sitting on one of the floor mattresses writing in my journal and only glanced up briefly when they first entered. Now I felt compelled to watch this odd little procession of two as it slowly, slowly passed, emitting a strange music in bass and treble, the moans of the woman underlying the higher pitch of the child's persistent questions, alternating with his whines.

She began halfway to mutter to herself, I could not say what about — the subject discussed with Sahr in passing? her pain? the boy's endless singsong?

241

'Gran'ma, I want ...' — 'Jiddeh, biddou halwa.'

Then she stopped by a large wooden china dresser where dishes not used everyday were kept. On its sideboard was one of several ashtrays that were carried from room to room almost daily, wherever the men went with their coffees and conversations and card games. Tarik was now adding tears to his whines. I thought surely she could answer, if only to send him away. I felt frustrated for him, for his being too young to understand that pain drove him from her consciousness. It seemed she hardly knew he was there beseeching her. He was a marginal annoyance. Whatever her grandchildren meant to her, when she was in pain they were like everything else, only at the outer edge of her awareness.

She leaned on the sideboard with one hand.

'A-biddak halwa?' (You want a sweet?)

His eyes lit up and all the hope and expectation of the world were concentrated into the softness of his single utterance.

'Na:am.' (Yes.)

She moaned again as she turned back and concentrated her attention on the sideboard. She muttered a few words that I later interpreted, looking back, as something like 'You want sweets? Here's sweets. I'll give you sweets.'

'Close your eyes and open your mouth,' she said to him more clearly. 'Put out your tongue.'

And he did as he was told. She passed her forefinger quickly across her own tongue, dipped it into the ashtray, pressing hard, and then onto his tongue. It took a moment for him to register. A long moment of silent absorption, in which I sat staring, my pen in my hand, motionless. Then it came. A great wail, followed by loud sobs and tears as he went running to his parents. She continued on her way through the room, at her pace, with her stick. 'Obaiyeeeeeah ...'

A Mystery Actor

A sideboard. An old refrigerator. The wardrobe that Omar had installed the day after my arrival. An old wooden table. A bookcase. Apart from these, there was no furniture in the house.

Except, of course, for the television set. Omar had bought it on time payment soon after returning from the US and taking up his teaching post. At first he kept it at Mu'tah, but in the second summer he brought it back to the village, and let the family keep it while he worked off payments for another new one for himself.

In Kufr Soum the 'old' television sat in one corner of the small guestroom, and spent the day under cover of a white cloth that hung down on all sides, concealing the screen entirely. It was mostly the younger members of the family who gathered in that room in the evening when the cloth was pulled off: Randa, Bilaal, a neighbour or two, the cousins from next door or from Abu Kariim's at the other end of the village. Sometimes Na:aameh or Aisha and their families joined us. Sometimes Saleh. Or Omar if he was there. And me.

Hearing only village dialect all day I found the evening News one of the most helpful programs for my Arabic, especially if I had recently seen the English or French versions, which were broadcast daily. Even though a large part of it was devoted to the Jordanian royal family, the News referred to a number of other things I had some knowledge of, so that I could focus more closely on the language. It was always clearly articulated in standard Arabic, enabling me to make the distinctions with the language around me. Then there were the foreign films, nearly all British or American, with Arabic subtitles, which Omar often watched with me. And there was a whole channel established and controlled, ostensibly at least, by an American religious sect, and available throughout a large area of the Middle East. My disgust was surpassed only by my amazement that it could not be in some way prohibited or curtailed. We rarely watched it.

And we hardly ever watched Israeli television, though it, too, was easily available. The exceptions were those rare occasions when a good foreign film was showing with subtitles in Hebrew and Arabic. Most of the time we flicked past the programs in Hebrew, but I was fascinated to hear, in those few moments, just how much the two languages have in common, orally at least, if not in their script. Sometimes I mentioned this and other Arab/Jewish similarities to Omar.

'They are our cousins,' he used to say to me, always heaving out the statement with a long sigh.

There was another saying he repeated a few times, one that had a centuries-old ring to it and seemed to me to sum up the Arabs' relations with the two major non-Arab, non-Islamic groups they have had contact with throughout their history. 'Sleep with a Christian, eat with a Jew,' goes the adage.

What Christian? What Jew? I wonder. And, for that matter, what Arab is being addressed? National leaders? Monarchs? Ordinary people? Eating is surely less of a problem. The White House must know not to serve pork and crustaceans at banquets for leaders from that part of the world. But then I try to imagine any of the Arab leaders of the past twenty years bedding down in the same room with, say, Reagan, Thatcher, Bush, Chirac, Clinton. 'Goodnight,' they say to each other as they switch off their bedside lamps and stare into the darkness.

Perhaps that's what they should do. But it's only ordinary people who ever have the opportunity, rare even then, to sleep with the 'other'. Or does 'sleep' refer to relations with women? You may sleep with a Western woman, according to the dictum. Where does that place me on the scale of things? Me, Omar's wife, here in this village? And now my mind toys with the omissions. 'Eat with a Jew' (but not with a Christian). 'Sleep with a Christian' (but don't sleep with a Jew). I fly back to the beginning, the very beginning.

'Wrong! You are wrong!' storms Abraham in a change of heart, 'and besides, who are you, woman, to tell me what to do?'

'A serving woman, a slave!' cries Sarah who turns on her heel and looks away as he hurries out, calling, 'I will have Hagar back in my bed this very night.' He goes into the desert and throws himself on his knees before their weeping servant, begging her to pay no attention to Sarah, and to come back. But no, what patriarch will do such a thing? And before a slave? Even if he does, what written word will attest to it? No, what really happens is that he sees Hagar in the distance, her tears forming the well that will quench the thirst of her children and of all the tribes that will be her issue. God is already looking after her, he perceives. And to bring her back would mean strife in his own household. Didn't he hear her vow loudly, in her grief (and make the boy beside her vow too,

245

as his cupped hand reached out to scoop up the fresh water), that her children will never sleep with Sarah's? He realises the wisdom of not bringing her back now, and, though it was not written, recognises his own deep, deep regret.

Jordanian television is full of programs of Arab music, song and dance, from contemporary dance troupes from different Arab countries to replays of films of the great names in song — Umm Kalthoum, Feyrouz, Fariid Al-Atrash, and those beautiful and noble dancers like Samia Gamal and Naiima Akef. The old Egyptian films are regarded as classics throughout this part of the world. The dancers are always dressed in elaborate, colourful costumes, and the type of dance ranges from folk or *baladi* to a more modern or cabaret style. Group dancing prevails over solo performances.

I could have watched these programs all evening, restraining myself with difficulty from getting up and dancing in front of the television set. In Perth I have taken up *raqs sharqi* lessons with one of the best performers of Middle Eastern dance in Australia. But in Kufr Soum, except for the wedding *dubkeh*, women do not dance in front of men. I could not help thinking, on the hot nights when Omar and his brothers brought the television outside the house, what a beautiful backdrop to the dance this gate, garden and tiled courtyard would have made. If I could not dance, then I wanted the troupe to leave the screen and perform right there before us.

When Na:aameh and Aisha came, their husbands, Adnan or Moussa, would help Omar move the set. They went to a lot of trouble for one night's viewing, especially considering that it was usually interrupted by visitors. They even climbed onto the roof and fiddled for ages with the aerial to obtain a good picture. We would all call up to them over and over to let them know how the screen was looking until everyone was satisfied.

But the news, the singing and dancing, the best film could not rival my favourite program, a Jordanian television serial — broadcast just before the news — that widened a little more the crack through which I had a glimpse of another world, another history, and with it some glimmer of understanding. In poetic cadence and in dazzling period costume, actors declaimed the good and evil on both sides of the story of the crusades. Here I found Richard I, that 'French' king of England, receiving the same measure of respect and admiration accorded to Salah al-Diin (Saladin). I can even imagine, on the basis of this program, the 'Lionheart' lying down beside his enemy, no lamb from all accounts, both of them sleeping soundly. In the morning they find themselves physically safe, with their characters and their political honour 'intact'. On waking they are ready and able to fight in frankness, or to negotiate an honest and meaningful truce, which is, historically, what they did before Richard returned to the West to be captured and ransomed, and then killed in some paltry, lurking European battle.

Neither of the two, it seemed to me, was central to the program's story, and I wonder if it was intentional, or owing to the outstanding quality of the actor, that another character was given pride of place in this historical drama series. I never quite understood who he was supposed to be, or what his function was. An advisor to the great general and sultan? Was he good or bad? Sometimes I thought he was the villain of the piece, he seemed so shrewd. Not tall and statuesque, but lithe and wiry, with a neat moustache, and always, I thought, telling one thing to one person and to another something else. His subtlety made me think of Shakespeare's master of deceit and evil, Iago, but when I asked, all the family told me he was a good, a great man. Was it my lack of all but the most rudimentary Arabic that had led me to make such an interpretive blunder? Or did my mistake come from a cross-cultural misreading of his tone of voice, of the looks he gave, of the calculated appearance of his thoughts, of his body language?

The actor, Randa said, was the best in Jordan. His Arabic was so excellent, his diction the clearest, and he was playing a 'good character'. Surely, I resisted, his very eloquence should make us suspicious of the character he plays. No, they all returned nearly in chorus. This was a famous historic personage, and his eloquence matched his strength of character. And this was the best actor for the role. Although Randa mentioned the names in passing, I did not take them in at the time, and to this day I do not know who the actor was or what character he was playing.

Randa said I should hear this actor recite poetry. Everyone in Jordan loves him, she told me.

'No one, Michèle,' she added by way of example, 'pronounces the letter *qaf* as he does.'

It was so. Although I understood next to nothing, I recognised all the sounds of the Arabic language, all the letters he pronounced, and I repeated them aloud or in my head. The program became a must as I tried to put his verbal and non-verbal language together, tried to understand how those around me perceived him. Now *qaf* is my favourite letter of the alphabet.

I will always love the sound of Arabic. I know this now. My feeling for it will not go away, whatever happens. I love its life-mimicking contrasts of the soft and harsh, long and short, earthy and majestic, ordinary and rhetorical, full-blown. They echo the contrasts I find in this country, pulling me every which way, surprising or bemusing me, and keeping me in the moment. I love its repetitions of 'and' at the beginnings of sentences, creating litanies. And its cadences, even without the formal rules of poetry. The *Qur'aan* sounds beautiful when simply spoken, no chanting needed. Rhyme and rhythm are invoked there, not given. Invoked, like everything meaningful, not in the language, but through it. No wonder Arabic speakers say the *Qur'aan* loses in translation.

The simplest words, when strung together in certain ways, can tell us far more than precise, sophisticated language. They invite us to play, and to make our own patterns with the strings. Simple yet complex, changing yet constant patterns of meaning. The power of one short simple word is infinite. Was it 'be!' that came with God's breath, rippling the cosmos into being?

Mu'áwiya

I had a special liking at first for Mu'áwiya's name. I had found it difficult to pronounce and remember, and once I'd got it right I enjoyed repeating it, feeling the Arabic consonants and the glottal stop of the *hamza* like a new taste on my tongue, an embrace my throat loved to make. It also resembled, for me, the word *'qawi'* (strong), which he was, right from babyhood. He was only a few months old when I first used to visit Na:aameh, and while Manar played with my hair and Nasser played with a toy, I would hold Mu'áwiya in my arms or on my lap. Already I felt the powerful kicks and stretches, the desire to be on the move, to follow up what the curiosity of his eyes was singling out, and so it should not have surprised me that he bore the name of someone else considered strong.

That someone was the fifth caliph, second of the Umayyads, who defeated his enemies in battle or politically destroyed them. I have always seen him as a military man more than anything else, who perpetuated the notion of rule by soldierly might. He had to win his position through battle.

All those caliphs that went before him lasted only a few years, eleven at most, but it was under Mu'áwiya's long 'reign' of twenty-two years that Sunni Islam was endorsed as the new order of the day. Then Mu'áwiya's own temporal power was consolidated and the caliphate confirmed as a dynasty. The very same clan affiliations that Mohammed the Prophet had sought to overcome in his concept of the *umma* or community of Islam, had re-established themselves on a grander scale under Mu'áwiya, and in the Prophet's name.

Learning of these associations I thought that Mu'áwiya the boy had a gentleness with his strength and an affection tempering his energy that I could not have imagined in the ambitious general turned caliph. It was more than the contrast of child and man, innocence and power. I felt strongly that the balance of traits I observed in the boy would always be there, and would grow with him. This feeling was strengthened by the memorable visit I paid to Adnan and Na:aameh on my last trip, when I stayed in Kufr Soum. Na:aameh had made a special dinner of fresh fish cooked in a light batter, and at the very right moment, just as I had finished the meal, Mu'áwiya stood smiling before me, holding out an empty plate in one hand and a damp towel in the other. He said my name and invited me in Arabic to put my fish bones in the plate and then to wipe my hands. He was barely five years old.

I may have been mistaken to assume a love of power to the point of ruthlessness in the caliph. But although I still loved the sound of the name, at this point I found myself wishing the boy had been called something else.

Yarmouk

At Yarmouk University where I had obtained a post in Modern Languages teaching French, most of my students were eager and committed. The poor ones, especially the Palestinians among them, were highly motivated and learned quickly. A few of the students from wealthy families, both Jordanian and Palestinian, could not take their studies seriously, behaved like children in the classroom, and cheated in exams. But they were in the minority.

An important issue for the faculty that year concerned scholarships for students to spend a year abroad, at a university in the country of the language they were studying. Our head of department was trying to carry out a government policy of encouraging more students from the rural districts to a higher level of education through such overseas experience. The problem was that in the exams designed for these overseas scholarships the best of the rural students were constantly surpassed by students from the city, mostly from private schools. He wanted to set up two streams, so that one scholarship would always go to at least one rural student. My other colleagues, from different parts of the Arab world and from several continental European countries, were against this. The scholarships, they said, should go to students from the city or from private schools if they performed better than the rural students. The awards should be based entirely on merit. It appeared that I was the only one who disagreed.

I pointed out how different the village life was, how next to impossible it would be for an intelligent person from the villages to perform well in a modern international academic environment. One of my colleagues answered, 'I come from a village, Michèle, and it's not impossible for a conscientious student.' I felt that if this was so, then the villages must vary greatly from one part of the country to another, and his could be nothing like Kufr Soum. For me, Randa was a perfect example of the kind of student I felt needed the encouragement the government wanted to give. Intelligent, capable of learning anything, but without that essential exposure to the wider world. A year abroad would have taught her much of what she needed, without which she could never really have competed. But my arguments did not win them over. I believe that in the end some sort of compromise was reached, disappointing to both parties.

Later in the year I found myself on the other side, supporting my colleagues against the department head. They wanted me to join them in protest, and although something within me told me to stop short of action, that I had not been at Yarmouk, or indeed in Jordan, long enough to understand how their institutional politics worked, I agreed. Had I stayed longer, I believe I would have learnt how to cope better with group pressure, so much part of the life of communities here. But by that next summer Omar and I were in Scotland, and I did not see Jordan again for three years.

I did not know then that Scotland was to be our

destination. I had encouraged Omar to find out all he could about the universities in the UK, so we could be assured of attending a good one where there was also some familiarity with the problems of foreign students and where accommodation was provided for couples and families. I knew there were not many such places, not nearly as many as in the US, but they were there. One day Omar came back from Mu'tah talking about a Scottish professor who had visited there, and who was recruiting Middle Eastern students. A huge contract was being drawn up between the two universities, and Mu'tah would be giving scholarships for a year or two of study.

'What university are we talking about Omar?'

'It's called Glasgow University.'

'Glasgow?'

I felt cold as I repeated the word with a vague hope that I had misheard and a sense of dread that I had not. As a guest of family friends in Scotland years earlier I had been told not to bother with that city, that it had been as good as destroyed by the Industrial Revolution, the very same one that had built its wealth. The city had billowed and died with that great wave.

'Are you sure? Did you make enquiries about Kent University and those others we discussed?'

'There's no reason to now. With this contract, Glasgow is the only place Mu'tah will accept that we go to.'

'But what about accommodation? Do they have 'married housing'?'

'Yes, yes. I'm sure they must.'

'No, Omar. *Make* sure. You want me to go with you don't you?'

'Of course.'

'Then find out. It's very important.'

Omar said he would.

$\mathcal{A}dnan$

Sometimes, when I changed buses in Irbid on my way to the university, it was Adnan's bus that came by. Adnan, Na:aameh's husband (and Mu'áwiya's father), drove buses for a living. He worked for a good company and managed to obtain a route in the city that drew plenty of passengers. I don't know if he finally bought the bus or if it continued in the company's name, but he looked after it as if it were his own, and he did well enough to maintain his family.

Whenever I stepped aboard Adnan's bus he greeted me warmly and refused to accept my fare. He let me ride no matter how crowded it was, and that was often. There was always room for one more when it was me. No one ever complained about that, because everyone did it; looked after relatives and friends.

If the family had to go anywhere together, and if Adnan wasn't working, he took them in the bus. He brought it home to the village overnight and cleaned it inside and out. On my first trip to Jordan, when it was time for me to leave, the entire family came to farewell me at the airport, in Adnan's bus. On two of the three trips I have made since then it was Adnan who came with Sahr to pick me up and drive me the hundred-plus kilometres from Amman airport all the way back to the village. Then there were our day excursions — to Jerash, for example, or to the Dead Sea — in Adnan's bus.

That was why I found it difficult to protest when he stopped in Irbid at the beginning of those excursions to load a whole case of beer on board, which he kept on the floor beside the driver's seat. He shared the beer with Omar and Saleh, but the women did not drink. For myself, I would have preferred a bottle of cool Chardonnay, if such a thing had been available. So no one else drank, not even Bilaal, who at seventeen was still the little brother and not yet man enough to earn the privilege. Even Saleh had no more than one or two bottles, though Omar could hold his own. Still, the heaviest drinker was the driver, who simply reached down to the case when the whim took him, and that was soon after a bottle had been emptied, and picked up another with his right hand while his left held the steering wheel. He never drank on the job, but this was different. This was leisure time.

I wouldn't have taken much notice of a bottle or two. It was the case that bothered me. When the beer came aboard I thought of the children. Not only were Adnan and Na:aameh's own three small ones with us — Manar, Nasser and Mu'áwiya — but also Saleh's daughter, Amira, and Aisha's son, Tarik, and her two daughters who were still toddlers. All the family's children and most of the adults were on that bus, I said, and Aisha was pregnant too. Adnan had the lives of the entire family in his hands. Na:aameh always agreed with me, made some reference to alcohol being forbidden in Islam, and shook her head disapprovingly at Adnan.

'Yes, verry bad, Mishaal. Verry verry bad.'

She mentioned to Adnan what I had said, and he

would joke about it, or simply not respond. Na:aameh turned back to me then, shrugging and smiling.

'Verry bad. But ... do? ... what?'

And so I said no more and we went on our way. That Adnan drove well, all the time, every time, did not diminish my apprehension.

Adnan came often to the house with Na:aameh and the children. It was well into the winter when we were gathered around the oil stove one afternoon. Omar was in Mu'tah, Na:aameh had gone into the kitchen with Sahr and their mother, and the children had gone with her, so that for a while only Adnan, Randa and I were left. I had just taken up a book, and Adnan and Randa were talking. This was the year she was studying for her final high school exam, and being top of her class, Randa was pleased with herself.

The conversation between these two gradually worked its way round to a new topic: me. They did not mention my name, but they said no one else's either, and something in Randa's tone told me she was trying to work out the puzzle of Michèle. Then I heard a word I understood. I thought Randa was saying something like, 'There are times when she gives me the impression of being ...' and there was that word: '*khábileh*'. Stupid.

It cut deep. I sat there, book in hand, quiet, appearing absorbed, and the word cut the more easily through my stillness. It reached down into memory, childhood. Stupid! Dreamy!

But my childhood feelings of alienation within my own society had extended to believing that I would not feel any more 'different' in any other country than in my own.

257

In Kufr Soum I had thought Randa and I were enjoying each other's company well enough. I had already begun to help her with her English school work, but all she seemed to go by now was my slowness in bathing, making tea, washing dishes and generally getting things done. Yes, I annoyed her sometimes with my slowness, but then she seemed to accept me. With that word she uttered I saw that Randa did not understand me, counted my reflectiveness for nothing, had no time for it. And for a moment there came the frightening thought that she may have represented her village in this. But if I could not read others correctly, if Randa's impatience with me had been greater than her acceptance of me, and I had not perceived this, what about others in her family, in her culture? Or was this just the culture of the village? Certainly my kind of contemplation and reflectiveness were not much in evidence. But what time was there for anyone to reflect in this place, where sheer survival was paramount?

Would it be like this for the rest of our lives in this village then, between Randa and me, the girl who had greeted me so warmly when I arrived? Or was it that she really was trying to understand, and that was why she had told Adnan the word that hurt me so.

Part of me wanted to jump up and show my surprise and hurt. At first it was the stunning effect of her word that kept me so still. I did not speak or move. But then some instinct told me that Randa need not learn I had understood her, and that for once language difference might work in my favour, giving me time. I did not think this through. It was the understanding of an instant, and came together with a compulsion to listen further.

'La, la, msh khabila, lakin ... yá:ni ...' (No, no, not stupid, but ... you see ...)

Adnan's first few words were easy enough to understand. But now I embellish.

'There are different kinds of intelligence,' I think he told Randa, 'and hers is not like yours.'

My eyes did not leave the book.

I don't know what Adnan said after that. I'd like to believe he may even have added that the village was not the sort of place where my intelligence would shine, that Randa ought to be patient with me because I was new to the life there. Whatever he said, she seemed reconciled, and the conversation moved onto other things. I did not let them know what I had understood. Not then. Not later. I could have told them directly there and then. Or I could have jumped up with a smile and pointedly offered to make Adnan a pot of tea. No. The best would have been to ask Randa to make tea for Adnan and me because Adnan was such a nice man and she, Randa, was so clever at making tea. After all, I might let it boil over.

But it was still early days, and we all needed time to know each other better, so I said not a word.

Rihaab Dances

Wedding: At the Church

We have left the bride's house. Followed each other in groups along several more streets up and down. The bridal car passed us as we walked. We could hear it coming long beforehand, and paused often to look behind us for the source of the growing din. Then all at once the honking horn and welling ululations rolled through us in a wave.

And here is the church, domed, with a cross in the Eastern Orthodox style. Deep green trees spread out at the far end of the courtyard where we gather and wait to go inside. I am looking for you when you appear before me. Magic. You look glad to have found me. Even contented. And impressive too, in your neat grey suit. It is well tailored. In fact you are at your best. Beautiful. But already the gladness is fading, as though you have discovered I am not who you thought I was.

We go in. The pews are taken, so we remain standing, but I'm satisfied. It's the only way to see the ceremony. We are encouraged to come to the front. The family insists. So much honour …

I turn to you with a smile. But you do not return it. You stare straight ahead, and I see discomfort spread through you. *Áhlen*, Omar, *áhlen*. But you are not at ease. Your head is bent forward and I catch you stealing a downward, sideways glance at me. As soon as you register my own steady gaze that has lost its smile and taken on puzzlement, you look away again.

If I lose you I lose everything. Surely I do. I lose not just yourself, but your whole world. Not the world I imagined you lived in, but the real one I have come to know — the world that connects me, that suffices for me in each of its moments. And then, if I lose you, Omar, I lose all of you, I who came from a small family and discovered the capacity to love in a larger circle. What can my love attach itself to after learning to run both deep and wide? Don't you see what your world means to me? I'll die without it …

And there flashes into my mind the poem addressed to Kufr Soum that I wrote in Australia some weeks ago. Was it written in a moment of real clarity that I have since preferred to deny? Just as I have been unable to bear thinking about the woman who wrote to me six months ago, the one he took there last year, and introduced to his family. Another Western woman. Someone who may well have been drawn by the same things that drew me. Her going to that place — my learning of her going there — was a sword that pierced my innermost being.

I did not come as a coloniser
but as a friend
even though I am foreign,
Not as an invader
but as a sister
though I cannot be one of you
who accepted me as I am
as you accept all.

Yet when I found
it was you who entered my self
did I perhaps claim of you
some mandate of the heart?
When you became for my spirit
a deep and generous well
could it be that I set stakes about?
planted a flag before you signalling
'Territory of my Poetic Being'?
How strangely I've been taught to understand
I have no copyright
on Kufr Soum.

Tea for Two

Once I had begun teaching, my almost daily bus trips into the city were long, and as soon as I arrived in Irbid, I would change buses to go to the university. I spent the entire day there and always came home tired and thirsty. After a while Rihaab, who gauged exactly when I would return, began the habit of having tea ready waiting for me as soon as I got off the bus, and when the weather was clear we would sit together outside, sipping and chatting, communicating as well as we could. Sahr was always there too, and had a way of making herself understood.

The first time Rihaab made tea for me came as a surprise. She was so often in pain that no one expected her to do anything much. She needed help with most things, even the most personal. Sahr bathed her and washed her long crinkly hair, putting henna through it and later combing it out for her. As soon as it was dry, Rihaab had the dark wimple and headcloth back on; you hardly ever saw her hair.

Occasionally Rihaab prepared food for herself when she thought she could eat a little, always something simple, like the green leaf vegetable that Na:aameh or Aisha sometimes brought with them. She cooked it down and mashed it like spinach, in a bowl. It had a slightly bitter, stinging taste, but Rihaab liked it. I was told you could pick it wild in the wadi along with *seleq* and *khobeizeh*, the other green plants that grew in abundance there, and more than once Omar's sisters took me with them. We spent a large part of the day gathering these greens from muddy, shady places at the bottom of the wadi or on the lowest slopes. Na:aameh handed us each one of those large plastic shopping bags of different colours that were discarded in fields and streets everywhere, and could be seen from miles away, caught on thistles and waving among bushes, making the country resemble a refuse dump. But those we carried were the only ones to be seen here, under the low trees where water dribbled out from the ground and spread liquid fingers through the short young grass. A favourite place for the *seleqleq*, as Na:aameh liked to call it. We also found plenty of another leafy plant that resembled a very strong, wild coriander. We did not go home until we had filled one bag each.

Most of the time Rihaab hardly ate at all, and even more rarely drank tea. But on that first day, several weeks after I had begun teaching and when my routine had been established, I came home to find the small silver tray set out in the courtyard with teapot and glasses. It was surrounded by bread and small dishes of things to pick at — za:'ter, olive oil and tomatoes cut into bite-sized quarters — spread out on the large straw mat. Rihaab was sitting there on the mattress Sahr had put out for her. It was early spring, and she gestured to me to join her there, our backs against the cushions lining the sunny wall. As I sat beside Rihaab, Sahr, who was standing nearby, smiled at me and pointed to the tea.

'My mother, *shai illa* Mishaal, *ba:d* you teach. Love Mishaal, my mother.'

To Marry or Not to Marry

I was making things difficult for Omar. Too much excitement and enthusiasm over her approaching wedding day is frowned upon in a woman in this part of the world. Still, there are clear, if subdued, ways of showing your commitment, and I was not the eager fiancée. I even expressed doubts, and insisted on discussing this marriage with a lawyer in Amman to find out what I might be forfeiting.

With the effort not to fool myself, my thoughts became cynical. I would be my own devil's advocate. There's no denying it, I told myself, I'm the cheapest wife he could get.

Noble, but poor. That was the view of the villagers towards his family. He would never be able to pay the dowry required of the bride's people if he married a local woman from a 'good' family, not to mention the cost of the home and the furniture, and the solid gold bangles for the bride, worn pushed up on the forearm. Some village women seemed weighed down by them. It is the husband's responsibility to give these gifts to his wife at the time of their wedding. Married women carried all their own wealth — their 'insurance' — on their persons. When Mona's mother, Umm Khalil, visited from the other end of the village, she had three gold rings on one hand, two thick bracelets and several bangles on each arm, and, not to be outdone by her neighbours, six gold teeth in prominent display.

As oldest son, Omar had a duty to see to it that his younger siblings were taken care of first. Sahr would probably never marry. That at least was the assumption in the village, where at twenty-eight a woman was already considered to be past marrying age. Sahr maintained that she had no desire to marry. All she wanted was to look after her mother. Although young women were expected to appear disinterested, it was gradually accepted that Sahr was in earnest. She still took great care with her appearance whenever she went visiting or into the city. She even flirted humorously with the idea of marriage, continuing to joke about some distant male member of the family, or Dr Nabil, or one or two shop assistants, but she had no time to think about it seriously. Three of Omar's other brothers and sisters — Saleh, Na:aameh and Aisha — were married, but there were also Bilaal and Randa, still in their teens.

Then, too, Omar had suffered earlier refusals, especially that of his cousin, or rather, of her uncle, a man that Omar's father and most of his other uncles did not get along with. Now Omar was bringing a Western woman into the family, but one who was a real find, who was educated and already practising a profession, and to boot, she would cost nothing to wed. This would be more than his salvation on the marriage front. It would be his own personal revenge upon a village in which he had been spurned. At least this was one way of looking at it, but it seemed at the time that a little healthy cynicism was important, even necessary, to my own understanding of my position.

I felt Omar should know that I was aware of the practical gains for him and his family in this marriage, and that I was aligning myself with them by choice and by will. For me, the awareness of what I was doing added meaning to the act, was part of the intensity of the experience and the closeness of the bond. It did not have to cancel out romantic feeling; I could love him, could be *in love* as I was, without being a dupe of romance. Nor did Omar's own knowledge of the advantages I brought in any way diminish his belief in us as a couple. On one occasion, when we had parted for the day and I walked away, he told me later how proud and happy he had felt standing watching me. It was not just my height, he said, but the way I walk and carry myself. And then he spoke of an understanding between us, something I had sensed growing for a long time. He referred to it now as a way we both had of adjusting to each other's step. We are good for each other, he told me, and we 'walk together as one.'

In many mixed marriages that have failed, complaints centre around the in-laws who are often cited as the greatest problem for the European wife. In this regard I thought myself fortunate. Not only did Omar's family treat me well, something required by the rules of hospitality to strangers, but I felt that they also genuinely cared for me, and that his sisters, particularly Sahr and Randa, had developed a special affection for me.

I felt very close to Omar's family, but in spite of this care and closeness, the strain of village life was beginning to tell. I knew after an uninterrupted nine months that it would be impossible for me to continue there indefinitely. I accepted this initial period as necessary for getting to know the family and forming attachments. But I had come to Jordan on the understanding that we would live mostly in the city — at least in Irbid if not Amman — and now that seemed next to impossible. Omar expected me to stay in the village, and even though I knew he had little control over our circumstances, he was making demands on me that were too difficult to meet. This became clear shortly after I obtained my teaching position at Yarmouk University, when I still had hopes of persuading him that I would have to live on or near the campus.

The village was beautiful, the wadi a place I would always want to return to, and Omar's family I would have stayed with for weeks or months at a time. But I needed the stimulation and companionship of people who shared my interests. Some of my colleagues at the university might have filled this role; their gender or nationality was immaterial. As it was, I saw too little of them. There were also Omar's two cousins from Ramtha, the grandchildren of Uncle Abdullah and Aunt Khadija. They had recently completed their university studies, and came to the village one day to visit us. The whole time was spent in stimulating conversation. The many questions they asked me contrasted starkly with the idle curiosity I had been the subject of among many of the villagers. Abbas was an artist, and later he would do a portrait of Omar that I saw for the first time on my last visit, hanging in the same front guestroom where we entertained them that day. He and his brother combined a natural sociability with an openness to others, and a keenness of understanding that I had begun to miss. I remember that day feeling glad that Omar was very fond of these cousins.

I had a strong sense that by marrying him I would ultimately lose him. I would be brought within the confines of social behaviour that would take away from me that very thing by which I identified myself: the freedom to meet people with whom I could share both professional and leisure interests, to make and choose my own friends, to stay within my culture or move outside it, learning about different ways; the freedom that had been part of what attracted him to me in the first place. If it came, as I knew, from my own cultural background, I also wanted to enjoy what his world had to offer. I still desire this mixture of two kinds of living, of movement between two worlds, and continue to search for ways of bringing it about for myself. But at that time, the doubts caused by all these considerations and intuitions made me hesitant to go through with the marriage.

If I could not succeed in convincing Omar that I should live elsewhere and visit the village regularly, our marriage would not hold out. In that case, why go ahead with it? I found myself pinning my hopes increasingly on our trip to the UK, where we might have a chance of rekindling something of our intimate bond. If during that time I could bring him to see the wisdom of living differently in Jordan once we returned, we could return to a new life. I would gain the kind of freedom I needed in order to live and breathe, without losing the other close ties I had formed. Life in Jordan would then be more than bearable; it would be enjoyable.

Omar sent his brother Saleh to me one day to talk about it. I had been taking my time trying to set up some sort of legal contract, with clauses about divorce and children; I wanted to do it the Arab way, which was just what I felt Omar didn't want. Why marry a Western woman if you don't receive the accompanying advantages? Omar turned to one thing he knew well and felt secure in: mediation.

'Omar really wants you to be his wife,' Saleh told me. 'He cares for you.' What about afterwards, I thought to myself, will it be the same?

Looking back, I understand better now that what I wished was impossible: to earn my reputation by my own behaviour in spite of living so much apart from Omar and his family. I did not know then that the sheer fact of setting myself up separately would be taken as a sign of looseness. Women always belong to a family, have at least one male protector, and are never on their own. Even if I did earn a 'good' reputation, my living outside the family fold would be enough to reflect dishonourably on Omar. His male friends and acquaintances would see only that he had a wife who 'went free', one he could not control. 'His wife does what she likes,' they would say. 'He is weak; he is not a man.' And more to the point for me, the women would say it too.

Omar said to me one day, 'Let's go into Irbid and have a beer.'

I had to ask Omar to repeat himself.

'Yes, come. Get ready.'

'So there are places in Irbid where you can sit and drink alcohol?'

'Of course.'

It was in a dingy little room with a few metal tables and chairs thrown together that we sat down and ordered. Why come all the way into Irbid for this?

We chatted as we drank, but Omar kept ordering more beer for himself. He seems to believe that when he drinks, which is rare, it should be in large quantities, the whole point and purpose being to get drunk. After the first couple of drinks he began to talk to me about our marriage. He told me why he wanted to marry me, how much he cared, how strong we would be as a couple, that we would accomplish so much together. And he told me what I meant to him.

I played tough and mean, in accordance with all the

ways I had been forewarned by the lawyer that I might be disadvantaged. Tougher and meaner than I turned out to be in the end. I said there were conditions. The first, that I should keep my own name, was easy enough to meet, since Arab women keep their own names anyway, when they marry.

'Then I must have legal right of divorce equal to yours, Omar. That would have to be written into the contract.'

He was listening, deeply, and made no response.

'And the divorce payments, if we ever divorce, should be higher for every year we have been married, with another reasonable sum added for each child, if we have children.'

Now the corners of his mouth were moving slightly, as if he knew this was a part I was playing, and one that I wasn't used to.

'Yes, yes, but we will not need to write it out.'

'Oh yes we will!'

I think he was unable to take me seriously, probably because I was not taking myself seriously when I told him the part about divorce. I tried to, but somehow could not, would not project so far into the future.

The family did not doubt our commitment to each other, and so could not understand my hesitancy. At last I made up my mind. In the end, nothing was written into the contract. What is a contract but another wall of words? We live out our pledges and promises if we really care, or we try to, without all the fuss to devise them.

It didn't occur to me on that day that Omar had needed to drink before he could discuss these things with me. When we came home later that evening, he was very sick.

Little wonder, then, that when I finally agreed, Omar had first to turn the tables for a while, putting off the date himself and playing the doubter. My indefiniteness and extreme caution must have made him genuinely question the wisdom of the step he was taking, but I believe it was also a case of not appearing too eager himself. If he was tormented by the delays I requested, he must not show it. His community demanded this of him.

It is easy to ask me, with what I've revealed, why, in such circumstances, I had to go ahead and marry. Perhaps it is frustrating to see into my thoughts as I go over the past like this, knowing that I did it, threw all caution to the wind as it were. What can I say? He was beautiful, my Omar. Yes, in spite of all I've told you. The poetry did not go away. The enchantment did not leave, just because I knew his weak points or the demands of the social system, just because I knew what problems lay ahead. 'Such a romantic,' my mother's voice echoes within. 'Grow up!' 'Get real!' 'Earth calling Michèle,' chimes in the chorus backing her. 'You may have set yourself a challenge that is humanly impossible to meet,' writes my sister, 'or only possible in certain circumstances, which are not yours.'

Yes, but Omar and his family had come to know my weak points too: my absent-mindedness, my frustration with the gender roles or with the daily closeness of us all. They accepted me. Looking through these chinks in the wall, you can see them there on the other side. Omar, tummy out, chin in, nonetheless stands tall and slim and beautiful. His head turns slightly away; he is trying to look occupied, not waiting, or wanting anything. There in the group is Rihaab, calling to us both with her thin light voice, wishing we would see time pass and make up our minds before she herself fades away. Beside her is Sahr smiling at me, glad of the support and understanding I bring to her situation, wanting to build on the friendship. There are Na:aameh and Aisha together, with smiles too, beaming. I see they have wholly accepted me and look to my loyalty in return. And here on the side is Randa, full of impatience, simplifying everything through the way she leans against the wall, a hand on her hip, all sure, proud youth and energy. Behind them, further off, are the other men; Abu Omar and Saleh, and Bilaal with his easy-going young cousins.

'Why don't you just leave?' you ask. And they: 'Why don't you stay?'

Rihaab Dances

Omar's sisters came to me often during that time of doubt, at first to ask why I saw so many problems and did not just go ahead and get married, later to tell me to be patient because Omar would finally set the day. Even Rihaab brought up the subject once or twice. She wanted us to marry, especially now that she could not persuade Omar against going to Scotland. I overheard her asking him one day, over and over, why he was going away again. Hadn't he just returned from '*Amriika*'? They were in the courtyard, just outside the window of the large guestroom where I was folding some clothes. I felt I could almost understand her words: 'Don't go, son. What need do you have, really, to go again so soon?' But his mind was made up. We would leave late in the summer. She knew that it was partly at my persuasion, yet she did not seem to hold this against me. And although she could not change his mind, at least if we were man and wife, and I were with him, I could help him through his studies and we would return all the sooner.

Rihaab had been getting constantly weaker, and was particularly ill on the day when Na:aameh came to tell me that Omar had arranged a date for the signing of the marriage contract. How Na:aameh knew this while Omar was at Mu'tah I never learnt, but these small puzzles had become a part of daily life for me. When she brought this news I was glad of it, and glad to find all his sisters in such good spirits at hearing of his decision.

Na:aameh and I went to find Rihaab, who was sitting in a corner of one of the inner rooms, mute as usual, except for the intermittent soft moans. She was so rarely able to take an interest in anything outside her chronic pain. But she was all attention when we told her, her face lighting up. She smiled as I had not seen her smile before. Then Randa immediately put a tape into the radio-cassette player and started dancing. Sahr, who had been washing clothes, came and joined in too, while Na:aameh, holding onto her youngest son, Mu'áwiya, looked on and encouraged me to do the same.

As soon as I began to dance I saw Rihaab get up slowly and come towards me. She was moving and swaying to the rhythm of the music, and for an instant we all stopped in astonishment, transfixed like a group of people in a photo.

'My mother, my mother!'

Sahr uttered the words barely above a whisper, as if afraid to break the magic of the moment. Then Rihaab raised her arms to me, and we held hands, beaming into each other's faces as we danced.

Treasure

Sometimes when I went with Omar into the wadi he would point out a cave in the hillside and tell me that it was a likely place for finding treasure. As a youth he had inspected a few of these caves with his cousins, but they did not persevere and nothing ever came of it. He told me that Fariis, Uncle Ahmed's second son — the one they called 'Mr Whale' and who had accompanied us on one of our hunting jaunts — had spent several weeks digging out a particular cave where he was convinced there was treasure. He and his friends had worked on it almost every day, but on returning there one morning they found it had been dug deeper during the night. He gave up then, in the belief that if there was anything to be had from there, someone else had got to it first.

On one occasion, as Omar and I walked along the wadi floor following the dried up bed of some seasonal stream, we saw several caves in the rocky hillside that rose steeply on both sides. A few of the cracks and crevices that Omar pointed out had clearly been opened up, their entrances freshly dug out.

'What treasure, Omar? Do all the villagers really believe it's here?'

'It is heerre, from the Turks. They fled, and could not

278

carry all their wealth. They buried it, and made plans to return. Later they sent maps to the people in the villages and paid them to find it, or they promised to share whatever was found. But many people here have discovered by accident the places where the Turks hid these things.'

'Was it only the Turks?'

'Nearly all Turks. But this country is thousands of years old. Think of all the people who passed through it! Sometimes very ancient and beautiful things have been found here, believe me.'

'If they're antiques wouldn't it be illegal to keep them? I mean, there must be museums run by the government ...'

'Yes, it's the law, but there are always places to get money for these things. And do you think there are no people who would sell them for profit? Everywhere you go you can hear stories of treasures that have been reported and taken away in official trucks, and no one hears of them again.'

'Do you believe that?'

'Yes. No. I don't know. I'm just telling you what the people often say.' I couldn't draw him any further on the subject.

Looking around at the wild and rough terrain I found it hard to imagine people of great wealth passing through or visiting these isolated northern villages, yet such out-of-the-way, hilly areas were precisely, I was assured, where people came in the past to hide their possessions.

It was late in the afternoon and very quiet. As usual there was no one else about until, on the point of turning back, we noticed an old woman all in black riding a donkey. On its back with her was a large bundle of sticks. She was clearly very poor, and to me she looked lonely and vulnerable, but Omar took little notice of her, and I thought the sight must not be unusual. She headed off on a diverging track around a hillside, and I remarked on her travelling alone.

Most people, said Omar, were quite safe going about in the wadi during the day. It was at dusk that it became dangerous to be alone here, not only on account of the jackals and hyenas, but also because that was the time when the beings believed to inhabit these caves went abroad. They would never show themselves in daylight, since they were always recognisable and horrifying to see. They go about in dark garments and hooded cloaks, and they loom up before you out of the shadows. You know them immediately, he told me, because they have vertically shaped eyes, in deep pockets from the eyebrow to the cheekbone. I asked if they were guardians of the treasures. Or were they thought to be jinn or ghouls, or devils of some sort? He couldn't say. Only that they had occasionally been seen and were known to bring harm to humans.

Absences

'I am not interested in this.'

'You know I can't go without you.'

'Then don't go.'

'But he's a good old friend Omar, and I've not seen him in years. It would be lovely to meet his wife and see his child.'

'Yes. He is your friend. These people have nothing to do with me.'

'But you already agreed when I spoke to you on the telephone last week. Wouldn't it be rude not to turn up now, after I told him we're coming?'

'You see? You have done this. You accepted this invitation for me.'

'Omar, I've not asked you to come with me anywhere, not once since I arrived. Couldn't you do this for me once?'

'Yes. I will do it. We will go to this dinner with this ... *your* friend, but first we will go to Amman where I have business at the bank, and we will visit my uncle while we are in the city. Then we'll go to your friend's tonight when we come back through Irbid.'

'Isn't that all too much in one day? You were just saying you didn't want to be away too long.'

'Do you want to see your friend? We will do it this way or not at all.'

'All right, all right.'

'And be sure you are ready in the morning. We will leave early.'

In the back room Rihaab was rocking and moaning. She had been in and out of hospital several times in the last few months, and now Sahr and Randa were fussing around her as they always did in those periodical bad bouts in her illness. Rihaab had been worse again all week, and with Omar gone for two weeks we had both been looking forward to his return. When he called and I told him about the invitation, he didn't readily agree; it took some persuasion on my part. Then he asked what was needed at the house, and I told him tomatoes for sure, and that his mother was worse again, so anything extra he could bring for her ...

She waited for him as I did, as if his mere presence would be curative, a breath of life, reviving our reason for being. Such a fuss we made when he turned up that Tuesday evening, just when we'd begun to think he wouldn't come until the next day. She and I. Smiling at each other with perfect understanding as Randa came calling to us, 'He's here, he's just arrived.' I rushed out to the kitchen where I heard his footsteps on the tiles, and found him still holding a large paper bag full of ripe red tomatoes, carefully chosen, and other parcels Sahr was already taking from him. They included several things for his mother.

His whole face was glowing with the pleasure of seeing me. A gladness. A sense of coming home to the hearth. It was so strong it almost took me by surprise. A deeply felt reciprocation of my own glad greeting. Mutual, instantaneous. And then the words: he had missed me so.

And the shaking of his head with a slight frown at the thought of that two weeks of parting, the way he could almost not articulate how bad it had been, how good it was now.

And now this. Only the next night. As if he were already tired of it all. As if my request had been exaggerated, and a disappointment for him after all the joy. I was human, asking for things he did not want to give.

So it was that we left the next morning with no small share each of bad feeling. We did all we'd planned, his business at the bank, the visit to his uncle, for whom it was completely unexpected. They gave us lunch and we stayed on chatting until well past the middle of the afternoon. Then we left for Irbid, where we wandered among a few shops before arriving in the early evening at Nawaf's place. The sun was only just setting.

Nawaf. I knew him a few years before meeting Omar. He'd been a student of linguistics at the same American campus, one of a group from Jordan whose English was next to impeccable in spite of their accents. They were a sophisticated set of young men, some married, some not, all highly intelligent, and also clever. I hadn't expected to see Nawaf again, though I should have known I might; Jordan's population is small enough, and the proportion of university graduates smaller still. I could hardly be in an academic institution and not run into him.

Nawaf's wife had made a wonderful dinner. Relations between the two men were a little strained, but still more pleasant than polite.

We got a taxi home. Sixteen kilometres. The only time I remember taking a taxi all the way back from Irbid to Kufr Soum. It was well after 10.00pm when we came to the first outlying houses of the village.

Omar said, 'Let's see if Abu Kariim is at home. We'll stay and talk with him here for a while and walk home afterwards.' Omar told the driver to stop, but as we were getting out of the taxi we saw one of Abu Kariim's sons standing by the road, and he told us to get back in right away and go home.

'Why?' said Omar, waving the taxi away, 'isn't your father here?'

'No, no,' the young man called to the driver, 'don't go. Wait here a little.' Then he shifted from foot to foot looking at the ground as Omar questioned him jovially. He would not look up, as if preparing Omar by the forced change in mood. Then the words came quiet and low: 'Your mother died.'

At the house the noise was terrible. Crowds of people in nearly every room. Omar was ushered into the guestroom full of men as soon as he came in the front door. Sahr wanted to take me to the back room with the women, but I was all dressed up in a brightly coloured floral skirt and matching top with shiny red shoes and bag. I felt as if I'd deliberately chosen this moment to flaunt my evening-out clothes, which made so plain to me the irony of my position. Guilt and the beginnings of resentment made me so uncomfortable that my immediate thought was that Rihaab had died in a fit of pique at my going off with Omar that day and leaving her behind.

It was not until I had changed my clothes that I could also put off these thoughts in which I, and not Omar's mother, was at the centre. But once I entered the room full of women the full impact of the event was borne in on me. It was in Sahr that we all could see the grief and loss condensed. We knew she suffered most now, and would suffer most in the years to come. She was trying to continue in her usual role of housewife, looking after the guests, bringing and taking food and drink, keeping herself busy and her mind averted from the full face of the calamity. And for her it was a calamity. Way back in her childhood her mother's illness had begun, but she'd adapted, and from that time had devoted herself to her mother's care, the responsibilities increasing with the years. It was all she ever wanted to do. Now she was in her late twenties, and that reason for living was gone. She had known this time would come, but she had lived so much in the present, in each moment of each task. There was no looking into a bleak future. Why? What for? There was only then.

It was while she was pouring tea. The glasses were spread on the tray, some already filled. She set down the pot staring ahead of her with a horrified recognition. And all at once it broke out, her voice, her body, all in a rush. Words tumbled over each other, their pitch rising and falling as she doubled over, dropped, stood up, turned away, came down again. A group of us were by her side in an instant, wanting to hold her up, to go down with her, wanting to give something we knew we could not give, something now totally out of reach for her. A self she knew. The loss of the person dearest to her had shoved her across a border from one life into another, vague and uncertain. There was no zone of transition into this being without identity or meaning, both of which had been given, and given only, by the one who had died.

That night I did not see Omar's grief. Once from behind the closed door I heard his voice cry out above the others. Then it broke into sobs and was lost again among the consolations and renewed lamentations of the men around him. But it seemed right to grieve with the women over this woman's death. It was their loss I found greatest and wanted to share in, their grief I felt closest to. And I knew that was the closest I could come to Omar's.

For several more hours and late into the night I was disturbed by a sense of something missing. Only in the morning I realised what it was. Another absence. That of the body. Hers, Rihaab's, and of a place to go to beyond the house, a focal point for all this activity of early grief. I asked several times, unable to believe what I was told at first, not sure if I had understood correctly. Gone. All done. She had been taken to the hospital in Irbid and died around three in the afternoon, when we were at his uncle's. They had telephoned there only minutes after we left, and had no idea of where we'd gone afterwards. But the body had to be in the ground before sunset. She had not simply died while we were gone, she had done all her leave taking without him, going off early enough to be sure that all the rites were completed before his return. I wondered, since he was her firstborn and special to her, if she had chosen this way to spare him the process of her dying, and the hospital horror that only her daughters had the stomach for.

This was Rihaab, slipping out of his life as she had so often slipped out of a room when unbearable pain took over. Always disappearing into a corner, her going unnoticed.

$\mathcal{B}louses$

Well over a month had passed since that terrible night, and we were moving from spring into early summer. At the university we were coming to the end of the academic year, with all the attendant pressures and stresses.

I came home from Irbid one day to find two of my blouses disturbed in the wardrobe. They've been wearing them, I thought. Without asking me, or even letting me know, they've put them on while I've been gone. I felt surprise, violation, anger. And confusion.

They had done nothing wrong they told me. But they had. Surely they knew that. I was confused and upset because ... in spite of the misunderstandings and problems of adjustment, only to be expected after all, we got on very well most of the time. No. It was more than that. I loved them.

I had come as a complete stranger into Omar's family. But then I saw Sahr and Randa every day. I lived with them, ate with them, worked with them there in that tiny poor village, forgotten by the wide and powerful world. 'No self-respecting Western woman would live in such a place,' I was later told by a self-respecting Western woman who had been there, as if by accident. 'But I loved it,' I said, guessing that she had not felt any need to ward off the suburban life experienced by so many Western women.

I loved it. I loved drawing the water from the well. Wearing my long black *dish-dásha* with the red embroidered border around hem and sleeves, and the red embroidered belt tied around my head to keep the hair out of my eyes. The rope would become damper as I pulled, hand over hand. Then I grabbed the black bucket. It was malleable, seemed small, yet held so much — what was it made of? skin? leather? canvas? I poured its contents into a larger bucket before letting it back down into the well where it hit with a cool plop. Randa would call me over to the thick clump of mint where we picked some leaves to take back to the kitchen. *Na:na:*, one of the first words I learnt there. It goes into the teapot with the handful of tea-leaves just as the sugared water comes to a boil. You must remove the pot from the flame at the very same moment. Randa taught me these things.

If I saw more of Sahr and Randa than of Omar and, if I missed Omar during the week, the proverbial growing 'fondness of heart' through absence was not the love I was looking for. During the week I found it, in large part, with these women, and I loved them in return. I loved them for the lives they led, for what they did. I was with them when they washed the tiled floors; I was with them when they beat the carpet out in the courtyard; I was with them when they cried out at the sudden pain of a scorpion sting. They were Omar's sisters, but they were mine too now.

I loved them. And they annoyed me.

Some things had not changed. Randa was still sweeping the dirty kitchen water under the door of the bathroom before I was ready to leave it. Sahr was still shrieking at Randa and Bilaal to vent her frustrations, and her grief too now. Her voice was shrill, so shrill. I hoped the noise would end before anyone found me crouched in a neighbouring room with my hands to my head.

When Sahr decided to make bread she kneaded the dough the night before, very late, the last thing before sleeping. I sat with her and we talked. My Arabic was a poor equivalent of pidgin, hers a village dialect. I can't say how it is we understood each other, but we laughed and told stories full of gestures, I with my hands, she with her head and shoulders as she drove the heels of her hands into the dough in a large metal basin.

But when she got up early in the morning, before light, and went into the earthen-floored room to start up the oven, when she sat cross-legged in that cool back room deep in the house and shaped the loaves and baked them, then I was sleeping and didn't join her. One time I got up at dawn with her, out of curiosity. Not since.

When guests visited for the day, and long after we had drunk the coffee to greet them with — and tea or a whole meal that followed later — the time came for Sahr to serve the thick sweet 'Turkish' coffee in small cups. Then, sometimes, she read our fortunes in the grounds. Once she asked me to read them in her place. I saw fish and birds in the cups, mountains and forests, caves and treasure. I learnt the Arabic for these things, and entered the language of tales and legends, but I knew few verbs and no tenses. Nouns were all I had, so that the legendary past and the futures I predicted merged in the moment as I pointed and named them into being. I must have overplayed my role; the next time we had guests she asked me to read again, and another time, and another. After several such readings I grew tired, and once I refused. She was disappointed.

They loved me. And I annoyed them.

I loved the thick waves of their beautiful black hair. 'How can you do that to your hair?' I would whine, wringing my hands. Sahr would look up at me with a contented smile from the blanket where she lay flat on her back as Randa worked the iron from the ends of Sahr's hair right up almost to the scalp. '*Biddou* (I want) ... as hair Mishaal,' she answered, pointing at me, but Randa scowled. 'Michèle, this is what we want.' She jerked her head dismissively.

I, who know some things, was happy to inform and advise. I told Sahr and Randa about the dangers of 'Gleam Cream'. It was a blanching cream they wore under their make-up whenever they went on a visit or into the city. On the days of those trips I often found them in the morning hurrying to smear the cream on their cheeks before the pot of sweet water in the kitchen began to boil; they wanted to have the tea made for their father's breakfast and still be ready to catch the bus. The cream came in a flattish round container like a deep powder compact, accompanied by a small folded paper with a description and set of instructions in Chinese, Arabic and English.

> Make skin white like cream. All ladies will use this product all time when they sees effects on skin. Cream wipe off all spots and pigments if use daily, and make skin too young. Put on cheeks each morning and spread over face before other applying.

At the bottom, in even smaller print, were the words 'Made in Shanghai'. When I tried to persuade them to use it less, they flung back at me all they'd heard about foolish Western women lying in the sun all day to become darker skinned.

I reverted to lending a hand in a few chores, when they

let me. Soon it was Randa's hair that spread out in all directions away from her head, like Gulliver's after the Lilliputians had nailed the ends to the ground with tiny invisible nails. I smoothed down the blanket underneath as Sahr ironed.

And I made tea and coffee, helped prepare food, sewed, swept, washed. I tried to make the tea come out right. You can't make any old pot of tea there, especially when Omar is at home. One weekend (and he was there then), it was too strong, and he asked Randa to remake it. The next day it was too sweet, although — truth to say — Sahr and Randa both preferred it that way.

I loved them. Now they angered me.

Two of my blouses hung in that large wardrobe. One blouse was too good for everyday use. It was blue, and made of silk. I tended to keep it for those dream occasions that never happened — something my sisters-in-law would never do. The other was a bright cerise, also silky, but actually made of rayon. It looked more like a shirt, too casual and male for wearing there in the village, I thought, and certainly not for teaching in the city. Besides, it was a little big on me.

I was tired when I came home from teaching on the day of the blouses. The return bus ride seemed interminable. Getting off the bus and going up to the front gate, I would have loved nothing more than a quiet sit with Rihaab over the pot of sweet tea she used to make for me. As I entered through the gate I spied an empty mattress facing the garden.

I went to put away my bag and books and change into a light *dish-dásha* for wearing about the house. Opening the wardrobe door I saw my two blouses standing out from the other clothes that had been pushed to one end. They faced the opposite way, only

291

half on their hangers, as if returned in haste.

All my sense of property, of possessions as extensions of myself, of clothing as near and dear to my body and part of my inviolable space, was outraged. Sacrilege. I exploded.

They came running, as if they thought I had been stung by a scorpion or bitten by a snake. Their surprise and incomprehension at the cause of my outcry was real enough, although something in me would love to regard it as a piece of theatre to match my own drama.

But I was away, they said, and not using them. Besides, when had I ever worn them? They went to visit a friend and borrowed my blouses for the afternoon. Look, couldn't I see they were perfectly good and clean? Not a mark or a tear. Sahr took the cerise one and put it on again in front of me, as if to demonstrate. 'It's big on you,' she said, 'but it's just my size, and I had nothing else to wear today.' All this in Arabic, but I understood by the way she pulled and pointed at the blouse and at both of us. 'Give it to me Mishaal,' she added now, with affection and mischief in her eyes together, just like Omar when he wanted something from me. But I had to let them know they were 'caught'.

'You thought you'd put them back before I got home, didn't you? And that I wouldn't notice, but I could tell right away that you've been wearing them.'

It was Randa who responded now: 'Yes, Michèle, but we do not hide this. We put them back because we finished with them. We came home before you.'

'But you know I'd have let you use them if you'd asked me. Why didn't you ask me?'

'You were not here. But Michèle, you see me wear Sahr's clothes when she does not use them. And I do not ask her all times. Do you see her nervous and angry? And

Sahr the same with my clothes. Why are you so much nervous and angry?'

I did not answer. It seemed that two responses were going through me at once. I felt the alienation, the total lack of understanding of how they could have behaved in this way, and still more the frustration of not being able to communicate to them the way I saw this incident, why it seemed so terrible to me. Would I ever belong here? But I felt something else too. Scenes of many occasions when not only Omar's sisters, but his cousins and their friends had given me things that were clearly of value to them. This had happened especially in the beginning when I admired something they were wearing and they took it off there and then and handed it to me. I quickly learnt not to pay such compliments. I had not been able to understand those actions any better than what I was experiencing now: the other side of the same coin. And yet, though still outraged, some part of me was drawn by Randa's words into a space where I could see both of us from the same distance. An intermediate moment which passed, for then. A flicker.

There was a small commotion at the front door.

'Mish mish.'

Omar's voice calling. He was standing at the door to the guestroom where he had just arrived with a group of men friends, probably those who brought him home early for the weekend. This time none of us had heard the car pull up. I went to him as Sahr and Randa dispersed in other directions to make ready for the unexpected guests. 'Mish mish' he repeated, quietly now, his voice brushing lightly over the name. He had begun to use the diminutive soon after I arrived. It is the same as the Arabic word for apricot, which had been his mother's favourite fruit. I loved the name. It was right.

Like everyone, I am bitter and sweet.

The thought of Rihaab brought home to me that not six weeks had gone by. But if I missed her, what then of Sahr and Randa, reminded of her absence in small ways every day? ...

'Make us some tea, dear.'

'I might make it too sweet again, or too strong.'

'No, no. It's getting better. Make us some, dear. I'm sure your tea is very good now. Abu Hassan and Munir are thirsty, like me, after our long journey. Thank you, dear.'

My tea was very good. I enjoyed making it for Omar and his guests. I wished he weren't away so much, but then we would be marrying soon and leaving together for Scotland only a few weeks after that. I would have the opportunity to bring him round, step by step, to an understanding of our situation as a couple. He cared enough to make an effort. I cared enough to make an effort.

I loved my sisters. I would miss them.

I was attached to my blouses.

I hated washing in the tiny cold bathroom.

I loved drawing water from the well.

Marriage

Wedding: and a Marriage

'Probably' is a word I am constantly on the verge of saying. This is 'probably' my last trip, I almost think to myself. Something within me is surer than this, knows that the probable will be real. There are only a few more days to go, and people are farewelling me. 'We'll see you in another eighteen months,' said your friends Haroun and Muammar who came by the apartment yesterday. 'Probably not,' I was about to say, 'probably never again.' I stopped myself, afraid of bringing about the blank future by pronouncing it, but my refusal to speak it made no difference; I knew.

I stand here today, watching the marrying couple. You are by my side as the groom is by the bride's. We are behind them, almost in line, an imitation, a repetition like the patterns on the church floor. It is at this moment, when the couple's flowery crowns are being exchanged, their ribbons intertwined, that the matching in space becomes one of time. Long ago, when it was our turn, we also stood, you and I, in just such a pose, another rite taking place around us, ourselves at its centre.

In your mother's town. Samar. Not two months after her death. If we had been planning to keep our marriage a simple affair, the timing made this imperative. There could be no celebrating now, even if we had wanted it. In a way that was just as well for you, who could not have afforded it anyway.

Samar. It must be the only time I went there other than to visit your mother's family, which wasn't often. I loved the idea of being married in your mother's town, but I found it strange that Samar should be the nearest place with a *qadi* (judge), because it is such a small town. Kufr Soum is much bigger, yet it has no *qadi*. At least that is what you told me.

The office was like any other, with a large desk and some chairs, and a few clerks standing by or scurrying in and out. In a setting that to me appeared so secular, I felt reassured by the formality of the *qadi's* dress, especially the fez he wore on his head, although for a moment I wondered if I was in Egypt. He conversed with us for a while, first with you in Arabic, then in English with me. I told him I had not seen a *qadi* before, but that I was reminded of the Egyptian writer, Tewfik Al-Hakim, who had been a district judge, and many of whose stories had legal settings. The *qadi* appeared delighted that I had read some of these, and expressed his own admiration for Al-Hakim as a very model for those in the legal profession. After we had chatted a while longer he became more serious as he turned back to you and it was clear that the formal procedure of the marriage had begun.

When he had asked you a few questions that you were evidently answering in the affirmative, he said to me in English: 'Do you want to marry this man?' I said 'Yes.' His eyes grew wide with surprise for a moment, then he mused to me aloud on the way a Muslim woman would

297

have been more likely to respond. She would not have answered in my very definite, outspoken tone of voice, he said; she might not have answered at all, except by a downcast flutter of her lids and a shy movement of her head that could possibly be meant, and would certainly be taken, as an affirmative. He acted out the described behaviour as he told me this, looking down on the floor of the office and fluttering his own lids, and adding a tiny smile at the corners of his mouth, a smile in such a serious face that it was almost not a smile. He turned his head away slightly and back again. We laughed, all three of us, although I knew better than to believe that we were laughing at the women, since the object of our laughter, if there was one, lay in the extreme difference between their manner and mine.

Again he turned to you, and something happened then. For me it was the moment of moments, not our signing of the contract that followed immediately after, but your standing there beside me holding out your arms at the elbow, palms open before you as everything went quiet. It was not vulnerability. You were opening yourself up to your destiny; a receptacle of some divine intention, your hands a gateway, your words an invocation. I recognised the *Faatíḥa*, the opening prayer of the *Qur'aan*, which you uttered with all solemnity. It was then I knew that God was willing, and that we were married.

A Visit

Sitting in the courtyard facing the garden, propped up with cushions provided by several members of Omar's family, my mother puffed on the *naarjiileh* (hookah). She looked up with a smile as I called her name. For once the photo and my best memory of her visit coincide. I thought she looked lovely in her new *dish-dásha* of twilight blue that we had bought in Irbid that day. The sun was about to set, and its rays caught the gold edging around the deep pink flowers embroidered all down the front of the *dish-dásha*. She was enjoying the attention.

Aisha's husband, Moussa, had come round to the house with the hookah while we were out. Now he told my mother it was a gift for her from all the family. He and Adnan were explaining how to use it and set it up. Everyone in the family seemed to have turned up at once that evening, including Aisha herself, now heavily pregnant. She was expecting any day, but had not slowed down at all; in spite of a telling waddle, she spoke and moved about with the same vibrancy I had noted in her greeting to me on the day I arrived. Uncle Ibrahim was there too, adding his share to the activity centred around the hookah. His references to the 'hubbly-bubbly', spattered throughout his Arabic contributions to the

299

discussion, set my mother chuckling every time they came up. No one had said a word to me about the hookah. Canny, the way they knew how much she would enjoy this gift. She had been with us barely a week.

As with all flights from Australia via Singapore, her plane had landed early in the morning. Adnan had got up well before sunrise to make the bus ready for us. Omar's father, brothers and sisters and their families including most of the children were all coming with us to pick her up, and I had also invited Hind. At that time, although Uncle Ibrahim had taken his second wife, Hind had not yet left the hilltop house with the lovely garden, and she had been pleased to accept. The bus would be full.

We were about to take off for the airport when I had a small dispute with Omar about a neighbour across the street who wanted to accompany us. I had told her that I wanted family on the bus, that Hind had already accepted to come and I did not think there would be room. The neighbour had then gone to Omar who said she could join us. I was annoyed. It was *my* mother we were picking up after all … I did not understand that it was out of respect for me that our neighbour had wanted to come. Omar assured me there would be enough room for us all. As it turned out, when Adnan took the detour up the hill and stopped on the nearest road to Ibrahim and Hind's house, there was no sign of Hind. He tooted the bus's horn without turning off the engine, which chugged away quietly in the dawn light as we all sat and waited. But still she did not come, and so we took off without her.

It was not quite a month since Omar and I had been married, three since Rihaab's death. Maman would be staying with us in Jordan for two weeks on her way to France to visit my father's family, and Omar and I would go there with her for two weeks before travelling onto

Scotland. I knew she wouldn't have wanted to be present for the marriage. That would have been too difficult for her. As it was, I appreciated the effort she made to come at all and see something of our life here.

My mother's perceptions of village life struck me as a condensed reflection of my own, and seemed to produce as many contradictory reactions and responses squeezed into the two weeks she had with us. They also reminded me of my own first impressions that had begun to fade. She kept remarking on the beauty of the people, as if marvelling at them, unable to believe her eyes. She soon began to worry about the conditions, wondering how I would live that way indefinitely when she found it so hard for the short period she was with us. She was overwhelmed by everyone's generosity of spirit, the care and interest they took in her. She begged me, on about the fourth day, to make her a pot of tea without sugar. 'They drink it so sweet here, I can't get used to it.' She loved the sips of bitter coffee passed round when guests came. She felt the hidden grief over Rihaab's death and was saddened for them, especially Sahr who continued to work as hard as ever. She was delighted to accompany her on visits to other families, possibly more than I had done. Or had I enjoyed those visits just as much when I first came? ...

One day when Omar and I went into Irbid, my mother was feeling tired and decided to stay behind with his sisters. On our return in the early evening, we found everyone full of excitement, including Maman. 'Oh, you missed it Michèle! Aisha's had her baby, and I went to visit her with Sahr and Randa. We've only just come back. You should have been with us. You'd never believe Aisha had just had a baby. She might as well have woken up from her beauty sleep. She was brushing out her lovely long hair when we arrived, and she was full of energy. What a beautiful girl! And the baby daughter is lovely. If only you'd been there.' I did go the next day with them, and found mother and baby healthy and happy, but my mother seemed to think it was not quite the same. She still referred to 'yesterday' as if I'd missed something special.

They called the baby Shaima, and not long before it was time to leave, I told Aisha that because my mother had been a beautiful young woman, and because she had visited so soon after Shaima's birth, this meant that Shaima would turn out to be especially beautiful. She was Aisha's fourth child, and her third daughter. Everyone remembered my mother's visit that day, and what I later said, and the odd thing is that it has come true. All of Aisha and Moussa's children are lovely, but Shaima, with her curls and large limpid eyes and her smooth flushed skin, is truly striking.

$\mathscr{L}etter\ to\ \mathscr{S}cotland$

We were together in Scotland for well over a year.

Glasgow, the city: a terrible place. More dreary for me than Amiens had been those many years before. Must and mould in nearly every affordable dwelling. Stifling fumes from car exhaust on the streets. Dirt. Crowding. Exorbitant prices. Windswept high rise council 'estates'. And terrible poverty — of others, and of ourselves. For a snapshot of the future of humanity in its nadir of decadence and deprivation, look to this city. They can patch it up all they like; it will not make a jot of difference. It will always and ever be only 'patching' of a place irreparably damaged. A place in the north full of beautiful people, but used and exploited in the setting up of industry, now used up, discarded.

We escaped to the Botanic Gardens where we spent a large part of each day, keeping within the perimeter of sunlight on the lawns or wandering through the glasshouses where we kept warm, and where long-leafed and sinuous exotic plants nodded familiar greetings.

Omar wrote regularly to his family from Scotland and

they wrote back. While I was still there the following letter arrived, addressed to me.

Kufr Soum
Dear Michèle

I wrote to you before one month but we received no letter from you. I think to you many times and I am so long to see you. I do not write too much in English but all in English my thoughts to you. That is my English practice since I stopped studying two months before and until now I have no job. But here there is no many opportunities so I didn't find a work as English teacher. Perhaps I make some mistakes. Not many no? Here no one cares if I speak English or if I find a work as teacher of English or Arabic. They care only that I help to make the meals and clean the house.

At this time we all are quiet and many sleep after the meal in middle of the day. You know when. You remember. I also I will sleep after this letter. But Sahr will come soon and she will pull the blankets from me and she will shout Yelleh Randa get up my lazy sister and help me wash the floors. You remember we wash them every day Michèle because you helped us. All rooms in the house and outside also. Or did you forget we pour water everywhere on the ground before the walls and the gate? And we wipe with the broom of rubber, and when it is dry, before the sun goes, we put the mattresses and the big pillows and all people come to sit with us in this place. The neighbours and the family and the friends sit under the olive tree and the pomegranate tree and all drink shai. You made this tea to us many times. And many nights in the summer we sleep there outside the house. I am sure that you remember the morning that I waked you and said please get up slowly Michèle. You must get up too too slowly. I said this in this way because a big scorpion went under your blanket near to your foot and I do not want to make to you a fright. We lifted the blanket and it was too big and black. You said its tail long and fat like the pipestove. Pipestove yes? That is correct?

At that morning I said to you we ate our breakfast and I said Michèle I think that you will forget us. When you will go away you will forget us. And you said no and you seemed surprise and then nervous or angry. Michèle why were you many times nervous? Will Omar come back alone or will you come with him? You will come with us then to the wadi and I will climb the almond tree again and throw the *loz* to you to catch them. Remember the *loz* that our mother loved to eat? The almonds in their shells very soft and fat and green? You and Manar she is seven now and Nasser he is five you catched the *loz* I sent to you from the tree. Perhaps you will write to us soon. My English is good, yes? I do not write English many times now.

Sahr sends kisses to you, she is so long to see you. Please you write to us. You do not know I think to you every day. Will we see you again Michèle? Yes insha 'Allah.

Your lovely sister

Randa

He had a pale face and a quiet manner, in both ways seeming more English than Scottish, despite his Scottish name. He had begun in a low calm tone, but one that told me from the beginning that he expected trouble, a complaint of some sort that he would have to deal with. Sure enough it came, from both of us. Omar had said something, also quietly at first, but I added my share. Why had we not been informed there was no accommodation for couples. Why, under the circumstances could they not find us somewhere, anywhere, better than the musty apartment we'd been assigned to. True, they had all worked hard in that office to find us this place, but would they live there themselves? I couldn't imagine any of them doing so. Now we had managed to find somewhere else on our own, a place that we could bear to live in, although it would cost us the earth. But we had to pay, this man told us, for all three remaining months of our original contract. That was the lease we'd signed. Those were the rules.

Omar turned to anger, which came entirely from his disbelief that anyone could be expected to live the way we had been living for close to a fortnight. It was the anger of the righteous, the wrath and rage that is required of those who know themselves fully justified in their demands. I could feel the blood accelerating through his veins and past his temples when he saw that the other showed a meekness in defiance, like all those who know they do wrong. But then I turned to the young man again, his fair hair and pale skin with its pasty look as if he had been disoriented to the point of near panic, his own blood drained, by this display of vehemence. And I saw he would hold his ground before the onslaught. Did this

Middle Easterner really believe he could frighten him or make him give way by indulging in this disgraceful outburst?

By then I was well out of it as they stood off against one another like horned bucks, males of two related but separate groups of animals, with every pawing of the ground, twitch of the ears and nostrils signalling challenge, but understood by the other as a form of surrender without backing down. It raised their ire further. Each one appeared to read his shame in the other, an admission of responsibility, and I felt I could read their mutual reactions.

How can this man air his feelings in this way, for everyone here in the office to see? Doesn't he know what a fool he's making of himself or that his anger accuses him?

How can this one remain so puny in his refusal to cooperate? Why does he not stir himself to anger — the anger that becomes the just — before all these people? It can only be because he knows that he and those he represents are in the wrong.

We did pay both rents, and got through those months somehow. It may well have been the stress of living so badly that caused many of our problems. Our living conditions were worse than they had been in the village, so much so that Omar called Glasgow 'the fourth world'. It became a standing joke between us. All the rest between us suffered.

We felt punishment in everything we did and did not do. Now it was not just one of us yearning for a home, but both. We missed the States, in particular the time when we were first together, discovering each other. It had receded into such a nebulous past that I caught myself wondering if it had happened at all. I missed my mother and sister, left in France when we crossed the Channel for Scotland. By this time they were on their way back to Perth. Omar was missing his own family, and now so was I. It was something I had not expected, Jordan calling to me like this. And I began to feel that all the difficulties of adjusting to the life there had been nothing compared with our time in Glasgow. We tried to go out and take trips into the beautiful Scottish countryside, but it was next to impossible. The few we managed resulted from the kindness of friends who took us, usually other Jordanians who were better off because they had come alone. We did spend one lovely day — thank God we had one! — at the Pollock Estate just outside the city which we reached through a combination of walking and other transport.

During those early months of extra rents to pay I arranged for the few thousand US dollars I had left behind in the States to be wired to me. With almost two dollars to the pound sterling I lost half of it in the currency exchange (the buying power of the pound in the UK being no different from that of the dollar in the US), and then lost the rest of it keeping us alive. As for my hopes and plans that lay behind this stint of study in Britain, they were dashed. My very reasons for persuading Omar to come to another Western country seemed to have turned in some awful twist of irony upon myself.

I became increasingly frustrated with our situation, while he would fly into tempers, sometimes hitting out. The second time he struck me, during a very physical fight, I made a decision. Waiting until the next morning after Omar had gone to the library, to continue with his research on the representation of cultural difference among turn-of-the-century authors, I packed my bags and took a room in a hotel, refusing to return until he promised to curb his anger. I was there for two days. It might have been longer if we had not bumped into each other on the city streets. He was much better after I came back, but something had happened. A tension of mood was making stealthy encroachments on our closeness.

When women look at other women suffering in their marriages, they tend to wonder, 'How can she put up with that?' When it's yourself, you are in it. Others are not the ones who committed themselves to that person in the first place, so how could they understand? They did not go through the long involved process of choosing, for reasons peculiar to the self, that particular partner and of building that relationship. The story is not there for them, the story with all its entrammelling threads, to hold them as it holds you.

Soon after that incident came the distressing calls from Australia. It was becoming clear that for my mother time was running out. She had borne the chemotherapy well and was still in remission before she came to Jordan and France, having the trip to look forward to. Now it was behind her and depression interfered with her coping. There was the 3.00am call, my mother sobbing into the phone that it was suddenly all too much for her. And me sobbing back. There was my sister's call within a day: she could no longer manage the situation; she felt a terrible need for my support, and presence. 'I know. I'm coming,' I told her, and I left for Perth.

Sacrifice

Well before I received those calls from Perth, there was a visit from an old family friend. Did she feel in some way duty-bound to visit me? I had always admired her, and found myself taken aback by the changes in her.

It was just a few things she said. Phrases dropped into our conversation, after twelve years. Up by train from London, she had called me with her invitation to dinner, insisting on treating me. In the Glasgow restaurant she ordered a whole roast shoulder of lamb between us. And she talked. At first I hung on every word, knowing how I had always enjoyed her wit, her freedom from convention, the way she mocked at social norms. She had been very close to my parents, especially my mother, and had made a short trip to France to see her before Maman returned to Australia. In personality at least, she had not changed since Sydney days. The clever storytelling, the flouting, carefree manner were just as I remembered them, but they were pressed into the service of something different now, something ugly, and that touched me more closely.

'… worst train journey ever … compartment full of Muslim women … veils … crying babies … squealing toddlers scrambling about … high-pitched voices jabbering … oh, I'm sure it was Arabic …'

She did not let up, and with the rhythm of her talk I could almost hear the background rhythm of the train. The children's noise and the endless flow of Arabic swept over me with her own flood of English.

'… Australian population today … less than sixty percent Anglo-Saxon or Celtic …'

She was living in England now. What was the percentage there, I wondered.

As I sat dismayed at the change in her, at the complete overturning of my expectations, the waiter carved at our table. Under the pressure of the knife, driblets of juice oozed out onto the platter. My disappointment with the trend of her talk, during a meal she enjoyed heartily, was mixed with relief that Omar had been unable to join us; I wondered how she would have behaved in his presence. She said nothing disapproving of my marriage. She did not refer to it. Just the few phrases every so often, enlarged and expanded, made to stand out in the small talk.

'… those unhygienic practices … slaughtering sheep in the heart of the city … poor animals … blood flowing into the London streets …'

I did not argue. I had heard this damning litany of catchphrases before, usually gory, as if the distaste of the speakers could be explained by the lurid extremes of their descriptions. And there had been a time when I, too, had felt that everything close to death and blood was closer to barbarism, further removed from civilisation whose purpose is to hide us from ourselves. But I would have been wasting my breath trying to argue. Dirtiness, unhealthiness, primitivity, cruelty to animals flowed together in her stream of words.

How to pit against this the living meaning of spilt

blood? How to register my own disgust at the vapid cleanliness of a supermarket meat counter, where the meat, no longer a life exchanged for mine, has become a nothing? As I listened I thought perhaps the city *should* be muddied, bloodied, to be read again as *something*, for those sensing menace, the menace of loss, the loss of meaning, the meaning of life, that which you give it. Collectively they give it who ritually take life away. Perhaps better not in the city, but then where? Better in the city than not at all. And best of all if you had experienced, and could hold onto the memory of, that other best 'where'.

Under the olive tree I sit with the women, Omar's sisters and cousins and neighbours, looking across at the snowcap of the Jebel Sheikh, so near on a crisp day. We walked here from the house, less than a hundred yards away. Further down our street as it leads out of the village you can almost see the spot where it turns into a dirt track that will bring you to the edge of the wadi. This too, this wadi at the end of a street, also makes the Syrian mountain seem clear and close.

Still nearer to us is the knot of men gathered around Omar talking in low voices, quick and tense, that echo quietly through the olive grove. They are by another tree to which is tied with a long rope a handsome ram with a honey-coloured fleece and horns that begin to spiral.

After a while Omar moves towards the animal who does not seem to notice him at first, then backs off in sudden fright. It is trembling and it baas at nothing before it, eyes staring. But Omar is holding it now, and strokes it gently as he continues to talk, ostensibly to his friends, really for the sheep. To this one he has transferred all his attention. Every word and movement is focused, purposeful. Omar calls for water, and a large old tin full of cool wellwater is brought. The ram draws up the water in great draughts. The tin is filled again, and only when the ram has drunk his fill is it removed. Then Omar has an arm round his neck, almost hugging him. His talking to him and to them turns imperceptibly into a *Qur'aanic* prayer. It is not from stealth, but from care, that the knife is unnoticeable. So quick, then, so sure and deft, the economy of movement such that I hardly know when or how the ram's forelegs were raised and positioned for the plunge. The other men are suddenly right there, helping to hold the ram down as he kicks and quivers. The life spurts out, and flows fast, then slowly, seeping, but not quite losing itself, in the thick soil. A new resignation enters the ram's eyes as they hold onto him firmly, gently, and keep holding long after all movement has ceased, hugging him close. Omar's head and chest and arms are near-buried in his fleece, one with his subsiding warmth.

After the sacrifice, when the meat is being divided up to send around the village to relatives and to the poor, Omar says to me, 'I always give the sheep water to drink beforehand. All the water it wants. Did you see how he drinks? Not lapping with his tongue like cats and dogs. The sheep drinks like us.'

Return to Kufr Soum

When I left Glasgow, we both believed that our separation was to be temporary. We must have seen it that way for a long time. Omar even came to Perth the following year for the European summer, the long student vacation. I don't know how he managed to scrounge the money together for the trip, but I felt heartened that it meant so much to him. He was with us for close to three months, and enjoyed the places we took him to see — city, forest of karri trees, ocean — but he also said that Australia must be the most racist country he had ever been in. In the US and the UK he had been very much protected by his international student status, but in Perth he was staying with me and experiencing the day-to-day world of ordinary life. The few Aborigines he saw looked clearly like third-class citizens, and then he told me how terrible it was to treat the original inhabitants of a country in this way. It was unfortunate, too, that the media in Perth at the time was full of the story of an Australian of Anglo-Irish, Dutch and Javenese descent who had tried to start up a racist political party. This man had recently engaged in acts of violence and had been tried and sentenced to gaol.

When Omar left we were both feeling doubtful about where and how soon we would be together again. My mother was very ill, and for several months after his visit all my attention was concentrated on her. I also had a full-time teaching post in one of the universities. Over time my life became increasingly a Perth life.

I called him when Maman died. He'd been expecting it. Since it was the middle of the winter holidays in Glasgow he'd waited indoors most of the time after receiving my last warning letter. Maman had enjoyed Christmas and the New Year with her family around her, and had come through most of January. The Gulf War was about to break out when she lapsed into unconsciousness at my sister's home and we moved her to the palliative care unit of a neighbourhood hospital. She had said she hoped it wouldn't come to war, and she was gone by the time it did. For me, her last words were, 'You're a survivor Michèle.'

After Maman's death I was uncertain about whether to return to Jordan to live. Before the year was out I did go in the hopes that a visit would help me make up my mind. When I arrived, Omar had just returned from Scotland himself with his higher degree and the status it would give him. He seemed to have suddenly become wildly in love with that country, and had brought back videos of the lakes and highlands which he played over and over to family and friends, and even after visitors had gone. He had been to see many of these places himself, and though I knew from a trip made with my mother many years earlier that Scotland is beautiful, in Glasgow Omar and I had never had the means to visit other parts outside the city. He made some passing reference once, sitting in front of those videos with glistening eyes, to a woman who had been very kind to him. I asked a few questions, but did not press him. There was a vague feeling of not wanting to hear whatever he might have answered. I was not prepared to articulate anything then, but I must have begun already, on that last trip, to place good and bad impressions of my visit side by side with good and bad memories of earlier times in the village. Not consciously, but in the way that most people do, allowing each image, each stored moment or event to take its place among the others and offer its weight of worth. I was reminded of the dilemma I underwent at the time of my second trip to Perth, but the choice was no longer between Omar and my mother. It was becoming one of Omar or not Omar.

In the village Omar's safe return home and grand new achievements were still being feted by the whole community when I arrived. He was expected to entertain. That was when Sahr made those many meals from the whole sheep he brought home one day from the city. But it wasn't all one way. Friends and neighbours also invited him to eat with them. Abu Youcef's family was among several who laid on a feast for him. Of warm recollections, the evening meal at Abu Youcef's house is the one I remember best.

Abu Youcef worked for the Ministry of Education. He also wrote poetry. But he saw no hard and fast divide between the obligation of the one and the pleasure of the other. They mix and flow together, part of the current (or currency) of daily life in the village. I asked Abu Youcef if I could hear some of his poetry. He thought I might find it tiresome, since his poems are always only in Arabic, and lose too much in translation. But it was poetry in Arabic, I assured him, that I loved to hear, even though I understood next to nothing. This, I said, was how Omar had won me, reciting traditional poetry I did not comprehend. So meaningful, this listening to a language we do not speak, a language we have little or no familiarity with. In every language is another, different from that of its words, its poetry a gateway. I was glad when Abu Youcef consented to share a few of his poems with us after the meal.

We were many, so many that two long cloths were unfurled end to end on the carpet of the spacious room reserved for guests, and long shallow mattresses were disposed on either side. Until it was time to eat we had been sitting in large armchairs and sofas disposed around the edges of the room. Then Abu Youcef's wife and two daughters, who had been coming and going constantly with dishes, utensils and bowls of salad, brought in the three enormous steaming platters of *mensef*, and we were invited to move onto the floor.

When everyone became quiet, I recalled that it is not the custom to continue deep in conversation while eating. The few words spoken came from our host inviting us to a dish, or from a guest responding. We focused on what we were doing. Once in a while one of Abu Youcef's daughters, who sat beside me, urged me to eat, placing extra pieces of meat before me. Like the other women I spooned the rice into my mouth, but most of the men scooped it up in the traditional way, lightly squeezed in a fist, so that it was held together by the yoghurt and the momentary pressure of their curved hand. All the men — Omar, his father and brother, Abu Youcef, his sons, even the old grandfather of the family — brought each handful of pressed rice level with the chin and tossed it in one piece into the mouth.

317

I have sometimes thought of making this dish back in Perth, am glad it has been no more than a thought. Some things become nothing when you take them away from their home. There is the difficulty of obtaining the dried yoghurt, which should come in the form of small rocks that you rub in water until they are dissolved. Then you must have a huge pot like a cauldron to cook the yoghurt and the mutton in. And then, too, the enormous round platter to pile the rice high like a hill so you can top it with the meat and nuts and rivulets of yoghurt. But this dish could not be called by the name of *mensef* without the large group of people to gather round and eat from it.

After dinner Abu Youcef read his poems. Omar translated a line here and there, with Abu Youcef adding a word of description or correction. It was a long time since I had heard Arabic poetry, and as I listened, I could not help recalling those heady days when Omar first quoted Arabic poetry to me. The two men's voices, one present and one past, intermingled, became one voice in a pool of reminiscence.

One voice. Omar's, in his tiny room high up on the twelfth floor of an American building. The rays of the afternoon sun touched the pot plants in his window before glancing off the edge of the outer wall. I sat listening, nestled into the cushions he had propped up for me along his neatly made bed.

'... the pomegranate is next to it. Ohhh ... the olive tree is very healthy, very lovely. The form is beautiful, with branches that cover just enough to give all shade to this place. If you look at it you think it is old, and it is. The olive lives many years, many hundreds of years. Some of these trees, they are very ancient. It is important in the religion also, in the *Qur'aan*. The prophet, he loved this tree. The oil from it is pure. The light from the lantern lit by the oil of the olive is pure light. It burns slowly, softly. It is the purest ...'

His description of the grapevine, too, was a portrait. He did not give it life, but wakened me to the life it had, its life as part of the family of vines, its character as the particular vine that grew at his home. He sketched its leaves and fruit in detail, and told the story of its meanderings. And the pomegranate. With the rise and fall of his voice the blossoms of the pomegranate would swell into polished globes.

And before I knew it the accents were those of poems — the classical poems that everyone knows who speaks Omar's language — poems with their love, glory, astonishment, their battle cries, waterfalls, trysts and promises all straining to break out of that equal measure of words.

What brought me back to Abu Youcef's reading was the different sound of his poetry, in which I recognised the less strictly measured modern rhythms as compared with the classics. No one explained or interpreted. For my sake a little context was given, just enough not to spoil the effect of the poems for me, on that cold winter night, with all of us warm indoors after the hot meal.

As the cups of sweet coffee were passed around I looked across at Omar's father, who was chatting with Abu Youcef. Whilst his sons and youngest daughter have surpassed him in education, Abu Omar can recite the long classical poems, and like Omar he does so with all the feeling and sense of rhetoric they demand. I've heard him recite for friends in the course of a quiet afternoon's conversation. I suppose it's the way in the villages. Even a retired policeman knows his poetry.

At Abu Youcef's that night, as usual since his heart attack, Abu Omar took no coffee but drank plenty of water. His large, dark moustache, which Omar insists he dyes, seems never to come in contact with anything he drinks or eats. He appeared relaxed and happy. In fact, on that trip I found him in a better frame of mind than in the past, even though I did not see him often. We greeted each other warmly when we crossed paths in the morning, but that was rare, after he began to live in rooms apart with his new wife. When I think about it, I'm amazed at how he managed to do this in a house of only five rooms. Abu Omar and his second wife made it seem larger than it was since taking two of the rooms for themselves. I couldn't help liking the wife. Yet who could expect Omar to feel anything but resentment for this woman, and this new, unexpected family, these encroaching little half-brothers, sweet as they are, for whom he must one day bear the responsibility, if not already ...

Cheating

Only a few days after I was back in Kufr Soum, a number of visitors came to the house; two or three older couples with some of their children. I did not recognise any of them, and could tell from the formality of reception that they were not regular visitors.

They arrived early in the afternoon, and everyone sat outside the house on mattresses and cushions spread around the courtyard. The initial obligatory coffee was followed by quiet chatting for over an hour, then tea was served, and around that time the conversation became more animated, even loud and full of protest. I heard the word *towjiihi* several times, the name of the end-of-school exam that throughout the country the students take around the end of May.

You have to pass this exam, and pass well, to go onto any form of tertiary education. Even Randa, at the top of her class, would not easily have gained entry to a university, although she was accepted at the Teachers' College where she had applied. Being the best student didn't mean much in a poor village where good teachers and resources were hard to come by. What was most needed — exposure to urban ways of thinking — was even further out of reach. Now, as I looked enquiringly at

Omar, he explained that a number of pupils from the school in Kufr Soum had been caught cheating in the exam, and the government had decided to make an example of them by having them gaoled.

Poor Umm Mohammed, Omar said, indicating one of the more voluble women visitors, and Umm Satki also, and he motioned towards another woman sitting near her, because their sons are both in gaol. I noticed the fathers were saying little, but then, on the subject of their children's education the women always seemed to have more to say, and to be permitted to speak, as if it were understood that this was their domain. Or perhaps these men felt it was undignified to complain about their sons' fate.

So that was the reason, I thought, why the talk had taken on a tone of complaint. Omar began to translate for me some of the things the women were saying, about how the villagers didn't stand a chance alongside the city students, who only happened, after all, to cheat in more sophisticated ways. And even if they didn't, weren't they equipped with everything they could want ... especially those who attended the private schools? And that was the majority of middle-class urban residents. Didn't they have such a huge advantage that it was a farce to make the rural students compete with them? If our children don't cheat a little, Umm Mohammed cried out, how can they even begin to improve their lot, up against all that?

I wasn't surprised at the government's action, only that it hadn't come sooner. And I recalled with guilt and confusion my own situation three years before.

How frustrating it had been to watch Randa, during most of my first year in the village, rocking back and forth as she learnt her history lessons verbatim from the text, just as children learn the *Qur'aan* by heart. A murmured chant of dates and names over and over. On one occasion she was telling me about the history of the Arabs and kept referring to an Englishman named 'Mak-ma-hooun.'

'Who?' I asked, and she pointed to the name, in her history text, of the man in whose agreement with Sharif Hussein the Arab world had placed so much trust. It was written in English at the bottom, in a footnote.

'McMahon,' I corrected, thinking how typically unphonetic the name was. She tossed her head at me.

'No. That is English pronunciation, Michèle, but it is not the Arab. In Arabic: Mak-ma-hooun.'

And she heaved out the aspirate of the last, stressed syllable, following her amendment of my own pronunciation with an assured and pretty smile. I corrected myself.

'Very well. Mak-ma-hooun.'

I thought for a moment, and then said, 'But you pronounce my own name well, and it's not Arabic.'

'Yes. This is correct. I pronounce your name too well, like the French, yes? Better than Sahr, better than all people here ... except Omar. But Michèle, you are not in the Arab history.'

All through that first year I watched as Randa went from cleaning house with Sahr, or making tea for guests and washing dishes, to studying for the *towjiihi*. We talked often about *Animal Farm*, the major text set for the English course. When we read it together I had a vivid image of moustached men in the Ministry of Education congratulating themselves on this find. Here was the English language, some good literature, and a nudge in the right political direction, all rolled into one. Whoever had had the felicitous idea to use Orwell's story would have known

323

that the majority of village youth didn't think much about political systems and ideologies. That came later, in the tertiary institutions, for those who attended them, but this single text could reach them first, and would, with a little encouragement from the right teachers, help to shape and set young minds. I wondered what Orwell would have thought of this use of his narrative in a small Arab country trying to steer its way between the perceived dangers of Islamic extremism on one side and socialism on the other.

These observations I kept to myself, not wanting to jeopardise Randa's chances of doing well in her exam. I went along with whatever they were told, and from the reductive reading of the allegory as little more than a critique of socialism, I could tell what would be wanted from the students. It was a foreign-language text, after all, not studied purely for its literary value (the perfect excuse for reductiveness), and what mattered was Randa's ability to understand it, to reproduce in her own best English a few of its basic ideas and then come up with some not too complex ideas of her own on these.

Several times I edited essays for her, helped her answer questions on the text and asked her others. A few weeks before the exam she wanted me to write out a whole essay that she might learn and use, because her teacher had been talking about strong hunches as to what the essay question on *Animal Farm* might be. I refused point blank at first, until she and Omar kept at me to help her and I caved in under the pressure. Then I insisted she be with me and discuss the text as we went, so that we were writing it together. This she agreed to.

What I did after that was wrong, by any standards. And yet, strangely, I knew that I would do it again in the same circumstances.

On the day of the English exam, only about a month

after her mother's death, Randa took off for school in the morning, nervous but confident. The house and the street outside were abuzz with activity, as they had been for some days, ever since the *towjiihi* began. I went out and joined the others hanging about in the road. The young girl who lived across the street was taking the exam too, and her mother stood outside chatting with us. Omar was away in Mu'tah, but Na:aameh and Aisha had come from their homes to wait for news. Twice I walked with them between the house and the school, which was only a couple of streets away. Relatives of the candidates were gathered outside. There were constant comings and goings and excited comments on what must be happening inside. Some stood back from the enclosing wall, occasionally jumping as high as they could to try and see inside the room where the exam was taking place. A few even tried scrambling up the wall. Even Bilaal was lingering at the edge of the groups with his knot of young friends. A teacher, I was told later, came out once to send people away, but they stayed around, quietening down for a while until the tension exploded again as someone called out that they could see a student, a relative, at one of the windows.

I had gone back to the house again, and was sitting in the room near the kitchen, when Aisha hurried in with a note in her hand, a bit of paper with Randa's writing on it. She kept pointing.

'The question. The question. Quickly, Mishaal, answer.'

And she made a motion of writing.

In no time some paper and a pen had been thrust into my hands and I could not see past the bodies gathered round. I knew that if I wrote an essay now it would make little or no difference to Randa's results. Their faith in native-speaker competence under such circumstances was as simple and total as it was unrealistic. Randa had always had some difficulty understanding my writing, and used to ask me to print, which I could not do quickly. Now there was little time to write a whole essay, and I had more faith than any of them in Randa's own abilities. But it seemed the whole village had turned out to support Randa in the only way they knew, and also to test my loyalties. I looked up at Na:aameh who was standing among them holding her youngest child, Mu'áwiya. She had always seemed to me to be the most sensible and mature one in the family. She returned my look with a nod.

'Help, Mishaal, help Randa.'

I remember raising my eyes to heaven with a look between resignation and conspiracy. Aisha asked her a question, making that writing gesture again, then turned back to me, repeating her plea more excitedly, 'Writing, Mishaal, quickly, quickly.'

And I wrote.

I never did learn whether my page and a half of writing, which Aisha grabbed from my hands and raced off with before I had added the last full stop, reached its destination. How they could have got it over the wall and into the classroom, how Randa would have used it, were mysteries not to be fathomed by me or divulged by those who knew. I did ask later if she got it, but she answered me evasively, and I realised it was naïve to question her.

On that day, I could not imagine Randa, with all her energy, sitting in the classroom doing nothing while she waited. There were other questions in the exam paper to answer, and she may have tried writing her own essay anyway, in case mine did not come through. But what exactly she wrote, and whether she used my sheet or not, only she will ever know.

Noor

Wedding: and Dead Sea

It is just as well we can both be here now, you and I, enjoying this wedding together, someone else's wedding, taking place within a religion that is neither yours nor mine. But it is 'of the Book', and we feel its power.

We are so close to the front of the church we can see all the details of the ceremony. I feel that what has occurred between us heightens our sensitivity to this rite. We are both more aware. On my last visit I suspected nothing about the other woman in your life. Not until you spoke of the helpfulness of some 'kind Scottish lady'. You had not brought her back to the village. I think you were still in dilemma then, trying to convince yourself that you had parted with her for good. But I sensed something different and unsettling emanating from you. That was why I did not press. I already knew the gist of it, was already hurting. So much was wrong.

So much was wrong, on that visit eighteen months ago. I believe the weather had a lot to do with it. Rain, wind, and then the unexpectedly heavy snowfalls. There was more snow than the oldest people of the village could remember, more than had yet been recorded in those northern hills and wadies. But even before the snow came, omens began to lay themselves out before us. With the possible exception of the dinner at Abu Youcef's, the outcome of every action and decision was mishap. And every adventure turned into a nightmare, like that terrible trip we took with your family, the nadir of my visit. Looking back, I see it now as representing the turning point, though I didn't know it then.

It wasn't anything you did. That's the strange thing about it. Just the trip itself and the way it all turned out. Adnan took us in his bus, and so Na:aameh and the children came too. Saleh was there, with their daughter Amira. Then there was Randa, and others. So I wasn't alone to experience the disappointments, but it was only I who saw them as foreboding.

At first it was like any other day trip, an outing, something new to look forward to. For me, the delight of movement into the unknown. In Irbid we were held up for a long time — I never did learn exactly why — and while we waited there, the rain hit suddenly, flooding the streets within minutes and turning them to mud. Wind and water lashed at our bus.

It eased for a while as we drove south. In some small town in the Jordan Valley we stopped to buy the flat round bread we could watch being baked in a huge stone oven. Once back in the bus we passed it round and each tore pieces off the steaming loaves.

Further on, gesturing vaguely to the right, you indicated the direction of the bridges into another world, a country lying lengthwise beside yours, a neighbour and cousin made remote, the river a sword between them. Then the rain that had begun in Irbid turned heavy again. The gardens and orchards you eagerly pointed out, the pride of the country, were barely visible, their bright colours turning neutral behind the great swashes of water that a gale was dashing against the bus windows.

At last we came down into the deep white depression, and could see the huge expanse before us. It was supposed to be water. It was lead-coloured, and stretched into a distance that appeared enclosed, land and sky vaulted leadenly over it. The shrouded sun hung low and still, but the wind beneath it had not abated, though it now blew strangely warm, and as we approached the edge we found that the surface of the heavy, heavy water, deep in its deep trough, was moving, churning, raging like an animal. Where was the floor-like flatness you could lie on with a book and a parasol as I had seen in my childhood school texts? How could a dead place whip itself into such a fury? Almost everyone in your family had been here before, at different times, and now told me they had not seen it like this, in fact never anything but calm. We stared, amazed.

Among the dunes some way from the shore we began to light a fire and cook lunch, the bus serving as a windbreak. We gulped down seared pieces of lamb before the white sand could crumb them. Afterwards, going to the sea's edge, we were met with rapid-fire pellets of salt which burned my exposed arms with a fiery, punishing sting and hardened on my body like cement. I thought to defy the place with wit. 'Not dead, this sea,' I told the others in my awful pidgin Arabic, 'very, very angry.'

We left before long. On the way back you yourself added the finishing touch, as if in league with death and destruction, or driven by them unawares. 'Muslims believe that it is bad luck to come to the Dead Sea,' you said. 'This is the place of the cities in the plain. They were destroyed by God, and it is said that when you come here the devil enters your heart.'

Why did you take me there? But you had come before, and the others too, so why should your words affect me? I have tried ever since to forget that trip. Didn't you tell me, in a wiser moment, to forget the past? But I didn't listen, and like Lot's wife, I am still looking back.

Hotel

Standing beside Omar at this wedding, I sense how much of him I had begun to forget. Eighteen months since I last saw him, and within only a few days he has taken shape again for me, through those many small things about a person we absorb without noticing: the way he stands — is standing now — the way he walks and speaks and sips his tea. When I go again will I remember enough connected with him? Enough for what? The camp of the forgotten grows and spreads as we speed away from each other, the delicate thread of memory spinning itself out and stretching thinner as the years fall behind us like that road beneath the wheels of the car long ago.

Straight American roads all. Even when they began to wind through country places, past wildlife parks, around lakes and through forests, they were smooth and secure, the roads of our courting. At that time the future rushed up to meet us, its every moment of transformation into the present welcomed. Since we began to live in separate countries, I am not in a particular time. It is always only now, endlessly.

What happened over the last few years was bound to leave its mark. When I went to Perth from Scotland I gave the largest part of my time to my mother. Therapy

332

procedures had begun to take their toll, but we had a whole year together before she died, a very good year. That I would not change for anything. Still, it is during absence that usurping occurs, even among the animals.

Impossible to pretend the other woman does not exist, that she did not visit him at Mu'tah, more than once, and that he did not take her there to the village, even if only for a short while ... Here is the symbolic 'beating' referred to in the joke Omar translated a few days ago at Shareen's home. In that case I should translate it as: 'There was once a man who, in a moment of inebriated forgetfulness, was unfaithful to his wife. When he came to his senses and realised what he had done, he was unfaithful again, many times.' If the old woman had told me the joke herself, directly, I might have seen understanding and commiseration in it, but because Omar mediated, all the intent was coming from him.

A Western woman too. If she had been Arab ... If he had not gone so far as to take her there ... She met the family — his father, his sisters, his cousins, his uncles — and in letters and telephone exchanges they have told me about her, as they must have told her about me. Some liked her. Others wished I would return and take my rightful place.

Well before they found each other, there was Omar's trip to Perth. At least I had that. Or did I? Had they already met by then? At the time of his visit our bond had not been broken, was still strong. You can sense those things, always. But then, there was the sadness of parting. Yet another leave-taking. And after he'd gone, the emptiness. Restlessness. Nights of terrible nostalgia, when I tossed sleepless, assailed by images of his mother, his sisters, and him. He had brought a whole world back to me, and taken it away again, leaving only the images that invaded my thoughts without warning, reminding me of all I missed. The very sound and smell and taste of things came slapping into my mind the way scraps and fragments are dashed against the face in a whirlwind.

It no longer happens that way. The nostalgia, the intensity of recall, used to come partly from the thought that it might die away. And from the uncertainty, wondering how long it would be before I would see him again, be with them all. Then I made the third trip, that trip that went so wrong.

A year later came the letter with Jordanian stamps on it, that I thought was from him. Only after I opened it did I see that the writing was different. *I* am Omar's wife now, it read, not you any more. Just like that. And a few other things, minor things, like how wealthy she was and how she had shown him all the beautiful places in Scotland, and Ireland, and Jordan, and everywhere that he and I had ever dreamt of going together. It became clear that she had sounded out the depth of every one of our hopes and dreams and had driven her own stake into each, just exactly so deep.

'It is over, and it means nothing to me,' he told me when I called. 'She is angry that I rejected her. Write her a rude letter. Make it clear, as I made it.' I did write, sending back the stinging barbs she had sent me. But this could not go on. Another communication, and before there was still another I stopped, returning her letters to her. 'Over,' he had told me, but a deed spins out through time and space, its smallest ripples warping what might have been. Now it will not only be every time Omar and I part, but every time I see him, that I will be taking another beating. Have I omitted something? Who is this man I try to remember?

There was his anger. That was dark. Over the years it

found different objects. When Na:aameh and Aisha were about to be married he beat them, literally, in a self-righteous rage at their choice of husbands. As oldest brother, and still in his youth at the time, he had been sure of his role, certain it was expected of him. Yet he had admired Sahr for standing up to their father who tried to marry her off. 'My father and my uncle are forcing me,' she told the judge who was presiding over the marriage. The judge gently reminded both father and uncle that forced marriages had become illegal in Jordan, then gaoled them for a week.

It is very different now. Soon it will be Randa's turn, and Omar is happy for her; she is marrying a second cousin much loved by all the family, one of Abu Kariim's sons. While we were in Scotland Randa wrote to Omar often, and shortly after her letter to me, she sent another to Omar saying that a family had approached her father proposing their son for her. She did not want this man, but was pressured into allowing the contract to be made. Only the wedding itself remained to be held, but strong-willed Randa recognised her mistake and wrote to Omar: 'I am miserable. Please stop our father.' Omar replied to both of them, encouraging her to break the contract and upbraiding his father for trying to force her hand. It worked.

He was always angry with city people, with wealth, with the commercial world and its inroads into his own. Not because it was commerce. He loved to strike a good bargain any time. But when the genuineness of spirit went out of people's interactions, and he saw that individuals hid behind anonymity to rob and hurt, he had only wrath and contempt. For him the city was another faceless mask of that self-interest.

On a beautiful summer's day we met Omar's old friend, Maher, in Amman. It was just after our marriage and not long before my mother's visit. I knew Maher from our student days in the United States, and thought of him as one of Omar's best and most loyal friends. He took us to lunch on the roof of a big hotel. Not much of a view, but there were plants and hanging baskets all around us, and waiters in uniform. Something felt wrong about the place, and the food, when it came, was terrible. It was so bland as to be tasteless, and had been slapped onto the plates as if in contempt, or as if its poor preparation was a necessary condition of modernity. I wondered if this was what those who ran the hotel thought of Western taste. Was this how they catered to it? Maher had invited us there, possibly because he thought I might enjoy a little Western food after so long in the village; perhaps I would find some pleasure in the suggestion of luxury. A suggestion is all it turned out to be.

It seemed ungracious for Omar and me to complain, but we did, all the same. Our reaction was too strong to let it pass, and I suppose there was a compensation of sorts tucked away in our outspokenness, an understanding among the three of us. For my part, I felt embarrassed at first, knowing that Maher would be paying for a very expensive meal. Still, I told him that he did not need to cater to my westernness, because I loved things as I found them wherever I happened to be. I knew he detested as much as Omar the incursion of foreign ways in the name of modernity, and I said that I, too, deplored the imperviousness to the worth of what was already there.

But Omar was angry. He railed against both the

modern, Western style of urban life as it appeared in his country, the sham of it all, and against the Arabs for letting it happen. In full-blown anger he cursed them for keeping stubbornly to tradition and for not keeping to tradition enough, for retaining the worst with the best customs and throwing out the good with the bad. As if all the strands could be combed and sorted out. He knew they couldn't really, and that was the most frustrating knowledge. Maher, though less vociferous, was equally annoyed with the meal that had been dished up to us, and sympathised with our reactions. Later, as we enjoyed the afternoon walking along the colonnade, taking photos and wandering about in the old city, the bad taste left by that meal was forgotten. In its place was the sense of something shared.

Yes, more and more of Omar is coming back to me. Here at this wedding, my time with him, past and present, has played itself out in my mind again like a film. And with it the smells and tastes and images, the affections, the devotedness, the friendships ... the limitations. And some of the anger. In a few days I will go, and loss will begin again, the loss that began with our first parting and deepened with that letter six months ago. I will tread the same path from intense recall through mixed nostalgia and anger — my own anger — to a gradual fading out. That sense of him is here with me now, but the future is shaping itself away from the present, as the present has spun away from the past.

Auntie

Auntie had a high-pitched quavering voice, older than her years, almost like Grandma's. She was very close to Rihaab, and as they lived next door to each other, she came often. It was she, more than anyone, who understood what Rihaab had suffered, having gone through much of it with her. She was Uncle Ahmed's wife, and it was to her that Rihaab could confide when Grandma treated her badly.

It was a bad life for you if you were on the wrong side of Grandma in the old days when she was younger, a full-blown matron with daughters-in-law in every house to chide and chastise. And to compare with each other. With sickness Rihaab became weaker, and in Grandma's eyes more and more useless.

But Auntie knew.

Auntie did not have a heart problem like Rihaab, but she had developed diabetes with the years, so that their looking out for each other was more than a commiseration and sharing of confidences. Not that she was incapacitated. Her disease was not debilitating in the same way as Rihaab's. She could grind coffee, for example, and often did, in our house and theirs. Once, when my mother was staying with us in the village, I asked Auntie to make us some fresh coffee so that my mother could enjoy the tune of the coffee being ground in the great stone mortar. She indicated that she wasn't up to a performance for visitors, and I felt that I had asked too much of her; it was so easy to forget and slip into the skin of the tourist. But she began nonetheless, with a slow clicking and clinking. Meanwhile Temaam, who had come in with her, was sent to fetch her father next door. Uncle Ahmed was fortunately at home that day, and after a while he came, and she passed on to him the instrument on which she had been tapping out her peaceful rhythm. In his control the sound was faster and more forceful, with more frequent downbeats, different and yet similar. I have a tape of this music punctuated by bursts of dialogue from all of us gathered round, in English and in Arabic.

Auntie died just before the heavy snowfalls. I had landed in Amman on that fateful last visit and been taken straight to the village. I was told that Auntie was in hospital and very weak. With one of her older married daughters staying at their house next door, I knew she must be gravely ill.

The news came on the evening of my second day. That night and all the next morning we spent several hours next door, where the main room had been cleared of everything but the wall mattresses. It was the largest room and on both days it was packed around the edges with women who stayed for hours, going away and returning later to mix with a different group. I went in with Yasmine and Randa, sometimes with Na:aameh or Aisha, and every time we entered I made the rounds with them, the women getting up in turn to accept and return our hushed greetings and to kiss us on both cheeks or shake hands with us. Sitting against the wall, changing places occasionally, we chatted in low key with this one and that one, rising ourselves for more greetings when another group of mourners came in. After four years of knowing this family, here were more relatives I had not met, even another daughter of Auntie's who lived far away and had come for the funeral.

The men were in another, smaller room. It seemed good and right that the women were together, not least when I heard the voices of a few of them approaching from another part of the house, repeating in rhythmic unison: *'La iláh ill'allah.'* The words were accompanied by a shuffle of feet, all moving closer until in through the far door they came with their burden. Down in the middle of the room they laid her, shrouded but for her face, which we now came up to kiss goodbye in turn.

It struck me as a strange coincidence that I should be present to farewell Rihaab's dear friend and neighbour and sister-in-law where over three years earlier I had failed to farewell Rihaab herself. Strange, too, that when they carried Auntie to the cemetery, once again I was not there. Yet I had been waiting outside while the women of Uncle Ahmed's family made last-minute preparations indoors.

I was sitting on a stone at the foot of a light pole with Na:aameh and her children, the usual street rubble scattered around us. A voice was coming over the loudspeaker of the mosque. I thought at first that it was related to Auntie's death, until I realised that it sounded too vehement, as if full of invective. Then I recognised the words 'Amreeka' and 'Meesterrr Bhooush'. I looked at Na:aameh wonderingly. It was already a good year since the Gulf War, and a few more since we had left for Scotland. Before that time, I had found most Jordanians interested in Westerners, especially Americans. Even though all non-Arabs would always be called foreigners — *ajnab* — the people were open and welcoming. I would certainly not have heard this stream of bitter, denunciatory-sounding language coming from any village mosque at that time. Na:aameh looked embarrassed when I queried her. She managed to convey to me that it was Friday, when people go to the mosque and the sermon is given. But I had not heard such a loud and long sermon on a Friday before. Omar came up to us and she explained what I'd been asking. He turned to me.

'This is the way it is, dear. Go inside for a while. No need to listen to this. I will call you when they bring Auntie.'

I would have been just as happy to stay and wait, but I wanted to change my clothes and take a much-needed break from the hours of sitting which I had lost the custom of. I had been indoors for only a few minutes when Omar called from outside.

'They are leaving now. Hurry up if you want to see her on her way to the cemetery.'

He had explained that the men would be taking her. The women's role was done.

It was winter, and I was pulling on a pair of socks when he called. I listened. More shuffling, this time outside, around the entrance to their house. Within a moment I was out the door finding my *khofái*, but once in the street I found it silent and empty. Omar himself was gone, and I saw only Na:aameh and a few other women with their children sitting by the road.

'And Auntie?' I asked Na:aameh.

'*Dhahabat.*' (She's gone.)

Then as I sat down on the stone beside her, Na:aameh pressed my arm lightly. 'Quickly,' she said in English.

'Die, then go to the ...' she tapped the ground with her other hand, smiling at me.

'Ground,' I said. 'Cemetery.'

'Yes, to the ground,' she answered, and then pronounced fast the words: 'verry verry quickly.'

Noor

I must weigh things. Not all of that last winter trip was bleak. There were even moments approaching completion — though not immediately connected with Omar and me — moments where some things I had found puzzling and open-ended began to take on ... not certainty, but direction.

I had been back in the village a few weeks on that visit when Omar said to me, 'We will visit Majiid tonight, we are invited.'

When we arrived, I found the two wives together, but from the beginning it was clear to me that Ibtisaam received her due as first lady of the house. Ibtisaam was our hostess, while Khola, in her carefully ironed and spotless grey dress and head covering, silently brought in dish after dish of delicious food they had both spent all day preparing.

I asked Khola if she would be eating with us. She answered no, in bashful, reticent manner, and as she went out to bring more food Majiid and Ibtisaam told me in turn that Khola had to go to the little one, that she had to put the children to bed. I thought: was it always so? Or could Khola, at other times, be hostess to other guests? I found myself watching as she came and went, watching

343

closely and against my will, embarrassed and yet mesmerised, trying to tease out some meaning from every word or gesture of either woman. After greeting us, Khola herself said nothing, and soon went away to another part of the house, not to return. I wanted to ask honestly, forthrightly, whether she could not surely stay, but I felt the indelicacy of further questions. Majiid and Ibtisaam had already answered me with that sort of patience and kindness that is needed with foreigners. It struck me that their hospitality mixed with reserve and their very courtly gentleness, so easily mistaken for hypocrisy in my own country, had no more of ritual in it than the modern West's much-vaunted openness and informality.

Still I kept wondering what it was, then, to be a *darra*, a 'co-wife', which is any wife after the first. In Jordan, such marriages are less common and often less publicly broadcast than, say, in Saudi Arabia. *Darra*: a word that I am unable to fill with meaning. In these villages, where old and new come most into conflict, the meaning of *darra* is constantly poured out and composed anew, made both to fit and to break out of its mould. Many affect not to know the term. I found my thoughts wandering back to my childhood. A co-mother was unimaginable, an impossibility in my family life, where the European notion of the marital bond prevailed. But elsewhere, outside my mind and my community, the inconceivable is. Always elsewhere, and always in this same world.

Omar's sociability fully compensated for my over-carefulness. He was conversing on a much lighter note, and his mood of that night, well tempered between buoyant and serious, made the visit go smoothly.

Some days later, around midmorning, I heard Sahr and Randa greeting a visitor at the gate. It was Khola. She made no hesitation to sit with me in the front room of the house, where guests are received. There was nothing diffident about her. Though still subdued in voice and manner, she was poised and self-assured.

The sisters unexpectedly brought in sweet coffee, and amazed me by leaving us soon after drinking theirs. Left alone with her I realised it was me Khola had come to see. We talked of this and that, managing to communicate in spite of the language difficulty. Her English was far better than her former silences had led me to believe. After she left I remembered the words that had surprised me, though Khola had spoken them softly, as part of the conversation.

'I speak English Mishaal. I am a teacher. Yes, I stopped to have the babies, but I will teach again, *insha 'Allah*. I have my certificate, Mishaal, my certificate to teach English.'

Auntie's was not the only funeral that took place on that trip. There was also the uncle in Samar. And again, it came just before the snow.

It happened not long after Auntie's death. The day was already unusual in that Sahr did not take up her customary household chores, but on a whim spent the morning sitting and playing with her baby nephew. This was Omar's brother Saleh's little boy. Sahr had woken early to go to Saleh's house and pick up Odaiyeh, the son that Saleh and Nawal had longed for. They had had another daughter since Amira, and that was all. Then, some months before I made that trip, their son was born and their desire fulfilled. But a third child also meant that they both had to work. Even that did not make the difference it would once have made. They had just built their new house and begun to make the mortgage payments when the Gulf War brought a reduction in the value of the Jordanian dinar. Little Odaiyeh was asthmatic and the special-formula powdered milk needed for him was expensive. Then there was the question of who would look after him while they both worked. Although they considered themselves fortunate, as teachers, to find posts at schools in nearby towns, there were times when both of them had to teach the morning shift of classes. On those days Sahr arranged to bring Odaiyeh back to our house and mind him until his mother came to fetch him at noon.

Sahr had a special affection for this child, and had decided that today she would put *kohl* on his eyes. She called me when it was done, and together we were admiring his big wide eyes when Sahr stiffened suddenly as if listening for something. Then laying the baby aside she got up and went out, asking me if I could hear anything. I followed her into the courtyard, then out the gate and into the street.

'Yes. Someone calling from a mosque.'

It had not occurred to me that this was outside the times of the call to prayer.

Sahr nodded and pointed across the olive grove at the back of the house.

'Yes. *Min Samar. Min al jam:ah fi Samar.*' From Samar. From the mosque in Samar.

We walked to a vantage point along the street where you could see in the distance the roofs of Rihaab's home town, the top of its mosque and the minaret. It was smaller than our minaret, but older, and built of that pale pink-coloured stone that I had always found more attractive than the cement bricks of our mosque. She listened longer and said she thought she had heard the name of an uncle, an older brother of Rihaab. If so, he must have died, as he had been very ill.

'Old Mishaal, old. *Wa mariiḏ.*' (And sick.)

Samar was so near as almost to be a twin village of Kufr Soum, yet it was far enough to keep me wondering how news with all its details managed to travel so fast between villages. By the time Nawal came to pick up Odaiyeh the death had been confirmed, and late that afternoon we were all on our way to Samar in Adnan's bus, arriving just on time for the men to follow the body to the gravesite. I went with the women into the house of a sister of the dead man. His own house next door would later be crowded with men.

There was little light inside, as if the place had been deliberately left in the shadows, and there were already many women sitting around the walls quietly talking. Between Sahr and Na:aameh I moved around from woman to woman shaking their hands and offering a subdued '*Marhabah*' as each got up in turn to greet us. It was in the midst of these rounds that my glance was drawn towards a woman I could see moving about on the far side of the room. We did not catch up with her to offer a greeting. She had continued round the circle, helping to serve tea, and as she sat down again, a place was offered to Na:aameh and me on the near side by the windows. I could not understand why my eyes kept drifting in her direction, and began to think I must be staring rudely.

Then she happened to turn a certain way, and it came to me with an intake of breath, the something recognisable in the movement of her head, in the way she raised her arm. Seeing her across the room, her features not quite distinct in the obscurity, I had an overwhelming impression of looking at a younger version of Rihaab.

I found a moment to whisper to Na:aameh, asking who that woman was, sitting on the far side of the room, that woman like Rihaab. So much like Rihaab, I repeated, showing my astonishment. Na:aameh was pleased that I had noticed the resemblance. She told me the woman was their cousin, the daughter of one of Rihaab's sisters, and that her name was Noor, which means Light. Many people, she said, had remarked on the likeness. It was well known.

Some weeks later in Irbid, we were to come across her again shopping in the markets. Under the brightness of the day I could discern those details of features that differentiated and distinguished her from Omar's mother. But at the time of the funeral, in that darkened room, I saw only the overall facial structure which together with her manner, her movements and carriage, recalled Rihaab as if by haunting.

Though only in her fifties, Rihaab had been so thin and weak, and worn by pain, that she had looked old. Now it seemed I could see how she must have appeared when she was healthy. I found this woman beautiful, and her resemblance to Rihaab so striking as to be uncanny. And I felt a sense of honour and privilege, as if granted a glimpse, like a vision, of Rihaab's heavenly form. This thought probably came to me because Sahr had often mentioned that her mother was beautiful again, now that she was in Paradise.

Farewell

The wedding is long over. Forgotten. The guests dispersed quickly once the married couple had left the church. Even Mu'tah is behind us, and I have said my goodbyes to our friends there. We have come to Kufr Soum for a week before I fly back to Perth. And most of that week has gone by.

Omar's family always seems happy to see me, no matter how long it has been between visits. Sahr in particular has shown her affection and attachment. Already in Mu'tah her gladness was apparent, but now she has made it clear that I should not keep going away. 'You have come back,' she said in Arabic with gestures verging on sign language, 'why don't you stay this time? Stay with us, Mishaal … with Omar.' Sometimes Saleh and other members of the family asked me about Australia, and I had begun since the previous trip to talk with Omar about his coming to live with me there, but all his responsibilities would clearly make this too complicated a move. Still, he told me he would think about it and try to work out ways to make it possible. But that has all changed now.

Randa has been mischievous and within my first few days here she has asked me pointedly if I know about the other. I do not answer in words. I tell her nothing of the envelope in now familiar handwriting that I found on the top of the cabinet in Omar's Mu'tah apartment the day after the wedding. It was so obvious, no one could have missed it. Left there soon after it must have arrived. Left as if deliberately, in full view. Omar was out teaching his summer classes, and it was Sahr who came rushing in at the sound of the crash when my arm swept across the cabinet top. Only the clock was broken. She clearly had not known what had set me off so violently, and she was angry with me. Then she consoled and commiserated, and appeared sad and worried, for me, for him, for herself. Omar, on his return, did not appear to know whether to be annoyed about the clock, angry at my outburst or annoyed with himself. And I did not know by that time just how angry I really was with him, after my initial reaction. There was more a growing sense of futility, especially when his insistence that this was an old letter and that the woman meant nothing to him had lost any power to convince. We didn't argue much about it. Even that seemed pointless. A couple of his friends tried to persuade me to return soon to Jordan. 'This is the only way to keep the marriage alive,' they said. I agreed, but could not see my way to doing that. I felt it was all too late. 'Stay with us,' Sahr says again now.

But Randa keeps at me, trying to find out what I know. I do know very well by now my Arabic gestures of disdain, better than the spoken language. I respond to her questions by closing and opening my eyes with slow deliberation, the brows raised as I click my tongue and jerk my head up and away to one side. She can see that her question is disregarded. But she presses on. 'Do you know herr name Michèle? What is herr name?' It happens that the name is the same as one of the months of the year.

'July?' I offer with a half smile. 'May? No, I think it's Avril, right?' She laughs. Then I click and jerk my head again, this time looking down on her and then away. There are no more questions after that.

I am tired. The drive north to Kufr Soum was long, and I seem not to have recovered over these last few days. We hardly stopped anywhere along the way.

Tomorrow I leave.

I am more than tired. I am exhausted. Here in the village I always sleep well. Not last night. Last night, in deepest sleep I was woken by a distant noise just like the explosions the Syrians made when they were building a dam on the river. Another project that would take more water away from Jordan. I thought, as I heard another one, that the dam was undertaken years ago, when I was living here. No one would be planting dam explosives in the dead of night. I was fully awake now, and heard another. And another. I counted forty-three, and wondered.

In the morning, at breakfast, which Bilaal had fetched from the village shop, I asked about those noises. Omar's answer in a few brief words seemed almost dismissive. 'It's the bombs,' he told me between sips of tea. I stared blankly. Randa said something to Sahr, who turned to me with another word, spoken soberly.

'*Loubnaan*, Mishaal.'

Then with a shrug she put the dishes and glasses back on the large round tray and took it to the kitchen.

Having left Australia before this spate of bombing in southern Lebanon had begun, I had seen no newspapers or television in that time and was unaware of the renewal of attacks there. I knew Lebanon was near, but so near? It would have been pointless, meant nothing to them, to tell the family the thing I most wanted to tell them out of pure awe and amazement at the realisation of it: that

351

these were the first bombs I had ever actually heard. We finished clearing away the breakfast utensils and sweeping the floor. On the matter of the bombs nothing more was said.

I spent most of yesterday visiting and saying my farewells. This morning I went with Na:ameh and Aisha to see Uncle Ahmed next door and say goodbye to Waliid, Temaam and the other cousins.

The last time I was in their house, a few weeks after Auntie died, Uncle Ahmed had asked me in a half serious spirit whether I thought he should remarry. I remember being surprised at his question. Abu Omar's remarrying after living with Rihaab's illness so many years was no shock to me, especially as they had not got on so well. But I had always seen Uncle Ahmed and Auntie as a couple with mutual caring and esteem, and so much goodness for each other and for their children. When he asked the question I looked across at two of his older daughters who were there at the time and had been the most visibly upset at losing their mother. One said 'no' to me aloud, and both made several other negative signs.

'No,' I told him in the best Arabic I could muster, 'your wife was so good, so sweet.'

'Yes, she was so very, very good' he answered, and continued in a tone that I could only describe as an almost jocular submission to fate, 'but she's not here.'

This morning I found Uncle Ahmed, robust for his seventies, sitting on the front porch with his new wife. She was in her forties, I thought, and appeared very healthy, happy and full of good humour. All the family, it seemed, had accepted her.

Not so in our household. Sahr had always run the house for her mother, and on top of her grief, now felt pushed out by the healthy woman her father had married when we were in Scotland. Omar especially called his father foolish, because he could not afford to have another family. It had happened just when Omar was beginning to see his way clear of the burden of younger siblings. Randa was about to marry her cousin, and Bilaal was soon to marry too.

'See these,' he said to me only this morning in a moment of anger, and waved his hand at his father's two new children, two-year-old Ahmed and his baby brother, pretty little Saddam, 'I am responsible for them now.' He muttered a curse in Arabic. But this afternoon I sat with them all in that part of the house that Abu Omar and his new wife have taken over. She gave me a parting gift of her long and patient work with the needle. All through the week she has been sewing together dresses made from beaded fabric for my friends and family in Australia, and she has added tufts and a fringe of snowy white cotton round the edges of the red checked *kefiiyeh* I am to take back with me.

Aunt Khadija came by later and sat in the courtyard, puffing on her pipe. I sat opposite her and looked back at the wall of the house with its peeling paint. But the house shows no visible signs, at least not that I can see, of last year's strife, when a crowd of youths threatened to burn it and Omar, with electric wire, rendered the wall and gate forbidding. In fact the new pale blue paint of the gate and grill work gives the whole entrance and wall a peaceful, approachable look.

By this blue gate I stood for the photo that Randa took of me this afternoon. The children had all been playing here in the courtyard, the girls dressing in some of their mothers' and aunts' clothes. Aisha's youngest daughter, the lovely Shaima, born when my mother was here and now around four years old, was clacking about in high-heeled shoes.

Sahr was watching, and suddenly got up and took from the clothes line her father's *kefiiyeh* that she washed this morning, and began to play with it. First, she wore it the way her father sometimes did, with one end thrown rakishly over the top of her head, and as everyone laughed I ran to grab my camera. Randa and Temaam were with us, but there were no men in the courtyard at the time, and keeping one eye peeled out for them, Sahr did a delightful imitation of the men's *dubkeh*, with plenty of hopping and jumping and stamping, though she wouldn't repeat it for a photo. Then she wound the *kefiiyeh* round her head to make a *silik*, and I did the same with my new *kefiiyeh*. Sahr found one of her mother's old *shrsh* with pink embroidery and encouraged me to put it on. Randa asked dear old Aunt Khadija if we could borrow her wimple for me. The black cloth fell in folds across my neck. We laughed and giggled with the little girls, participating in their dressing-up game. Even Aunt Khadija chuckled along with us.

But when I stood by the gate for the photo, with my hand up at the bars for I don't know what reason, as if I wanted or were about to go out, I must have become more serious. Still smiling, but with the festiveness gone from my eyes. I think that look will be recognisable in the photo, to me at least. Was I acting out a real leave-taking, one that began a long time ago, possibly even before the other woman came into his life? It is beginning to feel as if these constant departures belong to something larger, set in motion during my second stay, when Randa had told me, 'You will forget us.' Was that what she meant?... that

I would not 'stay the course', would not meet the challenge of adjustment. But forget? No. And I will return. Surely I must. The laughter, the dancing at weddings, my learning new things about time and space, the knowing each other better with every word, look, movement, with every meal taken together, the loving, and the dying, cannot have all been for nothing.

You do not marry a person in this part of the world. You marry a family, a community, a way of life. Whatever you may not like about it, there are the things you love, the things that opened up a world to you, drew you in and now keep you. I became a link in a multi-dimensional chain — the chain of the family, the chain of women — so many interlocking loyalties and allegiances. When I was living here, my commitment rapidly became complex, intense and all-absorbing. I wonder about their own lives in all this. None of them has given any sign of disruption caused every time I come and go. They would never show it. They would be like the hero who fed his horse to his guests. But this sense of wrenching. Do they feel it too? That is the pang that came with the moment when Randa held up the camera. I wonder, will that show in the photo? There, by that peaceful-blue gate?

We have taken our late evening snack of tomato slices, fresh coriander, hummus and bread, and our tea with mint, out in the courtyard. I am ready to sleep now, in this room, beside Sahr and Randa. I wonder for a moment if I will be woken by bombs or brays. Anxiety or sadness. I will not be woken. The family have spread tranquility through the house, whatever they are feeling. They have covered me with ease. I will deal with tomorrow when it comes. Adnan will take us, as always, to the airport in the morning. But now, I will enjoy, to the fullest reaches of the unconscious, my last night of truly safe, safe sleep.

Epilogue

Music

On the plane, I stare at the back of the seat in front of me, pick up a flight magazine and flick through it. I'm half aware of the festooned camel loping across the cover and the great walls of an immense wadi rising at some distance behind him, but I can take nothing else in.

Time lopes with a peculiar gait, catching up with me one moment, then leaping ahead. From panicky flights into a jumbled past and future it lurches back into present banalities. A hostess passing out drinks. Snapping. Fizzing. The clink of ice in glasses. I am here now, hurtling away from that country. Was I there? An in-flight dinner. The syrup of the peaches is curling around the cream, refusing to blend. Will I ever see them again? 'Yes' is always specific, I think as I lift this spoon of contrary tastes to my mouth. 'No' is a yawning indefiniteness. But its certainty wells up somewhere within me and turns in curdling horror away from becoming a thought. It will not join with consciousness. Beside the clinging residue of hope it refuses to declare itself, waiting until it can be accepted, voiced.

I am standing in the aisle with the other passengers amidst the thumps and clicks of overhead baggage compartments being opened and closed. I pull down my shoulder bag. Time keeps on jumping awkwardly from scene to scene like a badly edited film. Now the Customs Official is asking about the *za:'ter*, but he is polite, even kind, a border angel checking my credentials to bring fragments of my self into heaven. He cannot know that I come from Paradise, where everything I saw and did was real, where desire and fulfilment were perfectly matched, where loss and disappointment were likewise intense and complete. Paradise, where it could be so hot that a cold drink burnt the throat. At the Perth Airport arrival lounge my sister is waiting, and drives me home. It is winter here, and raining.

As if in a day the season passes, and with the spring months come strange dreams, or one dream so powerful that it stays with me, a permanent resident of my spirit. It is a dream of jagged ledges stretching before me over a chasm, a hybrid of steep wadi and high reservoir where the water below is a bare trickle, just to show it has run dry. A frail old woman in a long black gown is standing watching me. I am about to attempt a crossing, but then I look back where her gaze directs mine. Behind me a group of female lions pace back and forth before a cave in the hillside. I turn to her for a sign, but she only gazes again, now at a male lion that is following me out onto the ledge, and is lightly flicking the tufted tip of his tail against my forehead as if to wake me from a trance. Then he places the soft pad of his front paw in the same spot, on the dent in the middle of my forehead, above my nose and brow. He strokes and he strokes and I wake up with the sensation of something having really rubbed at me there. I throw the blanket from me, move my fingers across my forehead in the same spot, smooth back my hair, look about for beetles, spiders … There is nothing.

There is no sudden ending. I mail a few letters to Omar, but longer intervals grow between. 'The lion in your dream,' he writes, 'it is me, silly!' I do not answer this. It is not you, poor Omar, silly. It's myself. That's the trick. Someone stronger than I knew.

When I begin to feel it will not be long before our letters trickle to nothing, that is when I ask him what he wants me to call him in my book. 'Call me by a classical Arabic name, either Omar or Khaled,' he writes in answer. 'The first stands for love and manliness and virility. The second stands for fighting in battlefields and for knighthood. If you do not like either, then call me Eihab or Haatem. They mean giving and caring.'

Omar. Still my husband, officially. Hardly in reality. I hardly know what to call him now.

In October I spend a weekend in the bush. Two thoroughly Australian days, yet even here, association uncurls on an instant before a herb or a plant, a rustle, a whiff on the hot wind, the shape of a rock.

January stings me with its dry West Australian heat recalling that of Jordan in July. My remembering is constantly jolted by an invasive present in unrelated, blinding stabs of meaningless clarity: the design on this teacup as I raise it to my lips, the heavy stamp of my steps on this slab of cracked, uneven pavement. These sudden moments speak to me in a language I do not want to understand. You are here now, in this place, they tell me, and now you are here.

The letters stop. There are no endings in Omar's part of

the world. Closure is childish. The sultana's tales weave in and out of each other, opening up and pouring forth here, holding back and containing there. My story of Jordan is one of many in life's more expansive tale. Our ending as a couple is not dramatic. It is a gradual drifting apart, reasons unspoken. Those reasons, like our other tacit understandings, lie among the many small things scattered about here. They lie with the bits of the wall, which has come down in spite of everything. Not completely, but enough to see past.

I will not be among those who deny everything that was connected with their pain. When something fails, it was not all bad, and remembering has its own sweetness.

I will not be debriefed. Why throw away all thought of Sahr and Randa and my other beautiful sisters, my life among the women, my trips into the wadi, my entering along new ways of thought, my sharing pain as well as pleasure, and so much more, just because I am no longer there? I'm still yearning for the sounds of Jordan. I enrol in Arabic lessons. The teacher is Egyptian, and the language doesn't sound the same. But then I edit a magazine for the ethnic and multicultural arts. It is run by my Middle Eastern dance teacher, and Arabic music and dance are among the many subjects of the articles. I also buy a wild thyme plant and begin to make my own *za:'ter*. I eat it for breakfast with olives, white cheese, *hummus*, flat bread and yoghurt, enjoying the fragrance of the past. My friends in the Middle Eastern dance courses say I make the best *baba ghanoush* in the land, though I still insist on calling it *mtebel*.

In spite of the lessons, my Arabic, what little I had, is fading. But in English I break the massive grief into fragments, break down and distil, saving the best.

Loss stays with me, is the thing that will not lose itself

in everyday activities. Because I have lost Omar, I will never again speak with Sahr, learn what has happened to her, how she has fared with her own grief, and in her own life, or learn whether Randa has children now, how Amira and Manar have grown, and Shaima, born during my mother's visit.

Forget the past, said Omar in the taxi that day as we journeyed home from Amman. Yes, you are right, Omar. I will forget. But not from bitterness. Rancour and regret are so much wasted energy, a movement of the heart that sends dark ripples through time and space, disturbing their cosmic balance. At this moment I am sipping sage-flavoured tea. It will always be delicious to me. That's my challenge now: to let the past go without rejecting, without betraying it. Here are the scattered bits of wall, and in its place my garden.

In the middle of some household task I switch on the radio, and turn to complete what I am doing, half attending. Arabic music bursts into the room. I rush to adjust the volume and check the station. A few years ago I would have had to travel halfway round the world to hear this. Last year, before that last trip, I listened regularly to the FM 'ethnic' station. Now, amazed that the dial is on Radio National, I feel pleased and tormented, haunted. And it does not stop. Anwar Ibrahim is followed by two of the greatest singers, both women. 'Give me the ney and sing, for song is the secret of being,' sings Feyrouz, 'And the lament of the ney lingers on, long after being fades.' She is followed by Umm Kalthoum.

I do not turn it off. That is impossible. Before I know it the old feeling surges through me, accompanying Umm Kalthoum's fluttering courtship of a note, a syllable. She has taken the *a* of *qalbi*, which means 'my heart', and is riding it up and down, and now she hovers, her winged voice vibrating.

Now she has come down low on a downbeat. It is over. Tears give momentary relief. And then I breathe. With the end of the song and the return of the announcer's voice, a woman's voice trying not to be impersonal, the gates on the past close and wait for another key to turn in their locks. The present spreads over my memories with the brightness of a rapid-rising sun meeting its zenith. It shortens their shadows.

The Levant and Neighbouring Areas

TURKEY

CYPRUS

LEBANON

Mediterranean
Sea

SYRIA

IRAQ

ISRAEL

JORDAN

EGYPT

SAUDI
ARABIA

Red Sea

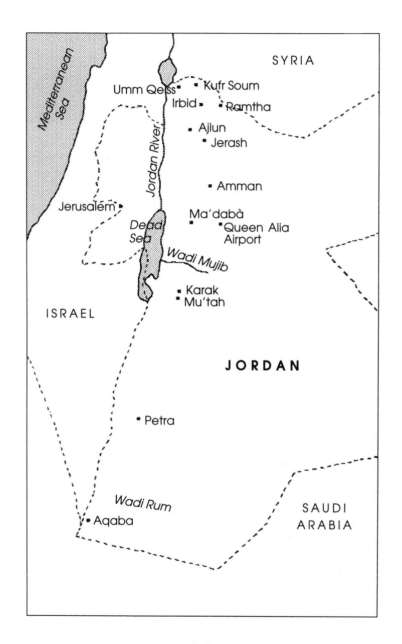

Note on Transliteration

In transcribing words from Arabic to romanised form, I have indicated the long vowels in Arabic by doubling the equivalent vowels in English. In the case of known words I have used the commonly accepted spellings in English, especially where an initial *:* or letter *:ayn* is dropped before words beginning with vowels. Stressed syllables are occasionally indicated by an accent over the vowel, as in *dish-dásha*.

The Arabic consonants that have no English equivalents are represented in the following way:

th (as in 'thin')

dh (like 'th' in 'this')

<u>*h*</u> (the throat is constricted as compared with 'h')

<u>*kh*</u> (like 'ch' in Scottish 'loch')

sh (as in 'ship')

* <u>*s*</u>
* <u>*d*</u>   (these four consanants bear
* <u>*t*</u>   slight resemblance to the sounds of
* <u>*dh*</u> the letters used here [*see below*])

**: (the letter *:ayn* – a velar or back-of-the-throat consonant)

gh (the letter *ghayn* – similar to French 'r' as in 'Paris')

' (the hamza or glottal stop, as it occurs in English before 'is' in 'Sandra is')

* Each of these consonants is strongly affected by the tight-throated velar vowel that invariably follows. Underlining indicates that the consonant is either produced from or associated with the back of the throat.

** I have departed from convention in using a colon for the letter *:ayn* instead of an opening apostrophe, which can be confusing for non-Arabic speakers in its similarity to the closing apostrophe used for the hamza or glottal stop.

Translation of Dialogue (pp. 45–46)

This is a rough translation of the romanised transliteration of Sahr's Arabic. The whole dialogue is repeated here for ease of reading.

'Why not marry Dr Nabil himself, Sahr?' I asked her, half seriously, 'he's not married.'

But my Arabic hadn't graduated beyond single words and names. I couldn't manage a sentence, much less a question. '*Enti ... zowaj ... Dr Nabil ...*' (You ... husband ... Dr Nabil) was all I could muster. She doubled up with laughter, as if I had added to the store of jokes on the topic.

'What?! Dr Nabil?! Do you think he's nice Mishaal?' She always pronounced my name with the long Arabic *alif*.

'You want to marry Dr Nabil instead of Omar?'

Sahr shot deliberate, meaningful looks at me as she spoke, which increasingly took on an air of mischief, reminding me of the looks Omar sometimes gave me.

'No. You, Sahr. You.'

Her high-pitched response was full of humour.

'Oh, me you mean? That will be when the cows come home' (lit. when Salah finds his cattle).

But after a while she became more serious. And just as I was wanting to understand her, the words came in rapid volleys.

'He's a very kind man, Dr Nabil. And I'm sure he's encouraging me to marry because he thinks it would be good for my health. People shouldn't be without a partner in life, he says to me. But he knows I won't do it. We've had this conversation before. There's just no way in the world ...'

'*La*. Stop. You're talking too fast. Again? *Kaman*?'

'He's a good person, but he knows I won't marry anyone. No way would I marry while my mother is so ill. My sisters can marry. But I just want to look after her. That's all that matters to me.'

Glossary

Some of the romanised Arabic words in this glossary belong to the local dialect and are not listed in a standard Arabic dictionary.

A

abu	father
abui	my father
abuk	your father
áhlen!	welcome!
áhlen wa sáhlen	welcome and be at ease
ajnabi (ajnabiiyeh, fem.)	foreign, foreigner
al 'aan	now
al-arba:a	Wednesday (the fourth day of the week)
Amriika	America (often used for the USA)
aqraba	scorpion
:assaaba	cowl-like head cloth used by women

B

b:ad	after
bandoora	tomato
beledi	of the country (as in '*beledi*' or folk music, poetry, singing and dancing)
biddou	I want
biddak, (*biddik,-itch,* fem.)	you want (-*itch* local dialect)
bidoun	without
boukra	tomorrow

C

couss omak!	your mother's cunt!

D

dish-dásha   long, straight-hanging dress, usually of cotton or synthetic material, coloured, worn in the home and informally

dhahaba (dhahabat, fem.)   go (he went, fem — she went)

dubkeh   traditional folk dance, used especially for weddings

dowali   stuffed vine leaves (usually with lamb and rice, sometimes other fillings)

ḏarra   co-wife (any wife after the first)

E

enta (enti, fem.)   you

F

Faatíḥa   opening prayer of the *Qur'aan*

fi   in; there is (there are)

Fooot!   come in

H

ḥabibi (ḥabibti, fem.)   dear, my dear

hadha   this, that

ḥajj   pilgimmage to Mecca that every Muslim should make at least once

ḥalwa   lolly, sweet

ḥimaar (ḥimaareh, fem.)   donkey

ḥolwa (ḥilwi, fem.)   sweet, pretty

ḥummus   a dip made of chickpeas

ḥoori   the beautiful spirit women waiting in Paradise to greet the faithful

ḥout   whale

I

illa to, for
illak (illik, -itch, fem.) to you, for you (*-itch* local dialect)
illi to me, for me
insha 'Allah God willing
ism name

J

jaama:a mosque
jaami:ah university
jalabiyeh full-length shirt or robe worn by men
jiddeh grandmother, grandma

K

kaalima word (*bidoun kaalima* – without words, without a word)
kaman again
kanaafet strands of pastry wrapped to form a crisp shell, filled with melting-hot white cheese and covered in syrup
kefiiyeh red-and-white-checked head cloth worn by men, or black and white as with Palestinians
khábil, (khábila, fem.) crazy; stupid (dimwitted, muddle-headed)
khobeizeh green plant that grow wild in the wadi
khóbuz bread (usually refers to the large round flat loaves)
khofái slip-on sandals, scuffs
kohl kohl, a black rock ground to powder and used as an eyeliner
kwáïss (kwáïssa, fem.) good

L

la	no
laban	liquid yoghurt (in the Middle East)
lakin	but
leysh	why
Loubnaan	Lebanon

M

majnoun	mad, crazy
mann?	who?
márhaba	hello (less formal greeting than *Salaam alleikoum*)
mariid (*mariida*, fem.)	sick
marra	time (as in once, two times, three times)
mensef	hot rice, mutton and yoghurt dish served on festive occasions, especially at weddings
min	from
mlokhiiyeh	a green plant eaten in many parts of the Middle East, known in English as Jew's mallow; makes a tasty viscous soup, often served with chicken
momtaaz	excellent
mustáshfa	hospital
msh	not (colloquial)
mish mish	apricot
mtebel	eggplant dip (in Egypt *baba ghanoush*)

N

na:am	yes
na:iïman!	a special greeting to someone who has just bathed, refreshed themselves
na:na:	mint
noor	light, day (light)

O

obaiyeh! — an exclamation of pain or suffering

Q

qadi — judge (the person)
qalb — heart
qalbi — my heart
Qur'aan — the Quran (or Koran)

R

raqs sharqi — Middle Eastern dance
raqsi! — dance!
romaaneh — pomegranate

S

seleq (seleqleq) — a green vegetable like spinach (*seleqleq* local dialect)

shahada — Muslim profession of faith ('There is no God but [the one] God, and Mohammed is His Prophet.')

shai — tea
shams — sun
shling — a coin of 50 fils or one twentieth of a dinar (probably from 'shilling' in the days of the British mandate)

shou — what? (colloquial)
shrsh — long, straight-hanging dress of a dark colour, usually of velvet or a synthetic substitute, worn by older, traditional women

shrob! — drink!
shwaiy — a little, a bit, slowly, a little while
silik — checked head cloth when worn by women in loose turban form

T

ta:abaan (*ta:abaana*, fem.) tired
towjiihi end of high school exam in Jordan

U

umm mother
ummak (*ummik*, *-itch*, fem.) your mother (*-itch* local dialect)
ummi my mother

W

wadi valley
wahed one (the number)
weyn? where? (colloquial)

Y

ya Oh (vocative address, eg. 'Oh Mary, where are you going?' — *not* a poetic stylisation, is used frequently in conversation)
yá:ni I mean, I mean to say, that is to say (an idiomatic expression used in conversation as 'you know' or 'you see' are used in English)

Z

za:'ter wild thyme leaves mixed with sesame seeds, used for snacks with bread and olive oil

Acknowledgements

To Jane Cousins and Jo Mead, the two dear friends, fellow writers and midwives who stayed by me throughout this labour, my heartfelt thanks, and my best wishes for your own happy birthings. Also to other earlier members of our writing group: Sarah Jones, Tanya Majourie and Carmel McDonald-Grahame for their advice and suggestions in the early stages, and their encouragement throughout.

To Marion Campbell, the first established writer to read my initial efforts during the wonderful semester when I took part in her creative writing course and began to believe, thank you. If I have re-invented myself, it is partly because of your unflagging faith and support. May your own brainchildren continue to flourish.

For the Goethe quotation that emboldened me, and for much, much more, my deepest thanks to Melanie Edwards, who showed me new ways of hope and faith and friendship, and whose first book, now in the formative stages, will be, I know, a gift to the world.

My warm appreciation goes to Mr Basem Kheis, Jordanian Consul in Canberra, for his help in providing information and details of Arabic names, words and terms. Also to Jasser Samardali of the Australian-Jordanian Friendship Association, who gave many more details and much of his time in reading this book and translating some of its passages, and to Mrs Alice Kirkbride for her kind help with the transliteration of Arabic words.

For their words of encouragement at different times in

the long process of writing, my thanks go to Kateryna
Longley, Bob Hodge, Kathy Trees, John Frodsham, Jenny
De Reuck, Gail Jones, Simone Lazaroo; also to Susan
Hayes for her advice and accessibility as the State
Literature Officer at the Fremantle Arts Centre; and to
Diana Clegg for her help and patience in the setting out
and printing of sections of the manuscript for different
purposes.

My warm thanks also to those who stood by me in
friendship and encouragement: Simone Scott, Teresa
Ashforth, Elizabeth McCardell, Wendy Duffy, Dori
Watson, Toni Ventriss and the members of my book club:
Wendy Beckhurst, Heather Cloudsdale, Di Dixon, Jill
Durack, Silvia Kinder, Maggie Mann, Genevieve Palmer
and Lillian Ryan. Also to Keti Susnjar, my Middle Eastern
Dance teacher and dear friend who has understood and
shared my interest in Arabo-Islamic cultures.

My special gratitude goes to those friends who have
read parts of the manuscript and offered further
suggestions with plenty of encouragement, in particular:
Joan (Justina) Williams and Vic Williams. Also to the
members of Toni Ventriss's book club who all provided
valuable assistance in giving their most honest
perceptions and responses, and in contributing much
needed editorial help.

Thank you to those who helped to 'launch' my work
before its official launching: David Britten and especially
Julie Rigg of the ABC, Radio National, who gave me my
first 'reading' on the 'Arts Today' program. Jan Teagle
Kapetas, Suzanne Covich and other members of the WEB
(Women Writers and Performers Network) committee,
who offered me my first public readings in Perth; and
Barbara Holland who published an extract from this book

as a short story in the anthology, *Sibling Stories*.

I am indebted to Ray Coffey for his initial interest and continuing faith, and to the many people at Fremantle Arts Centre Press who helped to make this book a reality, and to Wendy Jenkins and the other readers who contributed their responses and suggestions. Special thanks go to Janet Blagg for the depth and detail of her comments. Also to Helen Kirkbride and Cate Sutherland for their assistance and to Marion Duke for her skilful and creative work as artist and cover designer.

My deepest love and gratitude go to my sister, Geneviève Palmer, who maintained faith in me through some very difficult times, to my brother-in-law, Ben Palmer, a true believer and my first enthusiastic reader of the completed manuscript, and to my nieces Eliane and Lauren for their interest and input.